THE
JEWISH
PHENOMENON

SEVEN KEYS TO THE ENDURING
WEALTH OF A PEOPLE

STEVEN SILBIGER

LONGSTREET PRESS
ATLANTA, GEORGIA

Published by
LONGSTREET PRESS, INC.
2140 Newmarket Parkway, Suite 122
Marietta, GA 30067

WWW.LONGSTREETPRESS.NET

Printed in the United States of America

1st printing 2000

Library of Congress Catalog Card Number: 99-068572

ISBN: 1-56352-566-6

The best is yet to come.

Visit Longstreet Press on the World Wide Web at:
www.longstreetpress.net

Jacket and book design by Burtch Bennett Hunter

For my dad, Jack.

ACKNOWLEDGMENTS

I would like to thank John Yow, my editor at Longstreet Press, who immediately saw the potential of the project and made invaluable contributions to the book. I would also like to thank my editors who provided me a greater sensitivity and perspective: John Braun, Helen Gioulis and Rachel Silbiger, my mom.

Comments, questions? E-mail the author at: JEWISH7S@JUNO.COM

TABLE OF CONTENTS

INTRODUCTION

Steven Spielberg. Ralph Lauren. Michael Eisner. Michael Dell. They're all successful, at the top of their fields. They're all fabulously wealthy. And they're all Jewish. Those three characteristics – successful, wealthy and Jewish – are linked repeatedly in America today. And it is no accident. Jewish-Americans are, as a group, the wealthiest ethnic group in America. But the factors that work together to create Jewish wealth, which I identify in this book, can be applied to individuals and groups from any background.

Throughout 1997 and 1998 both *The Millionaire Next Door* and *The Gifts of the Jews* shared the *New York Times* bestseller lists. But despite this obvious interest in wealth, on one hand, and the Jewish people on the other, the two subjects have not been dealt with together. *The Gifts of the Jews* confines its discussion to the contributions that Judaism has made to American culture, including monotheism, the Ten Commandments and the Sabbath. But what largely defines Jews in the popular imagination is their economic success and the accomplishments that made it possible. Perhaps Jews and their wealth have not become a focus for discussion because whenever Americans discuss ethnicity and money, the conversation tends to become heated. It does not have to be that way. The extraordinary story of Jewish-American success contains lessons for all of us.

Many authors have written books about business success, trying to find a pattern that we can apply to all business organizations. What makes a company successful? Disney, Coca-Cola, Procter & Gamble, Microsoft . . . how have they overcome challenges and become so successful? In examining the phenomenon of Jewish-American success, this book reveals the principles that can be applied to your life. And it is important to note that the wealth created by Jews is much more than just money; it includes advances in the arts, sciences and the humanities that made the money possible.

A recent *Los Angeles Times* article describes the gap that *The Jewish Phenomenon* bridges. "The easy temptation is just to offer a laundry list of Jews and their achievements – a Hall of Fame of Nobel Prize winners, musicians and artists, a parade of business leaders, movie moguls, educators, journalists and entertainers who have influenced the American scene. Yet in searching for a deeper answer to the question – a theory that might explain the contributions of people as diverse as Jerry Seinfeld and Albert Einstein – there's a silence in the literature about Judaism and American life." The seven "keys" described in this book bring the silence to an end.

About half of American Jews marry gentiles, prompting experts to project that the Jewish-American community will shrink to half its size by 2050. This statistic lends urgency to the investigation of Jewish success today. As Rabbi David Wolpe of Sinai Temple, the oldest Conservative Jewish congregation in Los Angeles, explained to the writer for the *Los Angeles Times*, "The farther away you get from the source of your tradition, the less of a contribution you might be expected to make in a place like America. We could lose something precious."[1]

The Bell Curve, published with a storm of controversy in 1994, went down a slippery slope by examining the genetic IQ component of the success of Jews and other groups – an approach that alienated Jews and gentiles alike. During the debate over *The Bell Curve*, the Union of American Hebrew Congregations rightly stated, "As Jews, we know too well how these theories have been used against us . . . to justify hatred, discrimination, even murder and genocide."[2] *The Bell Curve*'s sharp rhetoric and dense statistics serve no useful purpose for two reasons: the science does not pass critical review, and there would be nothing to be learned if success lay in our genetic code at birth. *The Jewish Phenomenon* takes a positive position, that the Jewish people have been successful because of a combination of factors related to the Jewish religion and culture, and a collective historical experience. These are things that everyone and any group can examine and learn from.

Anti-Semitism has a long history, and it is by no means dead. Throughout that long history, the Jews' success has been decried as the reason for other people's problems. Even President Richard Nixon, in his Watergate paranoia, saw the Jews as his enemies. In the famed "Nixon Basement Tapes," Nixon told chief of staff H. R. Haldeman, "What about the rich Jews? The IRS is full of Jews, Bob. Go after 'em like a son-of-a-bitch!" While institutional anti-Semitism has been virtually eliminated in America, on a personal level anti-Semitism is very much alive.

Today an isolated anti-Semitic act such as the painting of a Nazi swastika on a synagogue makes front-page news and clergy from all denominations condemn it. The random shooting of three children by a madman at a Jewish community center in Los Angeles in 1999 brought worldwide outrage. But just seventy-five years ago Henry Ford, "Mr. Model T," conducted a propaganda campaign against the "International Jew." Ford believed that the Jews were involved in an international conspiracy to undermine the world economy. He spent millions of dollars investigating and publicizing his suspicions, but he could never uncover any evidence of the twisted plot.

Indeed, even today many Jewish people would rather reserve the subject of their success for private conversations rather than fuel the fires of anti-Semitism. Older Jewish-Americans, in particular, have downplayed their success and their Judaism in an effort to avoid unwanted attention and possible trouble. But in recent years the Jewish community has become less reluctant to trumpet its accomplishments. In *Schmoozing: The Private Conversations of American Jews*, younger American Jews expressed the opinion that "we debase ourselves when we hide our achievements out of fear of what the gentiles will think."[3] In December 1996, the Jewish magazine *Moment* published a cover story about the Jewish billionaires of the Forbes 400.[4] Such an article would have been unthinkable a few years before, and even today such reporting draws criticism. In any case, Jews remain much more defensive than the facts warrant. A recent study by Daniel Yankelovich and his staff revealed that 25 percent of Americans believe Jews have too much power in American business. But 75 percent of Jews think that others think Jews have too much power.[5]

The wildly successful *The Millionaire Next Door* concentrated on the factors common to American millionaires. That fascinating book actually inspired me to write this one because it began a discussion of wealth in America, but did not finish it. Conspicuously absent was any mention of religion or ethnicity. However, *The Millionaire* did list "The Top 15

Economically Productive Small Groups." Ranked No. 1 were Israeli-Americans with a productivity index of 6.8.[6] Those Jewish immigrants from Israel were seven times more likely to have the highest concentration of higher incomes and the lowest rate of dependency on public assistance than any other group studied. But that was all the book said. As I continued to thumb through the book, I thought that someone should take a closer look.

That closer look revealed a picture of a very small group with a great deal of economic and social success. Of course, that was no surprise to me. My parents raised me as a Jew with expectations of economic achievement, education and success. In addition, I had no shortage of role models from my family, my community, the media and the world. Economic success was the norm in my Jewish community.

Did I buy into a stereotype perpetuated out of ethnic pride, or was there a truth to it? Being critical by nature, I quickly uncovered some compelling facts that prove Jewish success is indeed a fact in America:

- The percentage of Jewish households with income greater than $50,000 is double that of non-Jews.

- On the other hand, the percentage of Jewish households with income less than $20,000 is half that of non-Jews.[7]

- "The Jewish advantage in economic status persists to the present day; it remains higher than that of white Protestants and Catholics, even among households of similar age, composition and location."[8]

- Forty-five percent of the top 40 of the Forbes 400 richest Americans are Jewish.

- "One-third of American multimillionaires are tallied as Jewish."[9]

- Twenty percent of professors at leading universities are Jewish.

- Forty percent of partners in the leading law firms in New York and Washington are Jewish.[10]

- Thirty percent of American Nobel prize winners in science and 25 percent of all American Nobel winners are Jewish.[11]

It didn't end there. In his book *Ethnic America*, Dr. Thomas Sowell, an African-American economist and senior fellow at the Hoover Institute, created a point-scale index that graphed Jewish economic success compared with that of other ethnic groups:[12]

ETHNIC HOUSEHOLD INCOME
(U.S. Average = 100)

JEWISH	172
JAPANESE	132
POLISH	115
CHINESE	112
ITALIAN	112
GERMAN	107
ANGLO-SAXON	107
IRISH	103
U.S. AVG.	100
FILIPINO	99
WEST INDIAN	94
MEXICAN	76
PUERTO RICAN	63
BLACK	62
NATIVE AMERICAN	60

THE JEWISH POPULATION IS SURPRISINGLY SMALL

The facts are extraordinary considering that Jewish Americans make up just 2 percent of the U.S. population, 5.9 million of America's 263 million people. The high media visibility of successful Jews in the sciences, the arts, the media and in business gives the false impression that the Jewish population is far larger than it is. Only in New York and New Jersey do Jews make up more than 5 percent of the state's population, and five states contain 68 percent of the Jewish-American population. At the bottom, there are only five hundred Jews in Idaho and five hundred in Wyoming, not enough to support a decent delicatessen.

JEWISH POPULATION OF THE UNITED STATES, 1996
By State (those over 100,000 listed)

State	Population	% of State Population	% of U.S. Jews
New York	1,652,000	9.1%	28%
California	921,000	2.9%	16%
Florida	644,000	4.5%	11%
New Jersey	435,000	5.5%	7%
Pennsylvania	325,000	2.7%	6%

State	Population	% of State Population	% of U.S. Jews
Massachusetts	268,000	4.4%	5%
Illinois	268,000	2.3%	5%
Maryland	212,000	4.2%	4%
Ohio	129,000	1.2%	2%
Texas	113,000	0.6%	2%
Michigan	107,000	1.1%	2%
Total	5,900,000		

(*American Jewish Year Book*, 1997)

In the world of six billion people, there are only thirteen million Jews, only one-fifth of 1 percent. Except for Israel, Jews are a tiny minority in every country. Jews live all over the world, but 93 percent of them live in just five countries. The former Soviet Union once contained more than a million Jews, who now live in many newly independent nations. Tahiti and Iraq have only 120 Jews each.

THE JEWISH POPULATION OF THE WORLD
(Countries over 50,000 listed)

Country	Number	% of all Jews
United States	5,900,000	45
Israel	4,600,000	35
France	600,000	5
Russia	550,000	4
Ukraine	400,000	3
Canada	360,000	3
United Kingdom	300,000	2
Argentina	250,000	2
Brazil	130,000	1
South Africa	106,000	0.8
Australia	100,000	0.8
Hungary	80,000	0.6
Belarus	60,000	0.5
Germany	60,000	0.5
Total	13,000,000	

(World Jewish Congress, 1996)

Even when it comes to the Jewish presence in any individual city, Jews are small in percentage of the population. Only a handful of cities outside Israel have a Jewish population of any significant size. New York and Miami have the largest percentage of Jews.

METROPOLITAN AREAS WITH THE LARGEST JEWISH POPULATIONS OUTSIDE ISRAEL

(Cities over 100,000 listed)

Cities	Jewish Population	% Jewish
New York, USA	1,750,000	13%
Miami, USA	535,000	15%
Los Angeles, USA	490,000	5%
Paris, France	350,000	4%
Philadelphia, USA	254,000	6%
Chicago, USA	248,000	4%
San Francisco, USA	210,000	5%
Boston, USA	208,000	8%
London, UK	200,000	2%
Moscow, Russia	200,000	2%
Buenos Aires, Arg.	180,000	2%
Toronto, Canada	175,000	6%
Washington, DC, USA	165,000	6%
Kiev, Ukraine	110,000	4%
Montreal, Canada	100,000	3v
St. Petersburg, Russia	100,000	2%

(World Jewish Congress and *Information Please Almanac*, 1996)

Beyond being a small part of the American melting pot, Jewish-Americans are relatively new arrivals. In many cases, Jews earned their American success in only one or two generations in the late nineteenth and twentieth centuries. For more than thirty years the Jewish-American population's growth has been flat, and Jews have become an ever-decreasing percentage of the total U.S. population.[13]

AMERICAN JEWISH POPULATION
1790 to 1990

Year	U.S. Population	U.S. Jews	% Jewish
1790	3,929,000	1,350	.03
1800	5,308,000	1,600	.03
1810	7,239,000	2,000	.03
1820	9,638,000	2,700	.03
1830	12,866,000	4,500	.03
1840	17,069,000	15,000	.09
1850	23,191,000	50,000	0.2
1860	31,433,000	150,000	0.5
1870	38,558,000	200,000	0.5
1880	50,155,000	250,000	0.5
1890	62,947,000	450,000	0.7
1900	75,994,000	1,050,000	1.4
1910	91,972,000	2,043,000	2.2
1920	105,710,000	3,600,000	3.4
1930	122,775,000	4,400,000	3.6
1940	131,669,000	4,800,000	3.7
1950	150,697,000	5,000,000	3.3
1960	179,323,000	5,500,000	3.1
1970	203,235,000	5,850,000	2.9
1980	226,545,000	5,920,000	2.6
1990	262,754,000	5,900,000	2.2

(*A History of the Jews in America*, A. Karp, 1997)

DISCOVERING THE KEYS

No doubt about it, the statistics of Jewish success – especially given the relatively small Jewish population – are remarkable. Of course, there are always individual exceptions to a general rule, just as individuals will vary within any group. However, when we view the complete picture, we see a big Jewish difference, and there must be some reasons for it. That is what *The Jewish Phenomenon* is all about. What secrets to success have the Jews learned that can apply to any life, any family and any community?

The research held the answer. A wealth of literature and data that chronicles the lives of Jewish people throughout the ages provides the clues. Countless individual Jewish success stories led me to the discovery of seven core values or beliefs that lay at the heart of Jewish achievement. In various combinations, these secrets have contributed significantly to the economic success of the Jewish people.

THE SEVEN KEYS TO JEWISH SUCCESS

1. Understand that real wealth is portable; it's knowledge

2. Take care of your own and they will take care of you

3. Successful people are professionals and entrepreneurs

4. Develop your verbal confidence

5. Be selectively extravagant but prudently frugal

6. Take pride in individuality: encourage creativity

7. Be psychologically driven to prove something

APPRECIATING THE KEYS

Listing them is not enough. Each has its roots in the history of the Jewish people. None of these secrets is independent of the others. They work together. Of course, education is very important, but a good education alone does not fully explain such success. As Dr. Sowell discovered, "Even when neither education nor age is a factor, Jews earn more." Among families headed by males with four or more years of college and aged 35 to 45, Jews still earn 75 percent higher incomes than the national average with the same demographics. Other qualitative and cultural differences not captured in the statistics contribute to their success.[14] If it were as simple as just getting an education or developing verbal confidence, just two of the keys, Jewish success would have been emulated years ago.

But nothing is to prevent non-Jews from learning about all seven principles and integrating them into their own lives, just as they already enjoy 75 percent of the $50 billion worth of kosher foods sold in the United States each year. Jews can also take a closer look and understand more about themselves. American society is rapidly assimilating its Jewish people, and a self-examination could be productive. This time the assimilation is not a matter of forced conversions, as had been the case in the Spanish Inquisition; it's a product of the openness of American society.

The Jewish Phenomenon is not a dry academic adventure. Flying in the face of political correctness, there will be a good Jewish joke where appropriate to provide insight to the Jewish way of thinking. I agree with Rabbi Joseph Telushkin that "People who oppose telling ethnic jokes would have us believe that the whole genre is nonsense, that alcoholics, neurotics, oversensitive people and shady characters are evenly distributed among all groups. However, tolerant as it sounds, this assumption makes no sense, for it implies that history and culture have no impact on human beings. But of course, they do. What makes Jews Jewish is a specific religious culture and historical experience that have shaped their values and strongly influenced how they view the world."[15] That's where the keys come from. In addition, all those Yiddish words that many Jews and non-Jews use and misuse in their day-to-day slang will be defined as well. Above all, the book is intended to be accessible so that when you finish, you'll have learned something. First you will learn about how a man turned $75 into a million dollars.

> Friedman learned about a tiny piece of worthless land, not more than a few feet square, that was for sale. It adjoined the city dump, and he could buy it for only $75. So he went to his brother-in-law and borrowed that amount, promising to repay the loan in a year.
>
> With the land now his, Friedman scouted the dump, and he found various items and was soon selling them to junk dealers. He bought a larger property and sold it at a profit. With the proceeds he built a couple of duplex houses and immediately sold them, too. Now only six months after he had borrowed the initial $75, he was worth $100,000.
>
> Then Friedman got an option on a large suburban tract, and tripled his money. On the very last day of the eleventh month since he started his junk business, he invested every penny he had, nearly twelve million dollars, in a fifty-story building with an appraised value of one hundred million. But just two hours after all the papers were signed and he took possession, an earthquake erupted and the building came tumbling down in ruins.
>
> His year was up. Sadly he went to his brother-in-law. "I am sorry, Max," he apologized, "but I guess I'm not much of a businessman. I just lost your whole seventy-five dollars!"

DEFINING WHAT A JEW IS

RACE, RELIGION OR TRIBE?

Despite the commonplace references to the Jewish race and the Jewish religion, Jews can best be understood as members of a tribe: "a cohesive ancestral group with particular customs, traditions and values. Those values can be religious and the customs linguistic." Bingo.

- ☐ An ancestral homeland: Israel
- ☐ Traditions, customs and values: celebrations, holidays, kosher foods
- ☐ Languages: Hebrew and Yiddish (a German/Polish/Hebrew mixture)

Unlike many religions, Judaism is more than simply a belief system that anyone can adopt. To become Jewish means enlisting in the tribe. The relationship or covenant is between God and the Jewish people, rather than between God and individual Jews. Judaism is a religion with a strong ancestral component. Furthermore, there is no evangelical aspect to the religion. Jews have had enough to worry about without inviting more people. Those who wish to convert have to study and pass through a local rabbi's approval process.

Only children of Jewish mothers are automatically considered Jewish, although in some Reform and Reconstructionist congregations, the father's progeny is considered Jewish as well. Otherwise a formal conversion is required. The State of Israel, in applying the "law of return" that makes any Jew an Israeli citizen if he or she returns to the Holy Land, defines Jews broadly, but it only recognizes conversions to Judaism performed by Orthodox rabbis.

There are approximately 150,000 converts to Judaism living in the United States. Some notable converts past and present include: Kate Capshaw, when she married Steven Spielberg; Sammy Davis Jr., after a serious car accident; Marilyn Monroe, when she married playwright Arthur Miller; Elizabeth Taylor, when she married producer Mike Todd; and baseball player Rod Carew. And let's not forget Ruth from the Bible, who said, "Your people shall be my people, and your God my God."

In the United States, the Jewish population has become much more liberal in its practices than its original Orthodox immigrant roots:

DENOMINATIONAL PREFERENCES OF JEWISH HOUSEHOLDS

Orthodox	7%
Conservative	40%
Reform	41%
Reconstructionist	2%
Others	10%

Furthermore, those Jews who are Orthodox are almost exclusively from Orthodox households.[16] The other denominations draw new members from outside their congregants and are growing.

WHY SO MANY COHENS?

An interesting inconsistency in Judaism's maternal lineage can be found in the determination of the class system within Judaism for prayer ceremonies. In particular, some special prayers are reserved for a group called Kohanim. Traced all the way back 3,300 years to the first temple in Jerusalem, a man with male ancestors who were once the temple priests is called a Kohen or Cohen. God chose Aaron from the tribe of Levi and all his descendants to serve as dedicated priests. The "father to son" connection in this case counts the Y chromosome.

A Kohen is authorized to bestow the priestly blessing while extending his hands outward, with the fingers forming a V shape. Leonard Nimoy, Jew not Vulcan, adopted it as the Vulcan greeting in Star Trek. Nimoy said, "I can call that salute my Vulcan shalom, my greeting of peace, my yearning for the blessed peace – the age-old quest of the Jewish people, my people."[17] (William Shatner, Captain Kirk, is Jewish as well.)

About 5 percent of modern Jewish men are actually Kohens. A Kohen-sounding name is not proof of the relationship. Many Jews outside of the authentic 5 percent have taken the names Cohen, Kahn, Kagan or Katz and are not entitled to perform priestly blessings. (Katz has its roots in the Hebrew word KohenTzedek, meaning "righteous priest.") On the other hand, many true Kohanim have totally different names, such as the Silbiger family.

The people who worked as the staff at the ancient temple in Jerusalem were called the Levites. Descendants often use names such as Levy, Levine or Segal. Again, the name is not proof of the heritage. The rest of the Jewish followers were named Israelites, and that is how most of Jews today are classified.

THE JEWISH RACE?

But aren't the Jewish people a race? No. The religion started more than four thousand years ago with Abraham, who was already a member of the Caucasian race at the time and who married a non-Jewish woman, Sarah. For more than forty centuries, generations of marriages and intermarriages have precluded a pure bloodline or race. There is no specific genetic code for the Jewish "race" like the genetic code for skin color. There may be a stereotypical look ascribed to Jews, including darker hair and eyes and larger noses, but these traits are common to all Semitic peoples, including Arabs, and the people from the Mediterranean area.

Let's talk about a big stereotype. How about the "Jewish nose"? Sociologists have shown that the "Jewish nose" is no more common to Jews than to Mediterranean people. In 1914 Maurice Fishberg examined four thousand Jewish noses in New York and found that only 14 percent were aquiline or hooked. The other 86 percent were either flat, straight or something other than the classic Jewish nose.[18] With the small total human population that existed in ancient times, it is no surprise that so many people today share similar genetic traits.

HOW DO JEWS CLASSIFY THEMSELVES?

When asked about what a Jew is, American Jews themselves are mixed on the subject. In the Council of Jewish Federations' National Jewish Population Survey of 1990 Jews were asked: "When you think of what it means to be a Jew in America, would you say that it means being a member of:

(a) a religious group
(b) an ethnic group
(c) a cultural group
(d) a nationality."

Given the opportunity to agree with one or more definitions, Jewish opinion reflected the multifaceted nature of Judaism.[19] Indeed, many simultaneously agreed with several definitions:

(a) a religious group	49%
(b) an ethnic group	57%
(c) a cultural group	70%
(d) a nationality	42%

What is interesting is that *tribe*, as defined at the beginning of this section, encompasses all four categories, including the nebulous "cultural group." Somehow Jewishness is something more than just a religious choice.

But however they define it, 87 percent of Jews polled considered being Jewish an important aspect of their lives.[20] The 1990 attitude survey asked:

HOW IMPORTANT WOULD YOU SAY BEING JEWISH IS IN YOUR LIFE?

Very Important	52%
Somewhat Important	35%
Not Very Important	9%
Not Important	3%
Don't Know	1%

In the context of exploring the success factors of *The Jewish Phenomenon*, the Jewish identity is clearly an important one to Jews, although it is not always clearly defined and sometimes taken for granted. Being Jewish brings with it a cultural, religious, ethnic and nationalist background that has enabled Jews to become successful in the United States.

THE JEWISH PERSPECTIVE ON MONEY

"WEALTH IS GOOD"

According to the New Testament, the Christian world has, at best, an ambivalent attitude toward money and wealth:

"Easier for a camel to pass through the eye of a needle than for someone who is rich to enter the kingdom of God."
> Matthew 19:24, Luke 18:25, Mark 10:25

"You cannot serve God and wealth."
> Luke 16:13

"If we have food and clothing, we will be content with these. But those who want to be rich fall into temptation and are trapped by many senseless and harmful desires that plunge people into ruin and destruction."
> Timothy 6:8–9

"For the love of money is the root of all kinds of evil."
> Timothy 6:10

For Jews, on the other hand, wealth is a good thing, a worthy and respectable goal to strive toward. What's more, once you earn it, it is tragic to lose it. Judaism has never considered poverty a virtue. The first Jews were not poor, and that was good. The Jewish founding fathers, Abraham, Isaac and Jacob, were blessed with cattle and land in abundance. Asceticism and self-denial are not Jewish ideals. With your financial house in order, it is easier to pursue your spiritual life:

"Where there is no flour, there is no Bible."
> The Mishna (a collection of books that outline the detailed laws for daily Jewish living)

"Poverty causes transgression."
> Hasidic folk saying

"Poverty in a man's house is worse than fifty plagues."
> The Talmud (a collection of books of rabbinical commentary on the Old Testament)

ANCIENT JEWISH HISTORY

As it has throughout the ages, their history of struggle and persecution continues to shape the Jewish identity today. The following is an extremely brief history of the Jewish people from biblical times to the present.

According to Rabbi Donin's *To Be a Jew*, "The terms Hebrew, Israelite and Jew have been used interchangeably. Israel was the alternate name for Abraham's grandson, Jacob. Hence his twelve sons and their descendants became known as the children of Israel or Israelite Nation. 'Jew' is derived from Judah, the son of Israel (Jacob), and one of the most prominent of the Twelve Tribes of Israel.

"'Jew' became the popular name used for the entire people when the Judeans, from the Kingdom of Judea, survived the downfall of the Northern Kingdom of Israel in 722 B.C. At that time ten of the Twelve Tribes were led into captivity. Thus today, the people are called Jewish, their faith Judaism, their language Hebrew, and their land Israel."[21]

The Jewish homeland of Israel has been in Jewish control on and off for about three thousand years. The Bible documents three episodes of peril and how Jews survived. In each case, Jewish holidays commemorate these trials and their happy resolution with the help of God. These three major Jewish holidays – Passover, Purim and Hanukah – annually remind Jews that they need to be on their guard and self-sufficient.

PASSOVER

In about 1300 B.C., the Egyptian pharaoh had enslaved the Jewish people and forced them to build the pyramids, the classic story in the Book of Exodus. God chose Moses to lead a revolt and take them back to Israel. When Moses asked the pharaoh to let his people go and the pharaoh refused, God sent the ten plagues to persuade him to change his mind. When the final plague, killing of the first-born sons of Egyptians, took the pharaoh's son, he finally agreed to release the Jews. This terrible plague "passed over" the Jewish households, hence the origin of the holiday's name. However, as the Jews began the trip to Israel, the Pharaoh reneged on his promise and sent an army to catch them. With the help of God, Moses parted the Red Sea, and the Jews escaped to safety. When the Egyptians attempted to cross, God drowned them. The Jews, in their hurry to escape, made flat bread that didn't have time to rise, called matzah.

On their trip home, Moses climbed Mount Sinai and God gave him the Ten Commandments. Unfortunately, while Moses was on the mountaintop, many Jews were rebellious and worshipped a golden calf. As punishment God kept the Jews wandering in the desert for forty years until the wicked generation died and a new generation was born. Finally the Jews eventually made it back to the Promised Land, but they never forgot those times of suffering.

Two Jews are sitting opposite each other in a train. Each recognizes a fellow Jew in the other but they sit quietly for several minutes.

Finally, one leans toward the other with a deep sigh. "Oy!" comes out in one breath.

The second leans forward and observes, "That's just what I was thinking!"

Today, the Passover story is read from a book called the Hagadah at the seder meal held in Jewish households each year. It's interesting to note that two millennia ago Jesus as a Jew led his disciples in a seder meal, the "Last Supper," the night before his crucifixion. The bread they ate was matzah, the forerunner of the modern communion wafer.

PURIM

In about 480 B.C., the mighty Persian Empire was ruled by King Ahasuerus. When his wife Queen Vashti disobeyed him by not entertaining the guests at his party, he took away her crown and led a kingdomwide search for a new queen. His chose Esther, the orphan niece of Mordechai, a wealthy Jewish leader. However, Esther's religion and her relationship with Mordechai were a secret. At about the same time, Mordechai gained favor in the king's court by exposing a plot to assassinate Ahasuerus.

The king's chief of staff, Haman, a would-be Hitler of his day, was intent on consolidating his power in the king's court. It was his command that everyone bow down to him and obey him, but Mordechai refused, threatening Haman's leadership. To do away with Mordechai and all the Jews who threatened his power, Haman convinced the king that the Jewish people were dangerous because they followed a different set of laws that subverted his royal authority. Haman asked for permission to kill all the Jews, and the king agreed.

Mordechai told Queen Esther of Haman's plot against the Jews and asked her to help her people. She agreed to reveal her religion and risk her crown and a sentence of death. Queen Esther planned a grand feast to ask the king to change his mind and even invited Haman.

Meanwhile, Haman was moving ahead with his plan by building a gallows especially for the execution of Mordechai. At the same time, the king had honored Mordechai for foiling the assassination plot and had given him royal robes, not realizing that his other order would bring about Mordechai's death.

At the feast Esther dropped the bombshell. She revealed her Jewish heritage and asked the king to spare all the Jews because they posed no danger to him. She told her husband that Haman's accusations were all lies and advised that Haman should be killed instead. The king's love of his queen was such that he believed her and did her bidding. As a twist of fate he ordered that Haman be hanged on the same gallows Haman had prepared for Mordechai. In addition the king ordered a death sentence for all of Haman's conspirators, including his ten sons.

Today's Purim holiday festival commemorates Esther's feast for the king and her courage. The story of Esther is written on a scroll, called the Megillah, and is read at the synagogue. (Jews often refer to any long story as "the whole megillah.") Whenever Haman's name is read aloud, the congregation, especially the children, drown out the sound of Haman's name with noisemakers called graggers. In addition, as part of the tradition Jews eat a three-cornered fruit pastry called a hamantashen that symbolizes Haman's hat or, morbidly, his head.

HANUKAH

When Antiochus, King of Syria, conquered Israel in 165 B.C., he refused to allow the Jews to practice their religion. The Syrians closed down the temple in Jerusalem and put out the "Eternal Light," a ceremonial lamp that had always remained burning. To protest this injustice, Judah Maccabee led a revolt with a small group of farmers. The Jews were outnumbered and poorly armed, but with the help of God they chased the army back to Syria. When the Jews returned to the temple, there was only one day's oil for the ceremonial lamp, yet it lasted for eight days. The Hanukah menorah (candelabra) celebrates this miracle.

These three historical events inscribe in the collective memories of the Jews a sense that the Jewish people must always be prepared for an attack.

MODERN JEWISH HISTORY

The modern history of the Jews began in 70 A.D. when the Romans completed their conquest of Jerusalem, destroyed the temple and forced a great migration of Jews out of the Holy Land, the so-called Diaspora. The Romans renamed their new conquest Palestine. By the time the State of Israel was re-established nearly two thousand years later in 1948, the descendants of the exiled Jews had spread throughout the world.

During the rise of the Roman Empire, Christians and Jews were two of many religious and ethnic groups living within the empire's boundaries. But Emperor Constantine converted to Christianity and decreed in about 300 A.D. that Christianity would be the official religion of the Holy Roman Empire, which covered most of the Western world. Romans compelled all non-Christian groups to convert or die. The Jews resisted and stubbornly maintained their religion, clothing, diet, customs and language, wherever they settled in the world. Consequently, Jews naturally lived in their own distinct communities, and their isolation bred mistrust and suspicion. In times of strife, it was easy for the general population, incited by those in power, to blame Jews for problems ranging from poisoned wells to diseases to economic disasters.

Throughout the Middle Ages and on into the fifteenth century, large Jewish communities emerged in Spain, Italy, Germany, France and Eastern

Europe, especially Poland and Russia. Governments throughout Europe barred Jews from owning land, so few were farmers. They gravitated to commercial and industrial occupations with trade skills. At the fringe of society and business, Jews were storekeepers, peddlers, artisans, bakers, tailors, small factory owners and middleman merchants. Dr. Sowell's research found that the historical prejudice against Jewish businessmen has also been experienced by other successful trading groups: "Where middle-men are an ethnically distinct group – the Chinese in Southeast Asia, the east Indians in Uganda, and the Ibos in Nigeria – that ethnic group is hated by the masses who deal with them."[22]

Jews often lived in officially mandated areas that were protected by nobility, kings or popes for their own gain. Government officials bene-fited from these communities by levying upon Jews a barrage of special taxes that Jews paid not as citizens, but as Jews: a tax on the right to travel, to pray with others, to marry, to have children, to bury a corpse in the cemetery. In addition, the nobility benefited from the Jews' wealth, commercial skills, international contacts and other technical knowledge. The Biblical injunction against money-lending pushed the Jews further away from the mainstream, when they filled the vacuum for this essential service for commerce.

Further stigmatizing the Jewish people, in 1215 the Fourth Lateran Council, convened by Pope Innocent III, decreed that Jews living in Christian lands were always required to wear a distinctive badge on their clothing. Governments periodically reimposed this requirement on European Jews for hundreds of years.

The gruesome myth of the "blood libel" was perpetuated during these dark days. It was said that Jews required the blood of a Christian baby to bake matzahs on the eve of Passover in a ritual re-enactment of the crucifix-ion. When the body of a child was found in a well in England in the 1200s, the authorities tortured a Jew and forced a confession that he committed the crime as part of a ritual murder. This incident led to the expulsion of the Jews from England in 1290. On two counts the charge is preposterous. Kosher dietary laws prohibit eating of even a drop of blood, and baking on the eve of Passover would violate prohibitions against working during the holiday.

At about this period, two forms of Judaism formed. The Jews of Spain and Portugal were known as Sephardic Jews – from Sefarad, meaning "Spain" in Hebrew. Today 20 percent of Jews are Sephardic. The Ashkenazic Jews evolved in Northern and Eastern Europe, and they account for 80 percent of Jews today.[23] Ashkenaz means "German" in Hebrew. They differed slightly in their pronunciation of Hebrew as well as in some prayers and ritual practices.

In 1492 the Spanish Inquisition compelled the Sephardic Jews to either convert, move or die. In this Sephardic diaspora a few made it to America. Some Jews, called Marranos or Conversos, acted as if they had converted, but lived as "secret Jews" in Spain and eventually emigrated or assimilated. Records indicate that Christopher Columbus himself may have been a Marrano. What is known for sure is many of his crew were Marranos, including Rodrigo Sanchez de Segovia, the voyage comptroller, and interpreter Luis de Torres. De Torres wrote in his diary, "[Columbus] thought that when he would reach China and the Far East, he would locate the exiled Jews from the Ten Lost Tribes, and he wanted me to be able to communicate with them." De Torres was not greeted by Jews in the New World, but his diary entry was still joyful. "And I, Yosef Ben Ha Levy Haivri – Joseph the son of Levy the Hebrew – sang with my friends a different song, a song of thanksgiving to God for leading us to place where we might publicly acknowledge our Judaism." Furthermore, the voyage was not financed by Queen Isabella as commonly believed; Abraham Senior was the primary financier of the historic voyage. In *Columbus and His Discovery of America*, Herbert Adams writes, "Not jewels, but Jews, were the real financial basis of the first expedition of Columbus."[24]

JEWS IN AMERICA

The first twenty-three Jews arrived in New Amsterdam on the Hudson River in 1654. These Jews had been living in Brazil when the Portuguese captured it from the Dutch. Instead of returning to Europe, they made their way to New Amsterdam. Until the end of the eighteenth century, the Jewish community in America remained small, and concentrated in a few of the larger cities on the Eastern Seaboard. In this new world Judaism was accepted as just one more religious denomination, a liberalism that was inconceivable in the anti-Semitic climate of Europe. Perhaps because there were too few Jews to create a visible Jewish presence, they were allowed to live in peace with equal rights. In 1791, just after their Revolution, France became the first European country to grant Jews equal rights.

Ashkenazic German Jews in larger numbers followed these Jews to America in the early 1800s. Instead of remaining concentrated in small communities, they ventured into the frontier as peddlers, tradesmen and professionals among the non-Jews. Many of these transient peddlers opened shops and businesses in the West, planting the seeds of department store empires. Levi Strauss began making jeans. The German Jews prospered but still amounted to only 250,000 of the fifty million Americans in 1880.

A massive wave of Eastern Europeans to the United States began in the 1880s. Unlike the limited early immigrations, two million or one-third of all Eastern European Jews moved to the United States by World War I. With the Russian invasions of Poland and neighboring Eastern European territories, the majority of Eastern European Jews came under Russian rule, and the Russians did not want them. The Russians conducted massive campaigns, called pogroms, to either convert the Jews or brutally persecute and kill them.

The size of the immigration swamped the existing Jewish-American communities, especially in New York City. These Jews came with less education and less money than the prior wave, and with highly distinctive Orthodox Jewish cultural traditions: the long beards, dark clothing, skullcaps, and hairstyles that the more cosmopolitan German Jews had given up in favor of a Reform lifestyle.

Despite their differences, the German-Jewish organizations made a great effort to aid their "poor cousins'" transition. There were caste-like divisions among the Jews, but they worked together when it came to their relationship with the non-Jewish world around them. At the turn of the century, the Jews developed the ready-to-wear clothing industry and employed most of the new Jewish immigrants in New York.

The last large wave of about one million Jewish immigrants came from Eastern and Western Europe as a result of the World War II-era persecutions by the Nazis. The Holocaust or Shoah has remained a fresh and cautionary reminder for Jews to keep vigilant and strong as a people.

The support of Israel as the ultimate refuge is critical in the minds of Jews. And even Israel has been under siege. Three times since its creation – at its birth in 1948, in the 1967 Six-Day War and in the 1973 Yom Kippur War – Israel has been on the brink of extinction, surrounded by hostile Arab neighbors. Each time Israel managed to overcome surprise attacks and overwhelming force to not only win the wars, but also to take the offensive and annex additional territory. For the first time in modern history Jews were not passive victims; they became recognized as a potent military power. Sol Linowitz, former chairman of Xerox, said, "The

Israeli victory in the Six-Day War in 1967 was the end of the image of the Jew as a loser."[25] In the 1980s and 1990s, much smaller Jewish migrations came from the former Soviet Union, directly or via Israel, totaling about 200,000.

This brief overview of Jewish history and the Jewish-American population provides the very broad historical and cultural context for the seven secrets and the success that Jews have enjoyed in America.

CHAPTER 1

Understand That Real Wealth
Is Portable; It's Knowledge

"My brain is the key to set me free."
Harry Houdini (born Erich Weiss), magician

A mind, as the slogan goes, is a terrible thing to waste. The best possible investment you can make in your future is an education. Even if you default on your student loan, nobody can repossess your diploma. It is such a basic concept, but the promise of education often falls on deaf ears. Getting an education requires the ability to defer gratification for a bigger payoff later, an ability Jews have had reason to develop. The value of an education is really not a secret; it is similar to the "miracle" of compounding financial returns given with every pitch for retirement savings. The Jewish secret is how they have come to fully embrace the idea of a good education and execute it. As just one example, after World War II, Jewish veterans took advantage of the GI Bill's educational benefits at a rate twice that of the general population.[1]

My father sat me down as a child and explained to me, as his father had done to him, "how the world works." "If you like to play around, you need to earn your free time. It takes a good education and good grades. Then you can get a good job and make good money. Having earned your way, you can play around for a much longer time with far more expensive toys. Now, Steve, if you get that out of order, the system does not work. You can play for a little while, but then you end up with a few inexpensive toys that eventually break. Then you're left working even harder for the rest of your life with no toys and no fun."

It may sound simplistic but it's true. I understood this very well even as a teen because my father took the time to show me the family checkbook, and show me what living in the United States cost in real-life terms. Clearly you needed a lot of money to pay bills, and an average job often could not provide enough. In the real world, the "toys" in my father's story translated to cars, houses, clothes, stereos, dining out and vacations. If you do not earn these "toys," or if you seek them out too early, the fun quickly comes to an unpleasant end.

Was my experience unique or common to Jewish children in the U.S.? A comprehensive study conducted in 1990 revealed that the educational advantage was very pronounced for both Jewish men and women: 87 percent of college-age Jews were enrolled in college versus 40 percent for non-Jews.[2] In addition, Jews enrolled in schools with higher academic standards.

Another 1990 study found that 78 percent of Jewish males twenty-five and older had at least some college education, compared to only 42 percent of all white males: 65 percent of Jewish men graduated, compared to 57 percent of all white males; 32 percent did some graduate work, compared to only 11 percent of all white males.

Jewish women have also had a great educational advantage over non-Jews, with a 69 percent college attendance record compared to 34 percent of all white females. That might explain why so many Jewish women were among the pioneers of the feminist movement. Betty Friedan founded the National Organization for Women. Gloria Steinem founded *Ms.* magazine. Congresswoman Bella Abzug, as well as other Jewish women, led the way in traditionally male jobs.

According to the April 1999 issue of *Biography* magazine, 50 percent of the "25 Most Powerful Women" were either Jewish or had Jewish parents. The list includes such notables as Barbara Walters; Sherry Lansing, chairman and CEO of Paramount Pictures; and Dr. Matilda Krim, who founded the American Foundation for AIDS Research (AmFAR).

HIGHEST LEVEL OF EDUCATION OF MALES ACHIEVED
By Religion and Age

	Jews 25+	Non-Jews 25+	Jews 25-44	Jews 45-65	Jews 65+
Less than High School	6	22	2	3	16
High School	17	36	9	14	33
Some College	17	18	16	17	19
College Graduate	28	13	35	30	18
Post-Graduate	32	11	39	37	14

HIGHEST LEVEL OF EDUCATION OF FEMALES ACHIEVED
By Religion and Age

	Jews 25+	Non-Jews 25+	Jews 25-44	Jews 45-65	Jews 65+
Less than High School	5	23	2	6	9
High School	26	43	12	28	47
Some College	21	17	19	22	22
College Graduate	24	11	30	24	15
Post-Graduate	24	6	37	21	7

(The CJF National Jewish Population Survey, 1990)

The movie *Scarface* offered a version of the natural order of social progression. The main character, played by Al Pacino, was a Cuban immigrant boatlifted to America in 1978. He explained to his handsome, sex-crazed boatmate how American society works. "In America first you get the money, then you get the power, then you get the women, and in that order." Of course, Scarface pursued a life of crime and died in a rain of bullets, perhaps because he omitted step one. Legitimately, the path to success for any group, including the successful Cuban community, begins with an education. The question in a Jewish household is not whether you will go to college, but where you will go, and which profession you will pursue there.

Gaining knowledge for knowledge's sake is a core Jewish value. But it's also true that wealth flows naturally from knowledge. In the U.S., the progression of income moves in lock-step with education. The values given in the following chart are median incomes since traditional charts of average incomes tend to overstate the truth, with very high incomes skewing the results. The medians are the middle values of all incomes put in sequential order, offering a view of what the "middle of the road" family actually earns.

EDUCATION AND INCOME

Education	Median Household Income
Less than 9th grade	$20,781
9th to 12th grade (no diploma)	$24,575
High school graduate	$38,563
Some college	$44,814
Associate's degree	$51,176
Bachelor's degree	$64,293
Master's degree	$76,065
Professional degree	$102,557
Doctorate degree	$92,316

(U.S. Bureau of the Census: *Current Population Reports, Money Income in the U.S.*, 1996)

My father's advice notwithstanding, Jews pursue education and wealth for much more than the purchase of "toys." Jews have been forced from their homes not just during the big expulsion from Israel by the Romans in 100 A.D., or during the flight from Nazi Germany in the late 1930s and 1940s, but also repeatedly throughout history. It has long been imperative that Jews have portable wealth and skills to survive.

A SHORT LIST OF JEWISH EXPULSIONS

The Crusaders en route to reclaim the Holy Land, 1000–1200s
Germany, 1182
England, 1290–1650
France in 1306, again 1394
The European Black Plague blame-inspired attacks, 1348
Austria, 1421
Spain, 1492
Portugal, 1497
Ukrainian Cossack murders in Poland, 1648
Vienna, 1670

Prague, 1744
Russian-occupied Eastern Europe, 1880s

RELIGIOUS ROOTS OF EDUCATION

For centuries Jews have been referred as the "The People of the Book." Jews bury religious books that have become worn with age and use, as a sign of respect for their contents and out of respect for the written word. From a very young age, Jewish children celebrate education. Rabbi Joseph Telushkin writes, "In Eastern Europe, both parents would ceremoniously lead their children to the first day of school and give them sweets when they learned their ABCs." Isaac Bashevis Singer, the Nobel Prize-winning novelist who grew up in Poland, claimed that the first day of school was more joyously celebrated than the Bar Mitzvah. The page from the Torah text in front of the child, Singer recalled, was sprinkled with raisins and candy to associate learning with sweetness."[3]

As part of their religious training, Jews intensely study the Bible or Torah, the Talmud and the Mishna. The Talmud consists of books of detailed rabbinical commentary on the Bible. The Mishna consists of books codifying the Jewish laws for prayer, religious observance and everyday living. The Jewish religion focuses on the individual and his or her own spiritual exploration and journey. It is therefore important that Jews are involved in spirited discussions and debate about the various stories and laws in their religious texts as a means of forming a personal and intellectual attachment to their religion.

At the core of the Christian faith is what is called the "Great Mystery" with regard to the Immaculate Conception, the birth of Jesus and the Resurrection. These events are accepted on faith, and in conservative Christian circles there is not a great deal of discussion or debate on the matter. As an old bumper sticker says, "God said it; I believe it; and that settles it!" There is also not much discussion about Jesus as a child or teen. This approach to accepting one's religious foundations without a great deal of debate is a major cultural departure from the Jewish tradition. Jewish teachers encourage questions as a way to get closer to one's faith.

In the 1990 Federations' survey, a large sampling of Jewish people were asked about their feelings toward the Torah or Old Testament Bible. The survey clearly reflects a more critical view of the Bible than the typical Christian attitude toward the Old and New Testaments. More than a divine religious book, the Bible is a historical account of the Jewish people.[4]

The Torah is the actual word of God 13%

The Torah is the inspired word of God, but not everything. 38%
should be taken literally word for word.

The Torah is an ancient book of history and moral. 45%
precepts recorded by man.

Cannot choose/Don't know. 4%

Beyond the context of religious readings, critical thinking skills are encouraged and developed in the Jewish community. These highly transferable skills also form the basis for many secular pursuits in the humanities, the sciences and business. It is therefore not so surprising that 40 percent of American Nobel prizes in science and economics have been awarded to Jews,[5] and Jews have won 25 percent of all the Nobel prizes awarded to Americans.[6] Despite a lack of secular educational opportunities throughout their history, the Jews' religious training created a literate and intellectual culture that celebrated academic achievement. When educational opportunities became available, especially in America, the Jewish people were prepared by their family and community environment.

A new flood is foretold. In five days the rain will be incessant, and the world will be wiped out.

The Dalai Lama addresses the world's Buddhists and says, "Meditate and prepare for your next reincarnation."

The Pope holds an audience and tells Catholics, "Confess your sins and pray."

The Chief Rabbi of Israel goes on TV and says, "We have five days to learn to live under water!"

At the turn of the century, Eastern European Jews who had emigrated to the U.S. pursued education to escape the tough industrial jobs traditionally available to new immigrants. The possibility of escaping the Jewish ghetto on the Lower East Side of Manhattan was much more plausible than an escape from the state-mandated ghettos of Eastern Europe. In 1908, 8 percent of

American college students were Jewish, even though Jews represented only 2 percent of the national population. These graduates often concentrated on becoming pharmacists, lawyers, dentists and teachers.[7]

In contrast to current calls for bilingual education, Jews knew that speaking English as soon as possible was critical to their success. At the turn of the century there was a vast informal adult education network where new English speakers would instruct the even greener immigrants about the baffling rules of English grammar and spelling. Karp's *A History of the Jews in America* describes it well: "A tenement house kitchen turned, after a scant dinner, into a classroom, with the head of the family and his boarder bent over an English school reader."[8]

From a sociologist's observation in 1905: "I have met very few wage-workers among Russian Jewish people who regard it as their permanent lot in life to remain in the condition of laborers for wage. Almost all are bending their energies to get into business or to acquire an education so that they may fit themselves for some other calling than that of wage worker of the ordinary kind."[9]

An interesting effort was made in 1884 to provide industrial education to poor Jewish immigrant boys from Eastern Europe. The Hebrew Technical Institute of New York City was founded by German Jews with the best of intentions; however, it was quickly rejected by the immigrants themselves. In Russia carpentry was looked down upon as lower class and parents wanted more for their children than being metal workers or electricians. Eastern European mothers sang lullabies to get their future scholar to sleep, and fathers worked long hours to produce a doctor, a lawyer.

The Jewish advancement in the professions was quick and dramatic. In 1890 there were few Jews practicing in law or medicine in New York City. By 1900, there were four hundred to six hundred Jewish doctors in the city and several thousand in teaching and other professions. In the 1930s, 55 percent of doctors, 64 percent of dentists, and 65 percent of lawyers in New York City were Jewish.[10] This was in spite of quotas restricting the admittance of Jews to institutions of higher learning.

The Jewish example of educational advancement and zeal was not lost on America's non-Jews. Other ethnic groups saw the Jewish education phenomenon and the social mobility it gave them. In the 1920s, an Italian immigrant commented on the progress of his group: "He has not yet learned the lesson which the American Jew could teach him so well; that in America the child of uneducated parents has not only the right but also the duty to rise to the highest rungs of the educational ladder, and thus achieve the success which his uneducated father failed to achieve."[11]

Leslie Cohen described what being a Jew was all about in the 1950s and 1960s: "70 to 80 percent of Jewish children started their school day in public school and attended a supplementary Hebrew school several afternoons a week. The whole process commonly ended with a lavish Bar Mitzvah, a ceremony recognizing a youth as an adult member at the age of thirteen, and led to the entry into high school and an abandonment of Jewish education. In postwar America, a Jew was more likely to get an extensive and intensive secular education than a religious one. One consequence, Jews have postponed marriage and reduced family size. During the 1960s and 1970s, Jews began to attain even higher formal education and greater average income than the rest of the population. This trend has continued into the present and has led sociologists to label Jews as America's most [financially] successful minority group."[12]

> A young stranger in New York was seeking Columbia University, but the many directions he had received only confused him, and he became lost. Luckily, he saw a scholarly old gentleman approaching with a load of books under his arm. He stopped the professional man.
>
> "Tell me, sir, how do you get to Columbia University?"
>
> The old man deliberated the question for a moment or two and then replied, "Study, young man. Constant study!"

JEWISH ROLE MODELS OF EDUCATIONAL SUCCESS

In the Jewish community there are numerous role models for whom a good education translated into high-paying professions. But one area where Jews are noticeably absent is in the world of sports. A running joke is that the book of Jewish sports heroes has only blank pages, but actually there would be a few. Of course there was Sandy Koufax in baseball. And there was Lipman Pike, who in 1866 became the first-ever professional baseball player when he paid twenty dollars a week to play for the Philadelphia Athletics. Mark Spitz won seven gold medals for swimming during the 1972 summer Olympics. Professional wrestler Bill Goldberg ruled the World Championship Wrestling alliance in 1999. There are well-known coaches such as Larry Brown (UCLA, University of Kansas and several NBA teams), Red Auerbach (Boston Celtics) and Marv Levy (Buffalo Bills). In the 1920s Jews dominated in the big Eastern clubs of the NBA.[13] Although not a player, Abe Saperstein took over the African-American team named the Savoy Big Five in 1927 and renamed them the Harlem Globetrotters, a team he then coached and trained. In the 1920s and '30s, Jews made up the largest ethnic group of boxing contenders in all weight divisions. Max Baer was the heavyweight champion in 1933 and wore a Star of David on his boxing trunks. Although he is often mentioned as a Jewish sports hero, he was not even Jewish. By passing as a Jew, though, he developed a loyal following of Jewish fans who supported his career.[14] But overall, yes, the list of famous Jewish athletes is small. For many reasons, including economic incentive, Jews have kept sports as recreational activities and have enjoyed them only when their schoolwork is completed.

From a purely economic standpoint, this lack of interest in professional sports has been a wise decision for the Jewish people. The probability of becoming one of America's five thousand highly paid professional athletes, two-thousandths of 1 percent (.002 percent) of the population, is pretty small. Take the expected monetary value of that outcome (the payoff multiplied by the probability of success) and you get a very small prize. Compare that to the total population of lawyers, doctors, accountants, business owners and professors. Getting a good education to pursue a higher-paying job seems like a sure thing by comparison.

Of course students can use sports to get a college scholarship, but again the odds are very long. How many star athletes does each high school have? How many high schools are there in this country? If the pursuit of educational excellence comes first and sports come second, the odds of success geometrically increase. With a good academic record – not an exceptional one – students have access to billions of dollars in loans, grants, campus jobs and work studies. These means of financial aid put college within reach of almost all Americans if they are strong students. Again, the "rules" of getting ahead in our society come back into play. An athlete's future is only as strong as his injury-prone bones or tendons, while an education, once earned, cannot be taken away from you.

When it comes to role models of Jewish success, there are far more examples than the few pages of this book permit. The following are stories of three Jewish boys who made good. They come from different generations, but with similar life stories that are grounded in a good education.

MICHAEL EISNER, CHAIRMAN OF DISNEY

Michael Eisner was born in Mount Kisco, New York, in 1943. His wealthy parents taught him the value of money, but as a teenager he turned away from a possible career in law or business. He once read a Maxwell Anderson essay that argued that what remains behind in societies are not the wars or the politics but the arts. This inspired Eisner to major in English literature and theater at Denison University in Ohio. Soon after graduating in 1964, he began to work at NBC as a clerk and quickly rose through the ranks at CBS and ABC to become a top TV programming executive. From 1976 to 1984, he was president of Paramount Pictures. In 1984 he took over Disney. Eisner's education in the arts served him well in his chosen career. He created opportunities for himself and was prepared to take advantage of them. *Forbes* estimated his wealth at $680 million in 1999.[15]

SUMNER REDSTONE, CHAIRMAN OF VIACOM

Sumner Redstone was born in Boston in 1923 as Sumner Rothstein. His father, Michael Rothstein, was a linoleum salesman in Boston's Jewish West End. After Prohibition, the elder Rothstein became a liquor wholesaler and nightclub owner, then bought a restaurant. In 1936 he bought one of the first drive-in movie theaters. Having earned enough money, he sent his son Sumner to Harvard, where Sumner studied languages. After serving in World War II, he returned to Harvard to complete his law degree. He practiced law for six years and then joined his father's company. In less than twenty years Sumner expanded the National Amusements theater chain from 12 to 855 screens by drawing upon his legal knowledge to pursue mergers and acquisitions. He made millions on takeovers of Twentieth Century Fox, Columbia Pictures and MGM-UA Home Entertainment. Redstone made billions in his 1987 leveraged buyout of Viacom, a media company that he greatly expanded. In 1998 Viacom owned Blockbuster, Simon & Schuster, Paramount Studios, the New York Knicks, the New York Rangers, MTV, Nickelodeon, and the USA and Sci-Fi Channels.[16] In September 1999, Redstone used Viacom as a springboard to make an even larger acquisition of CBS for $36 billion. *Forbes* estimated his fortune at $9.4 billion in 1999.

THE PRITZKER FAMILY: ABRAM PRITZKER

Nicholas Pritzker came to Chicago in 1881 at the age of ten. He went to night school and studied law. In 1901 he opened his own practice, Pritzker & Pritzker. His son Abram, born in 1896, earned his law degree at Harvard in 1920, and another son Jack, born in 1904, earned his law degree at Northwestern in 1927. Abram and Jack soon became the masterminds behind the successful real estate investments and business acquisitions that helped create a family empire, the Marmon Group. The first real wealth came from the takeover of Cory Corporation, a coffee percolator company. Abram believed in keeping their companies private, instead of subjecting them to the whims of investors: "We do not believe in public businesses, noting that shareholders are shortsighted and that obligations to disclose business deals can compromise the secrecy necessary to make the deals succeed."

Abram's first son Jay was born in 1922 and earned his law degree from Northwestern in 1947. His other son, Robert, was born in 1926 and earned an engineering degree. The two ran the family business for decades until Jay's death in January 1999. Jay avoided risk but loved deal-making, and likened it to boxing: "Hard and fast while in progress, but forgotten when finished." Under their leadership, Marmon bought the Hyatt hotel chain, Royal Caribbean cruise line, Braniff Airlines, Continental Airlines, *McCall's* magazine, Montgomery Securities and Ticketmaster, among many others. Jay's son Thomas took over his father's deal-making duties in 1999 and added thirty companies to Marmon's portfolio of manufacturers. Marmon had total sales of $6 billion in 1999. *Forbes* estimated Robert and Thomas Pritzker's net worths at $5.5 billion apiece.[17]

The stories of many other Jewish notables, high achievers in a wide range of endeavors, will be unfolded in the pages that follow.

SO, THE JEWS VALUE EDUCATION. WHAT CAN I DO?

1. Build your child's self-esteem

2. Build the ability to defer gratification

3. Choose the best education possible

4. Develop and demonstrate informed and literate habits

5. Create the education expectation

6. Keep your skills up to date

BUILD YOUR CHILD'S SELF-ESTEEM

If children value themselves as unique and talented individuals, they will be more inclined to strive for good things. All your lessons about education will have meaning to them. Make your children truly feel a part of a "chosen people," no matter their heritage.

Teach your own family history and teach about your family's ancestral homeland. If your family has many branches, try to concentrate on the two most prevalent so the identity is not diffused. Give your children an international view. Use a globe or maps to show them the world and where they fit into it. For Jews, one of the most profound cultural experiences is visiting Israel, much like Muslims who make their pilgrimage to Mecca.

Having a background and a heritage helps immunize children from negative influences. Those who believe that they live in a huge, chaotic world where they have no real place or purpose tend to be less focused and more susceptible to distractions.

BUILD THE ABILITY TO DEFER GRATIFICATION

Education is a gradual and lengthy process that leads to an uncertain outcome. The skill of deferring gratification is learned in small measures over time.

A parent must begin to provide long-term rewards for positive behaviors at an early age. Rewards can be offered to young children for doing simple household chores, and these can be followed later on by more substantial rewards for good grades. A chart with star stickers culminating in a pizza dinner or toy is just one idea. "Oh, I shouldn't have to pay for grades; they should want them." That is noble, but kids – just like adults – respond better to targeted rewards. Parents should of course warmly give emotional recognition, but there should be a tangible component as well. When an adult is honored as "Employee of the Month," we all know there is more gratification when the nominal prize has a material cash award with it.

"But the emphasis on grades may detract from the learning experience." The practical truth is that the rules of measuring academic success are based on grades, just as college admissions tests are based on numbers. Parents who deny the importance of grades are not being realistic with regard to their child's educational future – although I do not dispute that learning for learning's sake is extremely important throughout life as well.   Personally, I was a poor student. The only classes I made an effort in were the ones that mattered to me: science and history. Science had fun activities, and history was a collection of good stories that I had already seen on TV. Then in fifth grade, my father touched on something that interested me more than school: coin collecting. He promised that if I made the honor roll, he would buy a certain expensive coin set that I wanted for my collection. Unfortunately the goal included doing well in math and English. I hated those subjects and did not care how poor my marks were. During my "silver coin" semester, I actually had to study those subjects, which was not the case with the subjects that came more easily. I missed out on my playtime. But it was an amazing thing: when I studied, I got better grades. What a connection! (Like Oprah made her "connection" between exercise and weight loss.) Those hated subjects weren't that painful when I took the time to study for them. The "I'm not good in math, I'm not good in English" excuses no longer held true. In addition, those teachers who had treated me as an outcast because of my rowdy behavior began to treat me better. I did make my goal, but the prize itself was anticlimactic because I had figured out the school "game." I had acquired the study skills and academic self-confidence that have served me for a lifetime.

Another way to learn about deferred gratification is to invest money in a bank account or the stock market. Instead of your children spending their money on immediate needs, they can monitor their investment and watch it grow larger. The ability to defer gratification is a critical skill that will enable them to enter those professions that require lengthy educations. If children do not begin to learn this lesson at a young age, chances are they will be more apt to live hand to mouth as an adult.

CHOOSE THE BEST EDUCATION POSSIBLE

In his research for *Ethnic America*, Dr. Sowell found that "part of the reason for higher Jewish incomes is that Jews have not only more education but also better education – from higher quality colleges and in more demanding and remunerative fields." A bad mistake parents can make is to send their child to a college that is below his or her abilities. Since part of the education comes from the lessons learned from fellow students, seeking high-caliber students is important. The Talmud says, "As one piece of iron sharpens another so do two students sharpen each other [when they study together]." The child's social environment is also determined by college classmates who become life-long friends, business associates and, on occasion, spouses. The quality of the teachers will also be commensurate with the quality of students.

To find out if an intended school is on the desirable list, consult the latest college survey in *U.S. News and World Report*. The magazine lists all colleges and judges them by a variety of objective criteria. Restricting yourself to the top tier is not an absolute necessity and is not always economically or academically possible. There are great and affordable institutions in the second tier that provide an excellent education and do not require valedictorian status or perfect SAT scores. However, it is important to avoid the bottom two tiers. Junior college should be avoided entirely.

For many, the cost of college is beyond a parent's budget and savings. At worst a student will default on a student loan, but that student cannot reclaim his or her college years. A sacrifice of lifestyle by the student and family for a quality education is a trade-off that is well worth it in the long run.

DEVELOP AND DEMONSTRATE INFORMED AND LITERATE HABITS

Spotting trends and taking advantage of them creates business opportunities. Being aware of the world, locally and internationally, is critical to getting ahead of the curve. This does not mean a singular obsession with the business section of the paper, but a broad awareness of consumer trends, the arts, science, etc. Some of the biggest successes result from spotting a trend or technology and taking advantage of it.

David Sarnoff, founder of the NBC Radio and Television networks, realized early the promise of the new wireless technologies. He was born in Minsk, Russia, in 1891 and his family came to America in 1901. In 1906 his father died and the very young Sarnoff had to quit school and go to work for a cable telegraph company to support himself and his family. Without a formal education as an option, he studied technical books to raise his standing and became a wireless operator. He gained some fame when he was the first wireless operator to pick up the message that the Titanic was sinking in 1912. In 1915 he saw the possibilities of wireless mass communication, and proposed to his superiors the idea of the first radio set that he called a "radio music box." His superiors ignored him. In 1926 when his company was taken over by RCA, he founded NBC, the first radio broadcasting network. As early as 1923, Sarnoff saw the possibilities of television as well, and in 1928 he was given the authority to set up the first television station that eventually became the NBC television network.[18]

When parents demonstrate literate habits, they set an important example for their children to emulate. They show children the value of reading and being informed. Even reading is a form of deferred gratification; it takes time to enjoy a good book, and the pay-off is in the final chapter. Encourage them to watch the news and read the newspaper, and stress the importance of a world view. Parents should have frequent conversations about age-appropriate current events with their children. Your habits spur your children's imagination, knowledge and literacy. With Jewish children, the ties to Israel can give them a world view as they follow the current events of Israel and the Middle East with more than a passing interest. They will become familiar with geography, a foreign language and international events.

Encourage your children to develop a large vocabulary. It accounts for about one third of the SAT verbal section, a prime determinant of college admissions. Get a head start by reading to your child and providing a consistent explanation of new words when they appear in everyday life.

CREATE THE EDUCATION EXPECTATION

In a Jewish household, higher education is considered a natural progression from high school. As I mentioned before, the question should not be whether you will go to college, but where you will go, and which profession you will pursue. If you create a savings plan for college, let your child regularly see the statements. As the investment grows in value, the inevitability of a college education grows.

It may sound simplistic, but beginning a savings program at the earliest age makes the college bill much less burdensome. The financial cost of college is huge, but planning can help avoid decisions based solely on economics. An investment of just two hundred dollars a month, starting at birth, will yield more than one hundred thousand dollars over eighteen years at an 8 percent return. That is enough to cover the average cost at a public institution. If your child qualifies for a better school, there are loans, scholarships and more to cover the shortfall. The big problem is, just as with saving for retirement, the longer you wait, the more financially onerous the monthly savings become.

MONTHLY INVESTMENT REQUIRED TO HAVE $100,000 FOR COLLEGE WITH AN 8% ANNUAL INVESTMENT RETURN

Years until College	Monthly Investment
18 years	$200
16 years	$250
14 years	$325
12 years	$425
10 years	$550
8 years	$750
6 years	$1,100
4 years	$1,800

KEEP YOUR SKILLS UP TO DATE AS AN ADULT

If you want to be a professional in any occupation, you must keep your skills up to date. Just as any doctor, lawyer, accountant or teacher does, even tradesmen must keep informed. It's called life-long learning. With computer technology progressing so rapidly, computer skills are only useful for two or three years. A great Ivy League education without constant updating loses its value. If knowledge can be equated with power, then remaining ignorant puts you in a weaker position in the workplace. Executive education and skill-building courses are investments, not expenses.

Let your children see you continuing to learn throughout your adult years. It will reinforce the importance of education in their minds and will allow you to share with them the educational experience.

CHAPTER 2

Take Care of Your Own and They Will Take Care of You

To safeguard and enhance the health of their community, Jews zealously deploy their wealth and their time for both charity and social action. The numbers are incredible considering the small size of the Jewish population. In spite of the stereotype that they are miserly, Jews happen to be the most philanthropic ethnic group in the country. Their ability to organize and utilize economic power has been a prime source of the Jewish-American community's strength. Their charitable giving not only supports their expanded world community; it also helps individual Jews up the economic ladder.

It is written in the Talmud: "You're only as wealthy as the amount you are able to give." In the Jewish community as a whole, Jews' giving has made them very wealthy. The Book of Leviticus is even more explicit: "You are forbidden to reap the whole harvest; a remnant in the corner must be left for the poor." In addition, Jews understand that when the community serves itself, it also controls its own destiny. According to a Jewish proverb, "He who pays has the say." This philosophy of self-sufficiency applies to humanitarian assistance as well as government lobbying on issues of interest. Jews believe that if your group depends on the funding of others, it becomes subordinate to the funding group.

A short list of facts about Jewish-American philanthropy – and its politics – presents the picture of a wealthy, generous and liberally active community. The average American gives 2 percent of disposable income to charity, compared to 4 percent for the average Jew. The annual campaign for the United Jewish Appeal (UJA) collects about $1 billion annually, drawing from 2 percent of the total population. The United Way annual campaign, in contrast, attracts 32 million contributors and raises $3.6 billion.[1] With the possible exception of the Salvation Army, the United Jewish Appeal raises more money than any other individual charity in America, including the American Red Cross, Catholic Charities and the American Cancer Society.[2]

Total Jewish philanthropic giving totaled about $4.5 billion in 1997. This includes $1.5 billion to federations including UJA, $2 billion to synagogues, $700 million sent to Israel outside UJA (which came to be known as United Jewish Communities in 1999), and $250 million for educational, religious and community relations institutions and agencies.[3] Among the nation's most generous donors, Jews are prominent. *Worth* magazine's annual "Benefactor 100" contained thirty-five Jewish philanthropists in April 1999. The magazine's list is especially relevant because it counts lifetime donations that have already been put to work. Leading the list was George Soros, who has given more than $2 billion to charity. Bill Gates (No. 15 and not Jewish) was credited with $196 million, and Ted Turner (No. 23 and also not Jewish) with $172 million because their billion-dollar foundations remain primarily undistributed.

The impressive amount of Jewish philanthropy is due not only to Jewish wealth but also to well-organized and massive efforts to raise funds for Jewish causes. It serves as a model for other groups that want to create an effective fundraising organization to meet monetary goals year after year.

In the Jewish community, there is always a local Jewish assistance agency. According to the Talmud, a righteous scholar may not live in a town that does not operate a fund for charity. In Europe during the Middle Ages Jews maintained mechanisms to distribute food and clothing for the poor, rooms for travelers, dowries for brides, support for widows and orphans, and burial plots for the departed.

Jews would never have been allowed into America if they had not been self-sufficient. Peter Stuyvesant, the leader of the New Amsterdam settlement, refused to allow Jews into the colony until they promised to care for their own indigent and infirm. In fact, if Jews had not been major shareholders of the Dutch trading company that established the colony, Jews would have been turned away.[4] American Jews have maintained self-help institutions in America ever since, including the Jewish Federation, B'nai B'rith and Hadassah.

Indeed, the dependability of Jewish generosity has given rise to one of the enduring characteristics of Jewish lore, the self-confident beggar or shnorrer.

A shnorrer implored the lady of the house for a morsel of food. Pitying him, she invited him to her table and placed before him a plate heaping high with black bread and chaleh. The chaleh was almost twice as expensive as the black bread, and the beggar did not touch the cheaper variety. Instead he gorged himself on the chaleh.

The housewife, growing more irritated by the minute, finally asked, "Did it ever occur to you that the chaleh costs twice as much as the black bread?"

"I thought of it many times," answered the beggar agreeably, "and believe me, Madame, it's worth every cent!"

In many instances – sometimes in reaction to anti-Semitism – Jewish philanthropy created institutions that have benefited the entire community, including non-Jews. For example, when hospitals did not allow Jewish doctors to practice, Jews built their own hospitals open to all doctors and patients. Jews also started many country clubs and men's clubs because of other people's exclusionary policies. In fact, of all Jewish philanthropists, only 10 percent limit their giving to Jewish charities.[5] Jews are among the largest contributors to universities, libraries, hospitals, museums, symphonies and opera companies.

On the international side, the support of Israel is of paramount importance to Jews and receives very generous support. And when Jews around the world are threatened, Jewish-Americans quickly send money, as was the case with Ethiopian Jews facing starvation and the Russian Jews' resettlement needs after the fall of the Soviet Union. Sometimes the need is acute. The 1973 Yom Kippur War began with a surprise attack on Israel as Jews in America were getting dressed in the morning for High Holiday synagogue services. In a remarkable response to this threat, the UJA raised $100 million in cash in one week for emergency assistance.[6]

More recently, Jewish-American donors are increasing their direct support of Israeli causes and bypassing Israeli governmental agencies. The pace of the Arab-Israeli peace process upsets many, some considering the process too fast and others too slow. Also Reform and Conservative Jews feel snubbed by the requirement that only conversions conducted by Orthodox rabbis qualify the converted as a Jew under the Law of Return that makes all Jews automatic citizens of Israel. Direct non-governmental donations increased from $1.5 billion to $2 billion annually from 1993 to 1998. Meanwhile donations from the UJA to governmental institutions declined 21 percent from $275 million in 1985 to $217 million in 1997.[7]

CHARITY IS DIFFERENT FOR JEWS

Jews and non-Jews differ on their views of charitable giving. Jews are taught that charity is an obligation rooted in social justice, not in love or pity for their fellow man. The word for charity in Hebrew is *tzedakah*, from the root word *zedek* meaning "justice" or "righteousness." The word "charity" comes from the Latin word *caritas*, meaning "love." Likewise, "philanthropy," derived from the Greek, means "love of mankind." Support of social justice is a common theme in Jewish giving because of the Jews' long history of suffering discrimination.

"Upon what does the world rest? Upon a singular pillar and its name is: Justice."

The Talmud

"Jews cannot ensure equality for themselves unless it is assured for all."

American Jewish Committee founding statement, 1906[8]

Judaism is very practical; it focuses on the result. When it comes to a five-dollar gift of kindness or an obligatory gift of one hundred dollars, the larger gift is better because it does the most good. That explains why Jewish charitable institutions give so much public appreciation to the highest contributors. It encourages more giving.

In Judaism, the best donation is the one that aims to create an independent recipient. Moses Maimonides, a twelfth-century scholar and philosopher, determined that there are eight degrees of *tzedakah*:

1. The person gives reluctantly.

2. The person gives graciously, but less than his or her means.

3. The person gives the proper amount, but only after being asked.

4. The person gives before being asked.

5. The person gives without knowledge of the recipient, but the recipient knows the donor.

6. The person gives without making his or her own identity known.

7. The person gives without knowing the recipient and without making his or her identity known.

8. The person helps another by enabling that person to become self-sufficient through a gift or loan, or helping him gain a skill or find employment.

In addition, the Book of Leviticus describes a "holiness code": "Humanity is holy because God is holy, but our expression of that holiness is not, for the most part, through our actions toward God, such as worship, meditation, or sacrifices. The holiness code focuses on our responsibility toward other people."[9]

Another striking difference between synagogues and churches is the practical way synagogues support their institutions. Instead of a weekly voluntary collection, synagogues efficiently collect membership fees from each family much like a secular athletic club does. The annual needs of the temple are budgeted by their boards and the membership fees are set accordingly. Most fee plans allow for some allowances for young singles, new families and seniors in an effort to remain affordable. A 10 percent tithe is not solicited because, given the professional status of most synagogue members, the amount collected would exceed the synagogue's needs. A fee schedule also makes more sense than a weekly collection for synagogues because very few American Jews attend weekly services.

On the other hand, for many casually affiliated Jews and those not so well off, annual dues can be prohibitive. Furthermore, the most important Jewish observances, such as the services for the High Holidays of Rosh Hashanah and Yom Kippur, are often only available to paid-in-full members of the congregation.

It is Yom Kippur. A man comes to the synagogue in a state of obvious excitement. The usher is at the door looking at admission tickets. As the man tries to walk in, the usher stops him: "Let's see your ticket."

"I don't have a ticket. I just want to see my brother, Abe Teitelbaum. I have an important message for him."

"A likely story. There's always someone like you, trying to sneak in for the High Holy Day services. Forget it, friend. Try somewhere else."

"Honest. I swear to you, I have to tell my brother something. You'll see, I'll only be a minute."

The usher gives him a long look. "All right," he says, "I'll give you the benefit of the doubt. You can go in. But don't let me catch you praying!"

JEWISH FREE LOAN SOCIETIES

Another important way in which Jews have helped their own financially has been the creation of Jewish Free Loan Societies to directly help immigrants and others in need. There are about forty of these institutions around the country, and they make about $40 million in loans each year, interest free. Local endowments support these societies, exclusively funded by the Jewish community. As it is written in the Book of Exodus, "If you lend money to my people, to the poor among you, do not act toward them as a creditor; exact no interest from them."

These societies exist to make loans to people with no assets and with little or no credit history, and to loan smaller amounts than banks would typically bother with. At the turn of the century, it was a way for recent Jewish immigrants to go into business and to become self-supporting. In New York City, Jewish peddlers would use their loans to buy their initial merchandise for their pushcarts. Today these loans often go toward a down payment on a house or used car so that a recent Russian immigrant can get to his or her first job.

A surprising feature of these organizations is that most of them have a policy to also lend to non-Jewish people. It is a badly needed community service, and a powerful way to change ingrained prejudices, as illustrated in this story from the *Wall Street Journal*:

Mr. Pham needed money to fly his mother to the U.S. from a refugee camp in Thailand. He was working as a waiter and had little collateral, and a bank turned him down. So he headed to the loan society, which soon cut him a check for $2,000, interest-free. Such generosity was a revelation for Mr. Pham, a Catholic. He had never met a Jew before coming to the U.S. from Vietnam in 1984. Mr. Pham says he had been told that Jews were "mean and stingy" – yet he found the opposite to be true. "Nobody else gave me a loan."[10]

Unfortunately, high loan-default rates have caused several loan societies to recently reverse their nondiscriminatory policies and serve only Jewish people. In Phoenix the default rate reached about 10 percent a year in the early 1990s and nearly all the defaulted loans involved non-Jews. With the endowment in jeopardy, the Phoenix Free Loan Society reluctantly changed its policy to lend only to Jews, but most societies continue to lend to anyone.

For centuries Jews in America have found that similar lending to non-Jews could breed goodwill in the face of historic anti-Semitism. "Jews early on understood that charity was related to an ability to gain respect," said Jonathan Sarna, teacher at the School of American Jewish History at Brandeis University.[11] In 1671, Asser Levy financed the first Lutheran church in the early settlement of New Amsterdam, even though the church's German founder, Martin Luther, profoundly hated the Jews for not converting and persecuted them during the early years of his church. In 1543 Luther wrote, "What then shall we Christians do with this damned, rejected race of Jews? . . . Since they live among us and we know about their lying and blasphemy and cursing, we cannot tolerate them. . . . First, their synagogues should be set on fire. . . . Secondly, their homes should likewise be broken down and destroyed. . . . Thirdly, they should be deprived of their prayerbooks. . . . Fourthly, their rabbis must be forbidden under threat of death to teach anymore."[12] Fortunately, with the inter-faith goodwill first generated by Levy, the Lutheran church did not transport its active persecution of Jews to America. Haym Salomon, a Polish-born Jew, helped finance the Revolutionary War with interest-free loans to prominent colonialists, including James Madison and Thomas Jefferson. Joseph Seligman, founder of the investment banking firm J. & W. Seligman, was the person Lincoln trusted to convince European investors to buy Union bonds to finance the cost of the Civil War. Emanuel Lehman, one of the

founders of the Southern-based investment banking house Lehman
Brothers, went to Europe and raised a great deal of money for the
Confederacy.[13]

SUPPORTING THE JEWISH COMMUNITY
BY PATRONIZING JEWISH BUSINESSES

What better way is there to support your own community and provide people a way to support themselves? It sounds simple, but its effects are profound. Jews were secluded in ghettos of Eastern Europe and in urban con-
centrations in New York; as a result they patronized their own. From the
use of professional services such as medicine and law to meeting everyday
needs by using the local grocery, butcher, baker, tailor, car dealer or home
builder, Jews have a heightened sensitivity to doing business with their own.

The best example of a community business owned and operated by Jews
was the garment industry in New York City. Jews largely created the
American clothing production industry, replacing homemade clothes and
tailor-made clothing. Starting in the 1880s with the waves of new Eastern
European Jewish immigrants, the clothing industry absorbed more than
half of Jewish workers. The jobs were indeed sweatshop jobs; however, the
profits were being created for Jewish companies and for the Jewish community. By 1885, German Jews owned 234 of the 241 garment factories in
New York City.[14] Unlike other ethnic groups, Jews, through their labors,
created the equity that became the Jewish financial capital that supported
the progress of a wealthy and independent community.

Because of their particular needs for prayer services, their Saturday Sabbath
and their language differences, it was almost impossible for most new immigrants to work and live outside the community – adding to the community's
insular and self-serving nature. However, in the true Jewish tradition, parents
pushed children of the second generation toward an education so they could
leave the Lower East Side slum community and the manual factory work, to
become professionals and tradespeople as they had been in Europe.

JEWISH FEDERATIONS AND FOUNDATIONS

American Jews have developed a unique model of philanthropy, which has
greatly influenced America's philanthropic structure. It's the widespread
use of federations and foundations. The idea is to create a pool of assets
and provide mechanisms to fund annual needs, and to develop the infra-
structure to maintain those efforts. Charitable institutions that live hand to

mouth are likely to experience difficulties in the long run. The task of rein-
venting the fundraising wheel whenever funds run low is extremely burdensome. People are often motivated to build a building, but to maintain it
and maximize its usefulness takes a sustained effort.

The Boston Federation, the first of its kind in America, was founded in
1895; a century later there are 178 federations serving Jewish communities
in the United States. These federations are public foundations funded by
pooling individual donations for community services. They are organized in
a group called the Council of Jewish Federations (CJF). In addition, there
are now more than seven thousand independent Jewish foundations funded
by individuals or families with total assets estimated at $10 billion to $15
billion. Some of these private foundations have outlived their original creators, but in most cases the founder or his or her descendants still control
the funding. Twenty-four percent give more than $250,000 per year. Sixty-
four percent give $50,000 to $250,000 annually. The annual giving of all
Jewish foundations and federations totals $3 billion.[15] In 1999, to further
streamline the fundraising process, the CJF and the powerful United Jewish
Appeal (UJA) combined forces as the United Jewish Communities.

"THE MEGA GROUP"

In addition to traditional organizations and foundations, wealthy individuals
create their own special initiatives to give. In May 1998, the *Wall Street
Journal* reported on "a secretive and loosely organized club of twenty of the
wealthiest and most influential Jewish businessmen in America," called the
"Mega Group" or "Study Group." Leslie Wexner, the chairman of The
Limited, and Charles Bronfman, the cochairman of Seagram Co., founded
the group in 1991. Meeting twice a year for two days, members attend a
series of seminars related to philanthropy and Jews. Faced with the aging of
the immigrant generation, the blurring memory of the Holocaust, and the
high rate of intermarriage, the group tries to keep both the philanthropic
momentum and the Jewish identity going. This community of the very
wealthy enables its members to seek partnerships for their individual causes
and learn from one another about their successes and challenges.
Networking sessions exist in other faiths, but there are few from the highest
ranks of business such as this one.

Mega Group members keep a low profile because they do not want to
be in competition with established Jewish institutions. They take on special
projects that they think can make a difference, such as supporting Jewish

day schools or programs like the "Birthright Project," which sends to Israel any young Jew born on this planet who wants to go. In 1997, Michael Steinhardt, former investment fund manager, launched the Partnership for Jewish Education with the support of $19 million; $1.5 million came from six interested members of the Mega Group.

Mega Group members include Steven Spielberg of Dreamworks; Laurence Tisch, chairman of Loews Corp.; bagel tycoon Marvin Lender; Leonard Abramson, founder of U.S. Healthcare; and Lester Crown, investor and part owner of the Chicago Bulls.[16]

SUPPORT FOR ANTI-DISCRIMINATION CAUSES

Jewish support for justice extends beyond the Jewish community to embrace the broader cause of ending discrimination and promoting tolerance. Jewish liberalism stems from an acute awareness of a shared history of persecution and identification with the oppressed that goes all the way back to the time of Moses. In one sense, Jewish support of the liberal agenda is self-serving; after all, Jews continue to be discriminated against. But it also serves the larger community; by working for broad liberal objectives, Jews have made it much easier to form coalitions with other groups sharing similar problems. Jewish people tend to stand on the liberal side of any number of social issues: religious freedom, gay rights, church-state separation, immigration reforms and voters' rights. At the forefront of the fight for Jewish civil rights group is the Anti-Defamation League, a division of the B'nai B'rith organization.

AFRICAN AMERICANS AND THE JEWS

The relationship between the American Jews and the African-American community has been a close but strained one. At the beginning of the twentieth century the bonds were stronger, but the rise of Muslim religious leaders in the African-American community in the 1950s began to widen the rift between them. Some of these African-American Muslims have mistakenly used Jews as scapegoats for their own lack of progress.

Although there were a few Jewish slave owners in the South, Jews were not large players in the slave trade.[17] On the other hand, as early as 1915, Jews were involved with the civil rights movement of African-Americans. The National Association for the Advancement of Colored People (NAACP) was founded at the home of Joel Spingarn, a Columbia University literature professor and a Jew. He was elected board chairman of the NAACP in 1915 and served as president from 1929 to 1939. Arthur Spring, a Jew, served as president from 1939 to 1966. Kivie Kaplan, a Jew, served from 1966 to 1975. Only in 1975 did the first African-American serve as president.[18]

Black philosopher Marcus Garvey in the 1920s and 1930s saw many parallels between the Black and the Jewish experience. He was a proponent of ethnic pride. He researched ancient African cultures, promoted racial independence through competitive economic development, encouraged collective self-help and even called for the revitalization of Africa and repatriation to Africa. He saw the diaspora of African slaves as similar to the experience that Jews faced when they were forced from their homeland in Israel in the first century. Garvey was very close to the essence of The Jewish Phenomenon when he said, "Wealth is strength, wealth is power, wealth is influence, wealth is justice, is liberty, is real human rights."[19]

Garvey denounced discrimination against the Jews and ascribed it to others' jealousy of Jewish economic success.[20] At the same time, emphasizing his self-empowerment theme, he cautioned against relying on Jews, stating that the very racial solidarity he admired made Jews loyal only to themselves. Garvey's program of self-reliance ultimately fell into disfavor as the African American community began to embrace assimilation into the mainstream and social help via government legislation. Only recently has the public rediscovered and studied his ideas.

JULIUS ROSENWALD AND SEARS

Julius Rosenwald, born in 1862, was the son of poor Jewish immigrants in Springfield, Illinois. With his energy, vision and inventiveness, he rose to become president and major stockholder of Sears, Roebuck & Co. He built a regional department store into the largest department-store chain and mail-order retailer in America. With the obligation of *tzedakah* – specifically the type that gives needy people an opportunity to work to earn income – he became interested in the condition of African-Americans. In particular he became interested in the work of two men, Booker T. Washington, the founder of the Tuskegee Institute, and William Baldwin Jr., the founder of the Urban League.

Rosenwald believed that education was the only path for economic and social advancement, and he also knew that in 1911 the schools for African-Americans in the South were deplorable. Illiteracy was common, and spending on schools was at a minimum. In many states half of the blacks were illiterate, four or five times the proportion for whites. Inspired by the enormity of the problem, he financed the building of 5,295 schools by 1931. Often known as Rosenwald Schools in the South, these facilities cost $650 million in 1998 dollars.

But on a higher level Rosenwald's crusade was not against illiteracy; it was against racial prejudice. And he appealed for support from both the local black community (often in the form of the land to build the schools on) and from the white, non-Jewish establishment as a precondition for his support. It gave everyone a stake in the school's success. The words of his appeal were eloquent on behalf of all who suffered discrimination: "As an American and a Jew, I appeal to all high-minded men and women to join in a relentless crusade against race prejudice, indulgence in which will result in the blotting out of the highest ideals of our proud nation."[21]

During the 1940s and 1950s, Jews and African-Americans worked together to enact fair employment statutes via a state-by-state legislative campaign. In the courts, Jewish financial support was crucial during protracted legal battles. Jewish support was also critical in the famed 1954 Supreme Court victory in *Brown v. Topeka Board of Education*, which outlawed school segregation. According to *Jewish Power* by J. J. Goldberg, "The case was decided in large part on the strength of research that convinced the justices that segregation hurt African-American children. The research by African-American psychologist Kenneth Clark was largely funded by the American Jewish Committee."[22]

During the civil rights movement of the 1960s, half the Whites who went to the South during the peace marches were Jews. During the Southern crusade in the summer of 1964, in one of the most infamous episodes of the movement, three young civil rights workers were murdered in Mississippi: James Chaney, an African-American, and Michael Scherner and Andrew Goodman, two Jewish men from New York.[23]

Jews have been heavy supporters of the American Civil Liberties Union and the other civil rights organizations that were critical to the passing of the Civil Rights Bill of 1964 and Voting Rights Act of 1965. In addition, Jews supported fighting discrimination on a case-by-case basis, regardless of race, sex or national origin.

Unfortunately, in the 1980s and 1990s, Jewish opposition to affirmative action based on quotas has pitted Jews directly against many African-American leaders. Quotas have traditionally worked against Jews. Using quotas, the nation's medical and law schools have limited admissions of qualified Jewish applicants because Jews would be over-represented if admissions decisions were solely based on merit. Alan Dershowitz, in *The Vanishing American Jew*, concisely outlined the Jewish position on affirmative action: "Jews understandably have wanted 'pure' equality and are willing to take their chances with it, knowing that they have the inherent ability to excel and to live with it successfully. Centuries of persecution and adversity and discrimination have given the Jewish people this great attribute to compete successfully and with remarkable fortitude."[24]

In 1974 Allan Bakke, a white Christian, claimed that the University of California at Davis did not admit him to medical school because less-qualified minorities were admitted ahead of him. An affirmative-action policy had set a quota of 16 percent nonwhite admissions per year. In Bakke's 1978 Supreme Court victory, three of the largest Jewish organizations filed briefs on Bakke's behalf. All opposed the African-American leadership's position.

In 1998 African- and Hispanic-American leaders raised the issue of racial discrimination in the hiring of Supreme Court clerks, 30 percent of whom were Jewish. The *Wall Street Journal* quoted minority leaders as saying, "This is not ambiguous, this is clear discrimination." Of course, Jewish leaders opposed any quotas. They noted that minority representation among law clerks was in line with their representation in the applicant pool, the top five or ten individual graduates from the top five law schools.[25]

Regardless of the split on affirmative action, Jews were instrumental in the success of the civil rights movement that has provided African-Americans with the opportunity to make their broadest advances in their quest for equality.

EFFECTIVE LOBBYING EXTENDS JEWISH INFLUENCE AND POWER

Jews have been very successful raising funds from Jews and for Jews. But no other investment of time and effort has been as effective as Jewish lobbying of the federal government on behalf of Israel. President Harry Truman was politically instrumental in the establishment of Israel when he became the first leader to recognize the country just after its emergence in 1948. The lobbyist responsible was Eddie Jacobson, a friend and former partner of Truman's in a clothing store in Kansas City, Missouri. Jacobson implored Truman to meet Israeli advocate Chaim Weizmann to hear the case for a Jewish homeland. After the meeting,

Truman decided to recognize Israel over the strong objections of Secretary of State George Marshall, who correctly believed that it would upset Arabs and undermine U.S. influence in the oil-rich Middle East. Weizmann subsequently became the first president of Israel.

During Israel's first years as a nation, the United States offered it very little financial or military aid. The huge influx of direct aid occurred during the Nixon administration in the 1970s under the leadership of Secretary of State Henry Kissinger, the first Jew to hold the position. Aid skyrocketed from $300 million to $2.2 billion annually, making Israel the recipient of more U.S. dollars than any other nation. Today Israel receives 20 percent of U.S. foreign aid, despite being home to just 5 million people.[26]

Of course, this strategic U.S.–Israeli alliance was also a product of U.S. self-interest. During the Cold War with the Soviet Union, Israel supplied a key base for the American military presence and intelligence gathering that would counter Soviet influence in the Middle East. Nevertheless, since the Jewish-American lobby was aligned with the goals of U.S. foreign policy, the lobby's successes launched it into the spotlight. Its international lobbying apparatus, the American Israel Public Affairs Committee (AIPAC) grew from a staff of three to 150 with a budget of $15 million annually. It has grown exponentially in reputation, access and influence. From 1949 to 1996, U.S. aid, loans and grants to Israel totaled $77 billion.[27]

The Jewish lobby has been extremely effective in other areas as well. In the past two decades, the U.S. has established a government office to track down Nazi war criminals, has made emigration from the Soviet Union a central foreign policy goal, and has overseen the exodus of ancient Jewish communities in Syria and Ethiopia. In 1998 the U.S. aided in the return of Holocaust victims' stolen bank accounts in Switzerland. In addition the Holocaust museum, which was built using donated money, was given its land in the Smithsonian complex on the Mall by congressional mandate.[28]

In 1991, President Bush found out how strong the Jewish lobby was when, as he was trying to broker a Middle East peace settlement, he wanted to delay a $10 billion loan guarantee to Israel. "I am up against some powerful political forces," he said. About thirteen hundred leaders of local Jewish organizations from all over the country descended on Washington to lobby their congressmen. Bush went ahead and delayed the loan guarantees and won the battle. However, in the 1992 election he lost the war when Jews became very motivated to support the election of Democratic candidates.

VOTING TO ENHANCE JEWISH POWER
AND PROMOTE JEWISH INTERESTS

Although Jews are a small minority, they exercise their right to vote and thus magnify their voting power. About 80 percent of eligible Jews in the United States are registered to vote, compared to about 50 percent of all voting-age adults. In addition, registered Jews are twice as likely to vote.[29] Combining the two multiplies Jewish voting power by a factor of three.

Furthermore, 81 percent of Jews live in only nine states, making them a significant political bloc, especially on the national level. In presidential elections, those nine states cast 202 of the 535 votes in the Electoral College. Thus, the Jewish population could provide the swing vote in any close presidential election.

JEWISH POPULATION CONCENTRATION
AND PERCENTAGE OF THE TOTAL ELECTORATE

	% Jews	% of Electorate
New York	9.0	18.3
New Jersey	5.5	9.9
Florida	4.7	8.2
Massachusetts	4.5	8.3
Maryland	4.3	8.1
Connecticut	3.0	6.2
California	3.0	6.2
Pennsylvania	2.7	4.9
Illinois	2.3	3.9

(Goldberg, p. 30)

This concentration also extends to party affiliation. Wealthy voters lean toward the right. Yet despite their wealth, Jews tend to advance America's evolving liberal social agenda, thus aligning themselves with the Democratic Party. In fact, Jews are the only major American demographic group whose liberalism does not decline as its income goes up. While only 18 percent of Americans, overall, describe themselves as liberal, 41 percent of Jews so classify themselves.[30] Other studies have placed the liberal percentage as high as 55 percent. On a national basis, according to Goldberg, "about 55 to 60 percent of Jewish voters will vote Democratic almost no matter who is running. Another 10 percent or so will vote Republican, no matter what. The remainder (close to one-third) can be swayed by candidates and their positions."[31]

It is interesting to note that in spite of the Jewish community's deep connections with the Democratic Party, one of the most successful Jewish-American politicians was Senator Barry Goldwater of Arizona. He won the Republican nomination for president in 1964, the first Jew of either party to do so, and is often referred to as the father of the modern conservative movement. Nevertheless, regardless of Goldwater's contribution to the conservative cause, the majority of Jewish people are firmly in the liberal camp.

On the campaign trail Jews are energetic volunteers. According to James Carville, outspoken Democratic consultant, "All you have in Democratic campaigns are Catholics and Jews. I don't know why, but it's a standing joke. You show me twenty-five staffers in a Democratic campaign and you'll have maybe three Protestants."[32]

Beyond being generous contributors and motivated staff workers, Jews also have a greater direct representation to the houses of Congress than their population would dictate. In the 106th Congress of 1999, Jews were represented in the Senate at a rate five and one half times their representation in the population; in the House, the rate was three times greater. In the Senate there were eleven Jewish members (out of 100), one Republican, ten Democratic:

Barbara Boxer	D	California
Russ Feingold	D	Wisconsin
Dianne Feinstein	D	California
Herb Kohl	D	Wisconsin
Frank Lautenberg	D	New Jersey
Carl Levin	D	Michigan
Joseph Lieberman	D	Connecticut
Charles Schumer	D	New York
Arlen Specter	R	Pennsylvania
Paul Wellstone	D	Minnesota
Ron Wyden	D	Oregon

In the House there are 23 (of 436): one Republican, and twenty-one Democratic, and one Independent:

Gary Ackerman	D	New York
Shelley Berkley	D	Nevada
Howard Berman	D	California
Ben Cardin	D	Maryland
Peter Deutsch	D	Florida
Eliot Engel	D	New York
Bob Filner	D	California
Barney Frank	D	Massachusetts
Martin Frost	D	Texas
Sam Gejdenson	D	Connecticut
Benjamin Gilman	R	New York
Tom Lantos	D	California
Sander Levin	D	Michigan
Nita Lowey	D	New York
Jerrold Nadler	D	New York
Steve Rothman	D	New Jersey
Bernie Sanders	I	Vermont
Jan Schakowsky	D	Illinois
Brad Sherman	D	California
Norman Sisisky	D	Virginia
Henry Waxman	D	California
Anthony Weiner	D	New York
Robert Wexler	D	Florida

(*Jewish Bulletin of Northern California*, November 6, 1998)

In some cases their elections are Jewish victories, but not in all. Take the case of former House members Dan Glickman and Larry Smith. "One time Larry and I appeared on a panel together in Israel," Glickman recalls, "and he was asked what's unique about American Jewish politics. He said, 'Look at it this way. Here I am, a congressman named Smith representing South Florida with 200,000 Jews. And here's Dan Glickman with less than 1,000 Jews in his district. And boy, what we wouldn't do to trade names.'"[33]

The other piece of the puzzle that solidifies Jewish political power is its influential financial support. Jews donate or raise as much as half of all Democratic Party campaign funds, partly because Jewish-Americans are the only unified group of affluence supporting the Democratic Party.[34] Again, to quote the Jewish proverb, "He who pays has the say."

THE JEWS TAKE CARE OF THEIR OWN. WHAT CAN I DO?

The crucial point here is that taking care of its own exclusively does not provide a group with its greatest power and influence. A higher ideal, such as "justice," together with highly visible charitable institutions, creates the image of stature and strength. Still, from a purely economic perspective, it is critical to build the community's financial, educational and spiritual capital base. This builds self-esteem in its children and creates the means for them to succeed.

1. Support your own group's community-based and national charitable organizations

2. Create foundations and endowments for long-term self-help goals of your group

3. Minimize support of your local community by members of other groups

4. Organize, vote and participate in politics consistently

5. Patronize your own group's local businesses

6. Support general issues that also support your group's interests

SUPPORT YOUR OWN GROUP'S COMMUNITY-BASED AND NATIONAL CHARITABLE ORGANIZATIONS

The Jews have their local federations and the international United Jewish Appeal – a two-pronged approach to both taking care of their own and advancing their agenda. This approach energizes their base by delivering services and benefits and advancing their group's power by consolidating and coordinating their efforts.

CREATE FOUNDATIONS AND ENDOWMENTS FOR LONG-TERM SELF-HELP GOALS OF YOUR GROUP

Periodic charitable fundraisers are merely Band-Aids. Capital formation for charity is just as important as it is for businesses. For fundraisers, the adage that 80 percent of the money comes from 20 percent of the people is probably an understatement. The ratio is probably 90 percent from 10. By creating a capital base, groups can plan for and fund long-range strategic needs.

MINIMIZE SUPPORT OF YOUR LOCAL COMMUNITY
BY MEMBERS OF OTHER GROUPS

If your community is dependent on the charity of another, it is vulnerable to changes in the political wind. In addition, dependency breeds the schnorrer image that people make light of.

ORGANIZE, VOTE AND PARTICIPATE
IN POLITICS CONSISTENTLY

Money drives the American political system. Elections are getting more expensive and fewer people are voting. Those groups that meet the politicians' needs for money and votes become more powerful and the agenda they espouse takes a prominent position.

PATRONIZE YOUR OWN GROUP'S LOCAL BUSINESSES

In a cycle of community renewal, spending within the community builds the capital base and funds the community's objectives. Financially healthy communities can fund charitable causes and the educational needs of their people.

SUPPORT GENERAL ISSUES THAT ALSO SUPPORT
YOUR GROUP'S INTERESTS

In their quest for "justice," Jewish Americans helped not only themselves, but also many others. As a result, they have built coalitions, earned goodwill and increased Jewish power and influence.

CHAPTER 3

Successful People Are
Professionals and Entrepreneurs

Doctor, lawyer, businessman" is the commonly heard refrain among Jewish people deciding on an occupation. As American Jews have pursued higher education with a passion, many have naturally sought out professional occupations with the same fervor. Many others have become entrepreneurs and independent business owners. Both paths lead to higher-than-average incomes and a great potential for wealth accumulation. The Jewish value of delayed gratification I mentioned earlier – work hard now, go to school, and you will get your reward later – applies here. In fact, it seems that a young Jewish person's choice is not whether to follow a professional or business path but which path to pursue.

A Jewish mother is walking down the street with her two young sons.

A passerby asks her how old the boys are.

"The doctor is three," the mother answers. "And the lawyer is two."

By the middle of the twentieth century, 20 percent of Jewish males were professionals (double the national average), and 35 percent were proprietors (three times the national average). Fifty-five percent of all Jewish men were pursuing white-collar careers with high income potential, while the majority of non-Jewish workers were still in blue-collar jobs.[1] Sociologists characterize the Jews as the first ethnic group for which physical labor is thoroughly absent. By 1970, a scant one-third of 1 percent of American Jews were manual laborers.[2]

Jews have a disproportionately high representation at the nation's graduate schools, the incubators for white-collar professionals. Jewish women attend grad school at four times the rate of non-Jews. Jewish men attend at triple the rate of non-Jewish men. At Harvard Business School, which draws students from all over the world including Europe, the Middle East and Africa, Jews make up 15 percent of the eighteen hundred students. Twenty percent of professors at leading universities are Jewish, and 26 percent of law professors are Jewish.[3]

And the rate of Jews attending grad school is ever increasing. Nearly 40 percent of the younger generation of women and men under forty-five years old attend some postgraduate classes. This trend bodes well for a sustained Jewish income advantage.

HIGHEST LEVEL OF EDUCATION ACHIEVED

	Jews 25+	Non-Jews 25+	Jews 25-44	Jews 45-65	Jews 65+
Postgraduate – male	32%	11%	39%	37%	14%
Postgraduate – female	24%	6%	37%	21%	7%

(1990 National Jewish Population Survey, p. 10)

Upon completing their education, Jewish women seek professional occupations at a rate nearly five times that of non-Jews. In 1980, nearly half of thirty-year-old female Jews had professional occupations, compared to 20 percent for the prior generation. Jewish women were moving from clerical and sales positions to professional jobs when non-Jews were just moving from blue-collar employment into clerical and sales jobs. A 1980 study of Jewish female college freshmen found that 9 percent wanted to become lawyers, followed by elementary schoolteachers, 6 percent; business managers, 6 percent; doctors, 6 percent; and secondary schoolteachers, 1 percent.[4]

THE HISTORY OF JEWISH PROFESSIONAL CHOICES

Jewish occupational choices are not just an American phenomenon. In Eastern Europe, Jews suffered discrimination and were required to live apart from the rest of society; as a result they lived in cities and became professionals, tradesmen, shopkeepers or business owners. Their exclusion from the mainstream of European society – from agriculture, in particular – became the Jews' biggest competitive advantage when they came to America: they arrived with urban skills.

In Galicia, Poland, after World War I, Jews made up only 10 percent of the total population, but they represented 40 percent of the shoemakers, 50 percent of the merchants and 80 percent of the tailors. In Cracow, the region's largest city, 60 percent of the doctors and lawyers were Jewish. Similarly, 46 percent of German Jews were self-employed, three times the national average, and in 1930s Hungary, Jews made up less than 5 percent of the population but owned 36 percent of the retail stores and warehouses.

When Jews were forced to leave Eastern Europe in large numbers at the turn of the twentieth century, they came with less money in their pockets than the average immigrant, but with a distinctly different professional background. About 75 percent of the newcomers from Poland and southern Italy were farmers and manual laborers; 75 percent of the Jews were skilled workers.[5] Jews had been forbidden to own land in the old country but their non-agricultural skills served them well in America.

Seven out of ten Jews had been associated with commercial occupations before migrating, compared to about one in ten non-Jewish immigrants. As Joshua Halberstam notes, "Jews brought with them an ingrained understanding that money was essential not only for the good life, but for life itself. They were determined to manage their own fortunes, and the key to their economic ascent was to become entrepreneurs."[6] The European experience repeatedly taught Jews the value of owning transportable assets and transportable skills.

There were three waves of Jewish immigration before World War II: Spanish Jews before 1700, early German immigrants from 1700 to 1880, and the massive Eastern European migrations from 1881 to 1910. The early Spanish and Germans left Europe relatively well-off; they started out as peddlers in America and later opened stores and became merchants. They also sought educations and entered the professional ranks in great numbers.

The Eastern European Jews made a hurried departure and were much poorer. They poured into Jewish slums in New York, Boston, Philadelphia,

Cleveland, Chicago and Detroit. The Lower East Side of Manhattan was so densely packed that its conditions were considered to be worse than the worst slums in London. Tenement fires were common. Small two-bedroom apartments often housed twenty people, and the occupants slept in shifts. To afford the monthly five-dollar rent, it was necessary to share.

Initially these Jews became factory workers, primarily in the garment trade owned by other Jews. Later they educated themselves and their children and became professionals and businesspeople. The Jewish factory worker was a one-generation phenomenon. As the historian Henry Feingold observes in *Zion in America*, "The Jewish worker was neither a son of a worker nor would he produce a son who was a worker. Middle-class aspirations required that he earn more."[7]

JEWISH LAWYERS

The first Jewish-American lawyer was Moses Levy. He was admitted to the Pennsylvania bar in 1778, and practiced in Philadelphia. Jews were not allowed to practice law in most other countries until the early 1800s, when European governments started to grant Jews full citizenship and opened up the legal profession. Today 15 percent of the 740,000 lawyers in the United States are Jewish. Jewish representation is seven times greater than in the general population. In elite legal circles, the concentration is even more striking. Forty percent of partners in the leading law firms in New York and Washington are Jewish.[8] Jews hold two of the nine seats (22 percent) on the Supreme Court.

JEWISH SUPREME COURT JUSTICES

Louis D. Brandeis	1916–1939
Benjamin Cardozo	1932–1938
Felix Frankfurter	1939–1962
Arthur Goldberg	1962–1965
Abe Fortas	1965–1969
Ruth Bader Ginsberg	1993–present
Stephen Breyer	1994–present

Jews also sit on the bench of the people's TV courts as well. Judge Joseph Wapner, Judge Judy Sheindlin and former mayor Ed Koch are all Jewish. Such impressive statistics require further inspection. Alan

Dershowitz, practicing lawyer and professor, postulates in his book *The Vanishing American Jew* that "students who have rigorously studied the Talmud and other Jewish sources come to law school with a competitive advantage. At law school, the yeshiva alumni tend to be more familiar with modes of argumentation and with other ways of thinking like a lawyer. When I explain to my law students the role of hierarchical precedent in American law – the Constitution, statutes, regulations, practices – the ones who have studied Talmud immediately see the analogy to the Jewish hierarchical precedent: the Bible, Mishna, and so on. The nature of Talmudic argumentation, developed over centuries, parallels legal reasoning in many important respects."[9]

I've devoted a whole chapter to the value that Jews put on education. It follows logically that when Jews go into professions, the law would rank first. Law compares favorably to medicine in a number of practical respects. There are no undergraduate requirements for entering law school. There are many law schools, and a degree takes only three years. Unlike doctors, who deliver their services on a one-to-one basis, lawyers can hire young lawyers, researchers and assistants to help. That enables lawyers to take on large class-action suits, corporate litigation and many personal-injury cases simultaneously, enhancing their earning power. In the largest New York law firms, with their Wall Street clients, partners' average salary was $1,043,201 in 1995. It was $418,480 in Washington, D.C., and $311,446 in Chicago.

LAWYERS' INCOME DISTRIBUTION
(all lawyers)

More than $100,000	31%
$80,000 – $100,000	13%
$60,000 – $80,000	19%
$40,000 – $60,000	15%
$20,000 – $40,000	11%
Less than $20,000	11%

Median Incomes	
Law firm partners	$135,000
All lawyers	$72,100

(Andrew Hacker, *Money: Who Has How Much and Why* [1997], p. 124)

In this century anti-Semitism has been a constant problem for Jewish lawyers. Until the 1950s quotas limited Jewish law-school admissions to 10 percent.[10] Since the large prestigious firms did not hire Jews, Jews started their own firms and hired their own; in 1950, 85 percent of Jewish lawyers entered Jewish firms. Jewish firms were in turn hired by Jewish businesses and individuals. Many Jews went into specialties that were less appealing and less rewarding. These included taxation, bankruptcy, personal injury, estate work and bill collecting. The prestigious firms concentrated on corporate law. It was striking that when Justice Frankfurter was a top professor at Harvard in 1936, eight Jewish editors of the *Harvard Law Review* could not find jobs. He wondered bitterly "whether this school shouldn't tell Jewish students that they go through . . . at their own risk of ever having opportunity of entering the best law firms."[11] When he went to Washington to serve on the Supreme Court, he hired many Jews as his clerks. Many Jewish lawyers also went to work for the government in Washington, giving them an inside track to the growing and complex practice of tax law.

After World War II, the demand for lawyers began to outstrip the supply. In the big firms, however, old-timers continued to blackball Jews coming up for partnership, and change came slowly. The large firms that once served their clients' total needs began to require outside help for increasingly complex areas such as labor, securities and tax law. Corporations formed internal law departments to handle issues in-house, and these groups began consulting the specialists, bypassing their old law firms. Many of the specialties that Jewish lawyers had pursued became very lucrative, especially securities law. Skadden, Arps (Slate, Meagher & Flom) is a prime example of a prestigious Jewish firm that pioneered in and leads the field of securities litigation. Brooklyn-born Joseph Flom earned well in excess of $1 million annually during the 1980s. His family came a long way in one generation; his Eastern European father manufactured shoulder pads.

The Jewish family dynamic that fosters debate and argument also supports a career in law. Young Jewish children are encouraged to ask questions about their religion and just about everything else; the law requires similar cognitive and verbal skills. And not to downplay the role of money, the law profession's potential for high income and status has been a magnet for insecure Jewish immigrant populations wanting a way to climb the social ladder.

The law is not for everybody. Nearly a third of all lawyers leave the profession; however, legal training and skills are invaluable and transferable to business careers, as many of the biggest Jewish success stories can attest.

JEWISH DOCTORS

Jewish doctors have practiced medicine in America since colonial times. Jacob Lumbrozzo was the first Jewish-American doctor, arriving in Maryland in 1656. The American Medical Association estimates that there are now 684,000 doctors in the United States. Jewish physicians total about 100,000, or 15 percent. Like lawyers, this number is seven times higher than the Jews' share of the general population. Nine percent of 1988 medical school applications came from Jews. But Jews have had their share of barriers to obtaining degrees in the U.S.

In 1934, 60 percent of all medical school applicants were Jewish. But because of a discriminatory quota system in the 1930s, medical schools' student bodies were only 17 percent Jewish. Those students who were rejected often pursued careers in pharmacy or dentistry. Jews of that era used to joke that "D.D.S." after one's name stood for "disappointed doctor or surgeon."[12] Some years later, Monty Hall graduated in the top of his pre-med class and was rejected twice for medical school admission. He wanted to become a doctor, not the emcee of *Let's Make a Deal!*[13]

Until the 1960s Jewish doctors were confined, for the most part, to Jewish-sponsored hospitals. Since medicine is primarily pursued as an independent practice, anti-Semitism and exclusion did not significantly hamper the success of Jewish doctors. Jews built their own hospitals that served all races and creeds. When barriers to mainstream institutions fell, Jewish doctors joined faculties of prestigious medical schools. By 1969, Jews comprised nearly one-fourth of medical school faculties.

As in other professions, economics is a large part of the attraction of medicine. The investment of nearly a decade in one's medical education eventually has its financial rewards. When compared to a lawyer, a doctor's average income is higher, but the potential for extraordinary wealth is limited by the personal nature of medical services. In addition, the investment in education makes the profession a very difficult one to walk away from.

PHYSICIANS' INCOME DISTRIBUTION
(in private practice)

More than $400,000	5%
$300,000 – $400,000	5%

$200,000 – $300,000	23%
$150,000 – $200,000	17%
$100,000 – $150,000	27%
Less than $100,000	23%

Median Incomes

Private practice	$176,000
All physicians	$150,000
Salaried	$59,280

Median Physician Incomes by Specialty

Orthopaedic surgeon	$304,000
Cardiologist	$295,000
Radiologist	$282,000
General surgeon	$242,000
Anesthesiologist	$220,000
Pathologist	$215,000
Ophthalmologist	$215,000
Urologist	$213,000
Otolaryngologist	$207,000
Obstetrician/gynecologist	$200,000
Emergency medical	$185,000
Internist	$150,000
Psychiatrist	$137,000
Family medicine	$122,000
Pediatrician	$113,000

(Hacker, p. 126)

Income potential for physicians has recently become less rosy, as HMOs are hiring doctors for salaries averaging $100,000 to $150,000 a year plus bonuses. During years of residency, earnings are lower still, bringing the salaried doctor's average income to only $59,280 in 1995.[14]

JEWISH MEDICAL HISTORY

Jewish involvement in medicine goes back centuries. In medieval Europe, Jews frequently represented 50 to 60 percent of all physicians although they only made up 3 to 5 percent of the total population. To cite one example, the municipal records of Perpignon over a period of two centuries listed 67 Jews out of 120 total physicians.[15] A similar disproportion existed in fourteenth-century Aragon. It is possible that the occupation and skills were passed down as a family tradition from generation to generation. In 1881, 61 percent of Vienna's practicing physicians were Jewish and as late as 1938 the figure was nearly 50 percent.[16]

NOSTRADAMUS: JEWISH DOCTOR AND PROPHET

Although Nostradamus is one of the most studied prophets of the modern world, not many people know he was Jewish. Michel de Nostradame was born in France in 1503. His fame has grown from his uncanny predictions of the distant future, including the stock market crash of 1929 and the Kennedy assassination. From an early age, he showed a talent for prophecy and was a student of mathematics, astrology, Greek, Latin and Hebrew. Both his grandfathers were court physicians and were influential in Michel's education. They taught him traditional medical techniques and herbal folk medicine, as well as the forbidden arts of Kabbalah mysticism and alchemy.

When King Louis XII ordered all Jews be baptized, Nostradamus's family complied, but continued to practice their true faith in secret. Michel entered medical school in 1522, but was greatly dissatisfied with the ignorance of his teachers about such matters as personal hygiene and the dangers of bleeding and catharsis. Nostradamus graduated, but decided to use his own philosophies in his practice; he treated victims of the bubonic plague using his own prescription of fresh, unpolluted air and water and clean bedding. In addition, he ordered that corpses be removed and streets cleaned daily. He was at least three hundred years ahead of his time in his quest for sanitary conditions, noting their connection to disease and infection. He also prescribed his own folk medicine of herbal "rose pills." He was reputed to have saved thousands of lives in France, but he could not save his own family from that same plague in 1537.

His reputation destroyed, Nostradamus traveled throughout Europe, where he began his career as a prophet. In 1554 he wrote his first book of prophecy and became a favorite of Queen Catherine de Medici of Italy. His books are still scrutinized today as a source of amazing predictions, but few recognize him as the progressive Jewish doctor he was. Fortunately, his predictions of world war and Armageddon in July 1999 did not come true.[17]

JULIUS AXELROD: BRAIN PIONEER

Dr. Axelrod is a case study in how Jews have persevered in the face of discrimination and found creative ways to pursue their ambitions. Born in New York in 1912, Axelrod wanted to be a doctor, but restrictive quotas kept him out of medical school. Instead, he went into medical research. He earned his Ph.D. at Washington University in St. Louis in 1955 and worked at the National Institutes of Health in Maryland. He discovered the neurotransmitter, the basis for nerve impulse transmission. This discovery paved the way for treatments of all types of nervous system disorders. In 1970 he shared the Nobel Prize in medicine with his colleagues Bernard Katz and Ulf von Euler (not Jewish).

Many such stories exist, many discoveries and Nobel Prizes. As I mentioned in the introduction, 40 percent of all Nobel prizes awarded to Americans in science and medicine have gone to Jews. A short sampling of Jewish people in the health field includes:[18]

Casimir Funk – discovered vitamins and coined the term (1912).

Waldemar Mordecai Haffkine – discovered the cholera vaccine (1892).

Baruj Benacerraf – established the area of transplant immunology (Nobel Prize 1980).

Robert Barany – pioneered in the area of modern ear medicine (Nobel Prize 1914).

Baruch Blumberg – discovered the vaccine for hepatitis B (Nobel Prize 1976).

Paul Ehrlich – pioneered in the field of immunology and hematology (Nobel Prize 1908).

Willem Einthoven – invented the electrocardiogram (EKG) (Nobel Prize 1924).

Karl Landsteiner – discovered the human blood groups A, B, and O (Nobel Prize 1930).

Tadeus Reichstein – discovered adrenal hormones, including cortisone (Nobel Prize 1950).

Jonas Salk – discovered the first live virus vaccine for polio, delivered by injection (1952).

Albert Sabin – discovered the first dead virus vaccine for polio, delivered orally (1956).

Selman Waksman – developed the first antibiotics, including streptomycin (Nobel Prize 1952).

Adrian Kantrowitz – performed the first heart transplant in America (1967).

JEWISH BUSINESS ENTREPRENEURS

The entrepreneurial spirit burns strongly in the Jewish community. Entrepreneurial business formation is not wholly separate from medicine and the law, because those two professions often lead to private practices, which in fact are small, independent proprietorships.

In general, American Jews have nearly twice the self-employment rate of other ethnic groups in the U.S., a ratio similar to that in Great Britain and Europe.[19] Only 4 percent of Laotian and Puerto Rican immigrants are entrepreneurs. At the top are Korean and Israeli immigrants, with rates approaching 30 percent. This entrepreneurial drive is crucial to Jewish success, as 80 percent of millionaires in the U.S. are self-made and did not inherit their wealth.[20]

What Jewish experience gives rise to entrepreneurship? The common theme here is the feeling of an outsider. Running your own business appeals to individuals who want to control their own destinies and don't want to be subject to the whim or bigotry of an employer. Also, traditional job opportunities often were not available for Jews generations ago, so it was imperative that they find another path. Jews were shut out of the traditional old-line industries of insurance, automobiles, steel, coal, chemicals and heavy machinery. Earlier in the century, most insurance companies would not even issue policies to businessmen if they were Jewish.

Jews were apt to take more risks associated with running their own business because of this feeling of isolation. As Halberstam writes in *Schmoozing*, "If you are less invested materially and psychologically in the status quo the more comfortable you feel to take risks to try something new."[21] Comedian Jackie Mason jokes, "A Gentile works so that he can get the key to the men's room; a Jew works to get a key to the vault." The "vault" he refers to is the wealth of knowledge about how the business operates, so that the Jewish worker can start his or her own.

Entrepreneur is used so often today in the popular press it almost loses its meaning. Entrepreneurism takes many forms in business. According to

Karl Vesper, there are ten types of businesspeople, and many Jews have been successful as each type.[22]

1. Self-employed individuals: tradespeople, store owners, jewelers and diamond traders, and personal-service professionals who do the majority of the skilled work themselves. Doctors, lawyers, accountants and dentists as sole practitioners are included.
2. Team builders: craftspeople or professionals who hire others to perform their duties in order to expand their business, such as law firms, medical practices and accounting firms. For example, Henry and Richard Bloch created H&R Block, the national tax accounting firm. (The spelling "Block" was used to avoid mispronunciation.)

3. Independent inventors and innovators:

   Levi Strauss – invented jeans.

   Lillian Vernon (Hochberg) – catalog innovator.

   Helena Rubinstein – pioneered the modern cosmetics industry.

   Paul Fireman – developed Reebok athletic shoes for aerobics.

   Reuben Mattus, Ben Cohen & Jerry Greenfield – pioneered the premium ice cream business with Haagen Dazs and Ben & Jerry's, respectively.

   S. Daniel Abraham (SlimFast), Jean Nidetch (Weight Watchers), Harold Katz (Nutri/System), Sid and Jenny Craig (Jenny Craig) – weight loss entrepreneurs.

4. Pattern multipliers: expand business by franchising and chain expansion.

   Bernard Marcus and Arthur Blank – started The Home Depot, hardware category giant.

   Leslie Wexner – started The Limited, a clothing store found in most malls.

5. Economy of scale exploiters: produce more products at lower cost to build a business.

   The New York garment industry was founded by Jewish immigrants at the turn of the twentieth century and quickly began to replace tailored and homemade garments as the primary way Americans clothed themselves. Mechanization and the development of industrial techniques speeded the process, which began as low-tech sweatshop production. In the garment industry today, Calvin Klein, Ralph Lauren, Liz Claiborne, Donna Karan and Guess? are all firms owned and operated by Jews. Calvin's first name was Richard and Ralph's last name was Lifshitz.

6. Capital aggregators: pull together capital to create a financial service business.

Salomon Brothers, Goldman Sachs – investment banking firms.

7. Acquirers: buy businesses as a means to expand or get into businesses. Ron Perelman – Revlon, Marvel Entertainment, New World Communications, Coleman, MacAndrews & Forbes.

Henry Silverman – Formed HFS and bought the Ramada hotels, Howard Johnson motels, Super 8 motels, Park Inn motels and Avis, then bought CUC International and formed Cendant Corp.

8. Buy/sell artists: buy and sell businesses at a profit.

Robert and Laurence Tisch – Loews Theaters and Hotels, CBS, real estate, CA Financial, Bulova, Lorillard Tobacco.

Carl Ichan – hostile takeovers of TWA, Texaco and USX.

9. Conglomerators: use the equity of an existing business to buy others.

Sumner Redstone – bought media businesses and Viacom based on the equity of his family's theater chain, National Amusements. Then he bought CBS with the equity of Viacom.

Ziff family – purchased multiple publishing companies based on humorous *Ziff's* magazine equity founded in 1923: *Car & Driver*, *PC Magazine*, *Stereo Review*, *Popular Photography*, *Flying* and many more; sold assets in 1994.

Samuel I. (Si) and Donald Newhouse – their father, Samuel Sr., started the *Staten Island Advance* in 1922 and founded Advance Publications. With the equity, he bought Random House, fifteen Conde Nast magazines (*Vanity Fair*, *New Yorker* and *Vogue*), twenty-nine newspapers, radio stations and cable channels.

10. Speculators: make money through investments of stocks, bonds, securities, real estate and commodities.

George Soros – international speculator in currencies and securities.

Michael Milken – saw the opportunity and created the market for corporate high-yield bonds, which supported the leveraged buyout boom of the 1980s. This was especially true for high-tech companies for which he raised $30 billion, including Turner Broadcasting, Viacom and MCI. After taking his good ideas to extremes, Milken briefly ended up in prison for numerous securities violations.

Sam Zell – bought Midwest real estate in the 1970s, rehabbed the properties and sold them for big gains. Through real estate funds, he buys $4 billion worth of properties a year.

JEWS AND REAL ESTATE

Some of the great Jewish fortunes have been made in real estate. Of the 1999 "Forbes 400" list of wealthiest Americans, 23 percent were Jewish, and of those, 20 percent created their wealth in real estate. Because real estate uses a high degree of financial leverage (borrowing with little capital), it has a huge upside potential if property values increase. It was fortunate for Jewish immigrants that they came to America as an urban people and settled in its largest cities. With the increasing importance of these cities for industry and commerce, especially New York City, property values skyrocketed and made many Jewish real-estate millionaires. In addition, Jewish real estate brokers used their large commissions as down payments on their initial properties. Then, using those first properties for leverage, they acquired many more.

As Jews moved away from the Lower East Side in New York, real estate opportunities also grew. Historically Jews had avoided fixed investments because of their many expulsions, yet real estate was far too powerful a magnet. "Jews had to be smart, quick and facile, with a head for numbers – and that's real estate," says Richard Ravitch, a former head of a New York construction company.[23] In some of the first suburban moves to Brownsville, New York, early in the century, lot prices increased from fifty dollars to three thousand in two years. According to *When Harlem Was Jewish*, "by the 1920s, 40 percent of New York City builders and developers were Jewish. Some had been carpenters or painters, others storekeepers or garment manufacturers who had invested their small savings to buy first one tenement, then another, ultimately graduating to construction on their own."[24] The founders of the Tishman real estate empire initially owned a tiny dry goods store, and the Rudin real estate fortune began with a single grocery store.

The other attractive aspect of real estate was that an impersonal market – rather than anti-Semitic and bureaucratic superiors – would judge a Jew's efforts. "Jews go where they can make a good living," said Walter Shorenstein, a very successful San Francisco real estate developer, in 1983. "Where were we going to go forty years ago – the phone company? We lived in a society where there were very few places on the corporate ladder where Jews could be coequal." Shorenstein grew up on Long Island and moved with his wife to San Francisco after getting out of the military in 1946. He worked as a broker of industrial properties. In 1951 he became a partner in his firm and in 1960 he bought out his boss. By 1999 he controlled 25 percent of San Francisco's downtown office space, including the BankAmerica tower, as well as large holdings across the country. In 1999, *Forbes* estimated his net worth at $800 million.

In the real estate industry, it is said that what is lacking is not money but ideas. There are plenty of investors available for a good deal. Abraham Levitt and his son William Jaird Levitt, both from Brooklyn, had the idea to mass-produce housing to meet the acute postwar need. Mass production would lower costs and increase the speed of construction. Levitt & Sons produced cookie-cutter–style houses in assembly-line fashion in large "Levittown" communities in New York, Pennsylvania and New Jersey.

Melvin Simon was born the son of a tailor in New York City. He went to work as a leasing agent for shopping centers in the early 1950s, drawing one hundred dollars against his commissions each month to live on. "Meshugener [crazy man] Simon," as friends call him, realized that building shopping centers with movie theaters would more effectively use the real estate, since theaters could use the parking lots at night after stores were closed. He went into business for himself in 1959 and has since built hundreds of shopping centers across the Midwest and the rest of the country, including the Mall of America in Bloomington, Minnesota, the nation's largest. With the 1996 merger of Simon's company and the DeBartolo Group, Simon DeBartolo became the country's largest mall owner. *Forbes* estimated Simon's fortune at $600 million in 1999. Other Jewish mall moguls include Guilford Glazer and Alfred Taubman.

In addition to shopping malls, Jewish businessmen have been involved in the hotel business. Isadore Sharp created the Four Seasons hotel chain. His father Max, with little money, would build a house, move the family in, decorate it and then sell it. By the time "Issy" was sixteen, his family had moved fifteen times. Beginning with a small hotel in Toronto, his company built a chain of forty-five luxury hotels in seventeen countries.[25] Henry Silverman's HFS entered the more moderately priced room market in 1990 by acquiring established chains. HFS bought the Ramada, Super 8 and Howard Johnson chains and subsequently merged with CUC International to create Cendant Corp. in 1997. In 1991, Barry Sternlicht began using the public financial vehicle called a Real Estate Investment Trust (REIT) to pool investors' money to buy lodging assets as well. His Starwood Hotels & Resorts had acquired seven hundred upscale hotels by 1998, with assets of over $20 billion – including Sheraton hotels, Westin hotels, Doral hotels, St. Regis hotels, the "W" hotels and Caesar's World casinos.

As with any ethnic group, Jews have not always been on the right side of the law. The book *Tough Jews* chronicles the rise of Jewish mobsters in turn-of-the-century New York City. One of the most famous was Benjamin "Bugsy" Siegel. In 1945 he saw his opportunity in the Nevada desert near the Hoover Dam, a five-hour drive from Los Angeles. Nevada was the only state to have both legal gambling and prostitution. On Highway 9 in Las Vegas near the New Frontier and the El Rancho Vegas casinos, Bugsy had a vision of turning a few seedy gambling halls into an American Monte Carlo. He had failed to get his own Hollywood career off the ground, so he saw this as his chance to get into show business and make a fortune. Siegel's underworld friend Meyer Lansky had made his fortune during Prohibition and later with illegal gambling. Lansky was sold on Siegel's vision and helped him buy the El Cortez for $614,000 in 1945. But because of management problems, Siegel had to sell it a year later for $780,000. In a much more ambitious project in 1946, with help from Lansky and the Italian crime families, Siegel built the Flamingo Hotel, which revolutionized modern gaming. His casino was intended to make gambling "sophisticated," mainstream and affordable. Instead of being a smoky poker hall, it included a luxury hotel, a nightclub with Hollywood headliners, a golf course, a shopping mall and the all-important casino. Bugsy allegedly skimmed casino revenues and was executed in 1947 gangland-style, destined never to see his dream fully realized. His idea, however, created billions in profits for others.[26]

Harry Helmsley started working for twelve dollars a week in the mailroom of a New York City real estate firm in the 1930s. He quickly moved up to collecting rents, then to brokering buildings. In 1936 he invested one thousand dollars of his brokerage commissions into a building, and soon began buying a series of unassuming properties. With Lawrence Wien he pioneered real estate syndication, in which large groups of investors pooled their money to buy larger buildings. He bought prime New York City buildings in the 1950s and the Empire State Building in 1961. In 1972 he married condo broker Leona Rosenthal, who later said, "Only the little people pay taxes," and spent eighteen months in jail for senseless tax evasion, prisoner No. 15113-054. He also became a Quaker. At the time of his death in 1997, Helmsley owned or controlled through his partnerships "100 million square feet of commercial space, more than 100,000 apartments and 5,000 hotel rooms"; his net worth was $1.8 billion.

Other Jewish Forbes 400 members in 1999 with real estate fortunes include:

Robert Pritzker	$5.5 billion
Thomas Pritzker	$5.5 billion
Marvin Davis	$3.5 billion
Donald Bren	$3.2 billion
Leonard Stern	$2.4 billion
Robert Tisch	$2.3 billion
Laurence Tisch	$2.1 billion
Samuel LeFrak	$2 billion
Sam Zell	$1.8 billion
Fisher family	$1.3 billion
Durst family	$1.3 billion
Mortimer Zuckerman	$1.2 billion
Carl Berg	$950 million
Alfred Taubman	$860 million
Sheldon Solow	$800 million
Guilford Glazer	$700 million

JEWISH FINANCIERS AND WALL STREET

Anti-Semites love to tell stories about evil Jewish bankers locked in sinister worldwide conspiracies to bring about world destruction. The *Protocols of the Elders of Zion*, for example, was a famous document that Henry Ford and others pointed to in the 1920s and '30s as proof that Jewish financiers worked together with Bolsheviks to take over the world. In fact, a Russian monk working as an agent of the Russian secret police had created it in 1900. Although the document was exposed as a hoax in the *London Times* in 1921, it is incredibly still in print.

Even before the "conspiracy," Jews were at the center of the modern banking system. The early Catholic Church issued rules against the practice of usury, charging interest for lending money. Because this function is central to commerce, it drove banking underground and into the hands of Jews. The Council of Reims in 1049 reiterated the ban on usury. However, the Council did not ban charging a fee for currency exchanges or creating equity agreements to participate in the profits of ventures funded with borrowed money.

Although the Jews played an integral role in early banking activities, they were excluded from the institutional, commercial banking system. The Medici bank of Italy made loans masquerading as "Bills of Exchange" and created an extensive network of banks across Europe during the Renaissance. By the late 1400s, however, the Medici Bank had become insolvent because of bad loans, especially to nobility and other well-connected people. The Bank of England became the next leader of traditional banks and filled the void left by Medici.

In the nineteenth century, European Jewish banking entrepreneurs emerged and actually created the "merchant banking" or "investment banking" industry. The House of Rothschild was the most prominent in the sale and trading of commercial obligations. These Jewish bankers pioneered the idea of selling state-backed bonds to finance emerging industries and railroads.[27] Other Jewish banking houses quickly followed: Bleichroder in Berlin, Warburg in Hamburg, Oppenheim in Cologne, Speyer in Frankfurt, the Sassoons in Bombay and Haym Salomon, a supporter of the American Revolution.

The distinction between commercial banking, a field from which Jews were traditionally excluded, and investment banking, pioneered by Jews, requires a bit more explanation if you are not part of the financial industry. Traditional banking includes taking in deposits and making loans to individuals and businesses in separate transactions. Investment bankers act as financial intermediaries by raising private investment capital and matching that with businesses in need. The investors directly fund these companies in exchange for equity ownership or a bond obligation. Investors make their own investment decisions rather than having a bank board independently loan their money on deposit. If the investors want to sell their holdings, the investment banker or an exchange provides a secondary market for the securities.

Despite the success of Jewish investment banking in Europe, the United States banking system remained distinctly non-Jewish in the late nineteenth and twentieth centuries, dominated by Harriman, Fisk, Morgan and Gould. J. P. Morgan was the undisputed leader of the industry for a fifty-year period from 1880 to 1930.[28] The only exception was Jacob Schiff, who did travel in the periphery of this exclusive circle as the head of the investment banking firm Kuhn, Loeb. The firm had been established by Abraham Kuhn and Solomon Loeb in 1867, and it concentrated on railroad issues.

Other Jewish investment banking firms established at about the same time by German Jews included Lazard Frères by the Lazard brothers in 1832; Goldman Sachs by Marcus Goldman in 1869; J. & W. Seligman by Joseph Seligman in 1840; Salomon Brothers by Arthur, Herbert and Percy Salomon in 1910; and Lehman Brothers by Henry, Emanuel and Mayer Lehman in 1845.[29]

An interesting example of these famous traders' legendary aversion to fixed assets is described in Stephen Birmingham's *Our Crowd*. "In 1867, Joseph Seligman was advised that all the land north of Sixtieth Street and west of Broadway [in New York City] – up to 121st Street, and including most of what is now West End Avenue and Riverside Drive – was for sale. The price for the tract was $450,000 – more than 3 square miles of Manhattan for a fraction of what a single city block would cost now. It was perhaps the best bargain since Peter Minuit's original purchase of the island from the Indians. Joseph had the money but said no. 'It is a bad investment.' Had he felt otherwise, the Seligmans today would easily be the richest family in the world."[30]

Most of these men arrived as poor immigrants. Marcus Goldman came to Philadelphia in 1848 and peddled for two years before opening a clothing store in which he made his initial capital. Henry Lehman arrived in 1844 and peddled in Alabama. He opened a store in Montgomery and, together with his brothers, opened a cotton brokerage. These firms had extensive family contacts with other Jewish firms in Europe, which gave them competitive advantages by providing fresh capital for a dynamically growing American continent.

Jews continued to be systematically excluded from the traditional banking system until the 1960s, when their investment banking firms' innovative new financial services catapulted them front and center. Leading non-Jewish banks were forced to work alongside the Jewish firms to put together deals. Then, and only then, did Jews begin to enter traditional banking in significant numbers. Senator William Proxmire said during Congressional hearings in 1974, "There is probably no industry in this country that has more consistently and cruelly rejected Jews from positions of power and influence than the commercial banking industry."[31] Even taking into consideration the discrimination that excluded Jews, Jews themselves were not drawn strongly to the field of traditional banking, perhaps because such companies had been notoriously loose with vice presidential titles but tight with their cash compensation. In comparison, investment banking provided more lucrative and more entrepreneurial banking jobs with higher salaries, bonuses and equity potentials, but without the ethnic issues.

Jews took the lead in the '60s with new investment banking techniques that helped introduce a conglomeration craze by using multipurpose holding companies. The well-established Jewish banking firms expanded way beyond their founders' imaginations and have become extremely prosperous over the past thirty years. The following are the best-known Jewish firms:

Lehman Brothers (acquired by American Express)

Lazard Frères

Goldman Sachs

Salomon Brothers (acquired by Travelers Insurance, merged into Citigroup in 1998)

Bache & Co. (acquired by Prudential Insurance)

Cantor, Fitzgerald

In the 1980s, leveraged buyouts became the rage. An LBO is executed by buying a business and mortgaging the acquiring assets to pay for the acquisition – analagous to buying a house with a large mortgage with little down payment. The debt level is supposed to be within the projected limits of the cash flow of the underlying business, just as a house mortgage is granted based on certain income tests. A Jewish investment banker named Michael Milken made it all possible on a grand scale. He and the firm he worked for, Drexel Burnham Lambert, created the LBO boom by raising funds and creating a market for the debt securities created by these transactions, also known as "junk bonds." These high-yielding bonds financed such startups as MCI. All the established investment banks followed suit to earn millions in fees for advising, underwriting and executing the transactions. As with any craze, it was taken to extremes, and deals were made based on overly aggressive projections of cash flow to support the debt of the ever-increasing prices paid for the deals. In 1990 the LBO craze crashed and Milken's Drexel failed.

A short list of other well-known Jewish Wall Street movers and shakers includes:

George Soros – global currency, commodities and equity investor.

Carl Icahn – investor and takeover speculator; owns TWA, USX, Continental Airlines, RJR Nabisco.

Laurence Tisch – investor and takeover speculator; owns Loews theaters and hotels, CBS.

Barry Diller – chairman of USA Networks, owner of the Home Shopping Network and Ticketmaster.

Michael Bloomberg – founder and owner of Bloomberg LP financial news service.

Ron Perelman – takeover specialist; owns Revlon, MacAndrews & Forbes and other companies.

Sanford Weill – co-chairman of Citigroup, owner of Salomon, Smith Barney and Travelers Group.

Abbey Cohen – widely followed investment strategist, Goldman Sachs Group.

Alan Greenspan – chairman of the Federal Reserve; determines U.S. interest rates.

Alan "Ace" Greenberg – chairman of Bear Stearns.

Stephen Schwarzman – founded Blackstone Group, investment banking firm.

Harvey Golub – chairman of American Express.

Saul Steinberg – chairman of Reliance Corporation, investor.

Asher Edelman – influential financial columnist for *Barron's*

Louis Rukeyser – witty host of *Wall Street Week* on PBS.[32]

The concentration of Jewish-owned securities firms created well-paying employment opportunities at all levels of the securities industry: securities analysts; portfolio managers; and stock, bond and futures traders, brokers and deal-makers. Among the equity holders of the Jewish investment banking and trading firms on Wall Street are hundreds of Jewish millionaires. Upward mobility based on merit and high salaries has made working on Wall Street a Jewish-friendly career choice. Note that 30 percent of all Jews in the United States and 13 percent of Jews in the world live in the New York City area. Again, Jews are not just the workers in this industry – they are owners, partners and directors. Although exact figures for the number of Jews are not available, they no doubt have a leading and disproportionate role on Wall Street.

JEWISH MERCHANTS AND STORE OWNERS

One of the basic avenues of entrepreneurism is to open your own store. It is a very risky venture, and the owner must possess many skills. However, the freedom it allows and the income potential have been very attractive to Jews. In the early Jewish migrations to America, many German Jews pursued careers as wandering general-merchandise peddlers and later settled down to become wealthy shopkeepers. The entrepreneurial peddlers provided a great service to settlers in the nation's interior who had no access to a general store. Leon Harris referred to these new shopkeepers as the "merchant princes" in his important book by the same name. "Moving into sparsely settled areas with few towns and shops, pioneers felt the need again and again for once-available, familiar goods – combs, needles, pots, clothing – and they welcomed the peddler, carrying a pack on his shoulders or maneuvering a wagon along rutted paths."[33] Many peddlers settled in towns and established stores. Since that time, American Jews have had an extraordinary concentration in the retailing industry, as they had in Europe.

DEPARTMENT STORES

Non-Jews were very successful in establishing America's largest department store chains, including Sears, Macy's, Montgomery Ward and J.C. Penney. Sears and Macy's, however, later became Jewish-owned firms. After achieving great success in the mail-order business as partners, Richard Sears and Julius Rosenwald had management differences in 1908, and Sears resigned. Rosenwald bought control of the company and built it into the largest discount retailer in the United States. In 1888, the Straus brothers bought R. H. Macy's, and Isador Straus later bought total control of the company from his brothers. He proceeded to expand Macy's into the world's largest department store.

Another big story of department-store history belongs to the Lazarus family. Simon Lazarus opened a men's clothing shop in Columbus, Ohio, in 1854. With the purchase of a Lazarus suit, a customer received free suspenders, and with shoes came fifty free shoeshines. But it was Si's younger brother, Fred Lazarus Jr., who had national aspirations. He revolutionized the clothing industry by organizing garments according to size instead of price, which had been the custom at the time. He also began acquiring other stores. In 1929 he bought Abraham & Straus of New York and Filine's of Boston to create Federated Department Stores.[34] Bloomingdale's was acquired in 1930, and total sales that year topped $112 million. Through a series of ambitious acquisitions that picked up steam after World War II, Fred purchased chains across the country that characteristically were the strongest in their markets. The list includes Burdine's in Miami (1956), Goldsmith's in Memphis (1959) and Bullock's and I. Magnin in Los Angeles (1964).

In 1988 Campeau Corp. acquired Federated from the Lazarus family in a disastrous, overly leveraged buyout. Federated regained its independence in bankruptcy court in 1992, and in 1994 purchased Macy's, which also had gone bankrupt in a poorly planned LBO. Federated thus became the largest department store chain in the country, with more than 400 department stores and 160 specialty stores in 33 states and sales exceeding $15.7 billion in 1998.[35] In 1999, Federated also became one of the largest cataloguers as well by purchasing Fingerhut Cos., with sales of $1.6 billion. Imagine, it all started with a single shop in Columbus, Ohio.

The Jewish concentration in the department-store industry is striking. The list of chains owned or founded by Jews includes:

DEPARTMENT STORES

Macy's*

Sears

Bloomingdale's*

Neiman-Marcus

Filene's

Bergdorf Goodman

Saks Fifth Avenue

May Company

Kohl's

Lazarus*

Goldsmith's*

Rich's*

Stern's*

Loehmann's

* part of Federated Department Stores today

JEWISH CHAINS OF YESTERYEAR INCLUDE

I. Magnin**
Gimble's
B. Altman
Abraham & Straus**
Hecht's
Garfinkel's

** acquired by Federated Department Stores, but renamed.

OTHER JEWISH MERCHANTS

Jewish merchants have also established some of the biggest names in many specialty categories. For example, two of the most popular mall clothing stores, the Gap and The Limited, were started by Jews. Gap Inc. was founded by Donald and Doris Fisher and The Limited by Leslie Wexner.

Unlike many of the department stores, the Gap is new to the clothing industry. In 1969 the Fishers opened their first store in San Francisco. They originally sold jeans and records, but eventually dropped the records. They quickly prospered and opened stores in just about every shopping mall, specializing in private-label Gap jeans during the jeans craze of the 1970s, and expanding to a wide variety of apparel with a "basics" look. Gap bought Banana Republic in 1983, and started Gap Kids in 1986 and Old Navy in 1994. Today the company has more than 2,000 stores with $6.5 billion in sales.

After arguing with his parents about how to run the family clothing store, Leslie Wexner started a women's sportswear store in 1963 with a "limited" selection of high-turnover items. He parlayed a $5,000 loan from an aunt into first-year sales of $160,000. The Limited chain, which popularized the "baggy sweater" look, revolutionized the industry with a system for rapid overseas manufacturing and distribution to cut costs and to respond to fashion trends. The growth of shopping malls – also an area dominated by Jewish firms – made these mall chains hugely successful in a short period of time. You can hardly walk into any mall in America today and not see one of Wexner's stores. He soon expanded his business by acquiring mall chains that include Cacique, Lane Bryant, Structure and Lerner of New York. Wexner also developed his own businesses with Victoria's Secret and Bath & Body Works. There are now more than five thousand stores with more than $9 billion in revenues in the Wexner mall apparel store empire.

Not every Jewish business ends up successful, however. Barney Pressman opened a modest men's clothing store in 1923 and worked hard to make it a success. His son, Fred, took over in the 1960s and, using a disciplined approach and a flare for promotion, converted the sleepy business into a very profitable European design giant in New York, named not Pressman's but Barney's. However, the third generation – Fred's sons Gene and Bob, who had never really worked for a living – became enamored by the glitz and glamour they were supposed to be selling, and ran the company into bankruptcy in the 1990s.

In the "category killer" sector, where huge stores with the lowest prices drive competition out of business, Charles Lazarus (no relation to the Federated Lazarus family) was the pioneer in the toy industry with Toys 'R' Us. He started with a children's furniture shop in the corner of his father's bicycle repair business and eventually built the largest toy retailer in the U.S. with $11 billion in sales – accounting for more than 20 percent of all toy sales in the country.

Using the same concept, Bernard Marcus and Arthur Blank started the Home Depot in 1979 to put many mom-and-pop hardware stores out of business. Marcus, the son of a Russian immigrant cabinetmaker, started the company after he and Blank were fired from Handy Dan Improvement Centers. With only seven hundred stores, the Home Depot had $24 billion in sales in 1999.

Jews are also very involved with TV home shopping. Joseph Segel was one of the founders of the Franklin Mint, which sells commemorative coins, ceramic plates, jewelry and figurines by mail order. He then had the bright idea that he could team up with cable systems and provide twenty-four-hour live TV shopping on a network he would call QVC (Quality, Value, Convenience). He sold his QVC network to Ralph and Brian Roberts's Comcast Communications, and today QVC has revenues that top $2 billion. The Home Shopping Network, the other big home-shopping channel with $1.5 billion in sales, is run by Barry Diller, a media mogul and former president of QVC, through his company USA Networks.

JEWS AND JEWELRY

Although not as large an employer of Jews as the garment industry has been, the diamond and jewelry business still has a large concentration of Jews in positions of power. The many Jewish surnames beginning with "Gold," "Silver" and "Diamond" derive from the jewelry trade these families were once involved with in Europe and elsewhere. Jewelry and diamonds are international businesses in which Jews have exerted major control since the Middle Ages. They have been Jewish-friendly industries because the skills were taught through apprenticeship to relatives and friends, and their inventories were easy to move in times of persecution and expulsion.

Because diamonds were a rare and new commodity during the Middle Ages, the diamond trade was free of the restrictions that had barred Jews from other industries. Amsterdam was the major center of the diamond trade until the late 1500s. When Jews moved to England in the 1600s because of persecution, so did the diamond trade, but the diamond cutting remained in Amsterdam and in Antwerp, Belgium. In the late 1800s Jews accounted for 20 percent of the diamond workers and 75 percent of the diamond brokers and diamond factory owners in those cities.

Visit New York City's Diamond District at 47th Street and you will immediately feel the Jewish presence. South Africa's DeBeers Consolidated Mines controls the diamond industry and its "Central Buying Group." Jews have been involved in DeBeers from the beginning. Cecil Rhodes, a Gentile, and Alfred Beit, a Jew, were the architects of the DeBeers syndicate in 1888. S. B. Joel was its first president.[36]

In 1902 Cecil Rhodes died and Ernest Oppenheimer was sent by his London diamond firm to represent its interests in South Africa. In 1917 Oppenheimer founded Anglo-American Corp., a South African diamond mining company, and in 1929 became chairman of DeBeers, the distributor of the diamonds. DeBeers has controlled about 60 percent of the diamond production and 80 percent of the sales of rough diamonds ever since the big diamond discoveries in South Africa during the 1880s. Ernest's son Harry Oppenheimer, who converted to the Anglican religion, took over the company from his father and still runs it today.

The DeBeers diamond supply comes from about 150 "sightholders" who are predominantly Jewish. These elite dealers, wholesalers and cutting factories receive boxes of rough diamonds about ten times a year at 17 Charterhouse Street in London. The boxes may contain anywhere from $1 million to $25 million worth of diamonds. Unknown by the sightholder until he opens the box, the price and size of the shipment are not negotiable, and the transaction is cash and carry. The price is usually 25 percent off the prevailing wholesale rate for uncut diamonds to compensate these sightholders for their intermediary function. Unreliable sightholders and those quickly selling their boxes to speculators are summarily cut from this elite group.

Again, predominantly Jewish diamond manufacturers in Israel, New York, and India buy the raw goods, then cut and polish the diamonds. They resell them to jewelry makers, who then sell them to retailers and then to the public. At every step of the process, Jewish people have maintained their strong presence. At the end of the distribution chain, many small Jewish-owned jewelry stores and chains, such as Zale's and Helzberg's, combine their precious diamond inventory with widely available gold, silver and gems. Morris Zale started Zale's in Wichita Falls, Texas, in the 1920s. When the oil fields were discovered nearby, he had more business than he could handle, and his company soon grew into the nation's largest jewelry chain. The company is currently headed by Beryl Raff, who holds the titles of president and CEO. Barnett Helzberg founded the Helzberg Diamond chain, based in Kansas City. He sold out to Warren Buffett's Berkshire Hathaway in 1994 for $500 million in Berkshire Hathaway stock at 1998 values.

A group of American tourists at the tomb of the Israeli Unknown Soldier in Tel Aviv noticed this inscription on the tomb:

Here Lies Abraham Schwartz.
Died 1973 During Arab-Israeli War
A Good Soldier and Jeweler

"What's this jewelry business?" a tourist asked the guide. "This is supposed to be the tomb of an unknown soldier."

"That's true," said the guide. "As a soldier nobody knew him, but as a jeweler he was famous!"

This joke is also told with the punch line "a good soldier and furrier," as there is an equally large concentration of Jewish businessmen in the fur trade. It is a specialized trade with skills learned by apprenticeship and it is portable, just as the jewelry and diamond industries are. Adolph Zukor and Marcus Loew began as furriers before they went on to establish their respective Hollywood empires of Paramount and MGM, as I explain later in this chapter.

JEWISH COMPUTER INDUSTRY LEADERS

The wealthiest Jewish American is not a real estate mogul or financier; he is a computer entrepreneur. As in other industries where Jews have excelled, change comes quickly, rules are meant to be broken and creativity is at a premium. Michael Dell is the poster boy for entrepreneurial success. Dell was a driven college freshman in 1983 when he had a crazy idea: he thought he could be more efficient than IBM or Compaq by selling computers directly to consumers. He began at the University of Texas, selling PC upgrades from his dorm room, and then moved up to making entire PC clones. Dell assembled his computers from standard components and sold them through the mail. By using standard components, he kept his inventory costs low and his technology up to date, and he developed the ability to build a machine to the customer's specifications. In addition, by selling his computers directly to the consumer, he eliminated a high-cost distribution channel that delivered little value to technologically savvy consumers. With Dell's personal stake worth $20 billion in 1999, Dell Computer is the consumer PC industry leader that IBM and Compaq are trying to chase. According to Dell, "Compaq and IBM are assuming that price is the problem. The problem is that the dealer channel has fundamentally failed customers."

As Dell demonstrated, going in the other direction often breeds success. In 1982 a group of Texas Instruments engineers approached Benjamin M. Rosen to seek backing for their idea to make computer components. Rosen proposed that they produce "luggable" computers instead. The portable computer and Compaq Computer were born. According to the *Wall Street Journal* in 1999, "He [Rosen] was current with new technologies in the 1970s, and he's just as current today [as chairman]. With that he develops his own vision and sees things usually before most people do."

Even more influential is Hungarian-American Andrew Grove (Andras Grof), co-founder and chairman of the Intel Corp. The ubiquitous "Intel Inside" label demonstrates his company's dominance in the microchip industry, where they make 90 percent of personal computer microprocessors and have annual sales of $26 billion. From early on, the 8086, 386, 486 and Pentium have set the standard for the computer industry.[37] In 1978 there were twenty-nine thousand transistors on the 8086 chip, running at ten megahertz. The Pentium III had 9.5 million transistors running at five hundred megahertz in 1999. It would be easy to become complacent, but the computer industry does not allow it. In his book, *Only the Paranoid Survive*, Grove preaches never to let your guard down and to keep innovating regardless of what your competition is doing.

Larry Ellison founded Oracle Corp., which sells the preeminent database software used by businesses. He helped build the first IBM-compatible mainframe computer at Amdahl Corp., breaking IBM's monopoly of the market. He formed Oracle in 1977 after reading an IBM paper about the emerging database software languages. In fact, Ellison beat IBM to the database software market and has maintained industry dominance ever since. His stake in 1999 was valued at $13 billion. Always a competitor in his personal and business life, Ellison continues to lead a fight to topple his arch-rival Bill Gates's monopoly of PC-operating systems.

Jewish entrepreneurs are also very involved in the emerging markets created by the Internet. Their presence at the forefront of this growing industry is similar to their trailblazing entrepreneurism in the Old West, when Jewish merchants fanned out across the plains selling their wares. A *Forbes* article about the Internet in July 1998 titled "Masters of the New Universe" pointed out that there were thirteen corporate leaders of the Internet boom. Research revealed that four (30 percent) are Jewish.

A related fortune belongs to the landlord of Silicon Valley. By 1999 Carl Berg had created an estimated $950 million real estate and investment fortune by being smart and at the right place at the right time. As a landlord he evaluated potential new tenants and rented to and invested in those companies he found promising. His investments include stakes in over one hundred startups, including Sun Microsystems.

THE JEWS OF THE FORBES 400: OCTOBER 1999

It would be impossible to mention all of the successful Jewish businesspeople in America today. One of the clear benchmarks of success, however, is being listed in the Forbes 400. To make the list in October 1999 required a net worth of at least $625 million.[38] Jewish individuals accounted for 23 percent of the entire group, 36 percent of the top fifty and 24 percent of the billionaires – eleven, eighteen and twelve times their relative percentage in the U.S. population at large. And these percentages in the Forbes 400 have been consistent over time, although the players change from year to year; studies of the lists from 1982, 1983 and 1984 conducted by others reveal similar figures.

I have carefully documented the names of the Jewish members of the current Forbes 400 list. Beginning with a December 1996 article about Jewish billionaires in the Jewish magazine *Moment*, this information has been updated and expanded through public sources. Jewish charities, including the United Jewish Appeal, and prominent fundraisers were also helpful. I excluded about fifteen people who have made a point of keeping their religion private because it is not the purpose of this book to breach their privacy.

To make my list of the Jewish Forbes 400 more complete, I added the Jewish families from the family fortunes that *Forbes* lists separately each year. And to reflect the changing nature of the list, included as a footnote are those Jewish members who have fallen off the list in the past three years.

THE JEWS OF THE FORBES 400

Name	Millions $	Source
Dell, Michael	$20,000	Dell Computer
Ellison, Larry	13,000	Oracle Corp. (network software)
Redstone, Sumner	9,400	Viacom, National Amusements, CBS (1999)
Pritzker, Robert	5,500	Hyatt Hotels, Marmon Group, investments
Pritzker, Thomas	5,500	Hyatt Hotels, Marmon Group, investments, inherited from Jay in 1999
Arison, Micky	5,100	Carnival Cruise Lines, son of founder Ted
Newhouse, Si	4,500	Advance Publications, Conde Nast magazines
Newhouse, Donald	4,500	Advance Publications, Conde Nast magazines
Bronfman, Edgar Sr.	4,200	Seagram Co., Time Warner, MCA, Universal Studios
Icahn, Carl	4,200	investments, takeovers
Fisher, Donald	4,100	The Gap, founder
Fisher, Doris	4,100	The Gap, founder
Lauder, Leonard	4,100	Estée Lauder, CEO; inheritance
Lerner, Alfred	4,100	MBNA Financial (credit cards)
Annenberg, Walter	4,000	*TV Guide*, Triangle Publications
Broad, Eli	4,000	Sun America (insurance) sold, Kaufman & Broad (real estate)
Lauder, Ronald	4,000	Estée Lauder, inheritance
Soros, George	4,000	Quantum Fund, investments, trading
Perelman, Ronald	3,800	investments, Revlon

Greenberg, Maurice	3,700	American Intl. Group (insurance), Sun America
Davis, Marvin	3,500	real estate, oil
Bren, Donald	3,200	California real estate
Winnick, Gary	3,200	Global Crossing (telecommunications), Drexel Burnham Lambert, trading with Milken
Sturm, Donald	3,000	Peter Kiewit Sons (investments)
Crown, Lester	2,900	Material Service Corp., General Dynamics
Blaustein family	2,800	Amoco (F. Henry Rosenberg Jr., Louis Thalheimer)
Geffen, David	2,700	Geffen Records (sold to MCA), Dreamworks
Marcus, Bernard	2,700	Home Depot
Wexner, Leslie	2,700	The Limited
Bloomberg, Michael	2,500	Bloomberg news service
Stern, Leonard	2,400	Hartz Mountain (pet supplies), N.Y.C. real estate
Lenfest, "Gerry"	2,300	Lenfest Communications (cable), sold ½ to AT&T
Tisch, Preston Robert	2,300	Loews Corp., CBS
Fisher, John	2,200	The Gap, inheritance
Davidson, William	2,100	Guardian Industries (glass manufacturer)
Tisch, Laurence	2,100	Loews Corp., CBS
Fisher, Robert	2,100	The Gap, inheritance
LeFrak, Samuel	2,000	N.Y.C. real estate
Spielberg, Steven	2,000	Amblin Entertainment, Dreamworks
Haas, Peter Sr.	1,900	Levi Strauss, inheritance
Helmsley, Leona	1,800	N.Y.C. real estate of husband Harry, converted to Quakerism – (formerly Lena Rosenthal)
Zell, Sam	1,800	real estate, investments
Lauren, Ralph	1,700	Ralph Lauren fashion
Alfond family	1,700	Dexter Shoes (Harold Alfond)
Gonda, Louis	1,600	International Lease Finance (aircraft leases)
Blank, Arthur	1,500	Home Depot
Goldman, Richard	1,500	Levi Strauss, inheritance
Gonda, Leslie	1,400	International Lease Finance, real estate
Haas, John	1,300	Levi Strauss, inheritance
Jacobs, Irwin	1,300	Qualcomm (telecommunications)
Fisher family	1,300	N.Y.C. real estate (Zachary, Lawrence, Martin and Richard)

Durst family	1,300	N.Y.C. real estate (Seymour, Roy and David)
Ziff, Dirk	1,200	Ziff Davis Publishing (sold), inheritance
Ziff, Robert	1,200	Ziff Davis Publishing (sold), inheritance
Ziff, Daniel	1,200	Ziff Davis Publishing (sold), inheritance
Zuckerman, Mortimer	1,200	Boston Properties, *U.S. News & World Report*
Fisher, William	1,600	The Gap, inheritance
Weill, Sanford	1,100	Citigroup (Travelers Group)
Kimmel, Sidney	1,000	Jones Apparel Group, Nine West shoe stores
Levine, William	1,000	Outdoor Systems (billboard advertising)
Drexler, Millard	1,000	The Gap, CEO
Lewis, Peter B.	1,000	Progressive Corp. (auto insurance)
Rich, Marc	1,000	commodities trader, fugitive living in Switzerland for fraud and tax evasion
Fisher, Max	975	Marathon Oil
Berg, Carl	950	Silicon Valley real estate and investments
Diller, Barry	950	USA Networks (TV stations, HSN, Ticketmaster)
Green, Pincus	950	commodities trader, fugitive living in Switzerland for fraud and tax evasion
Kovner, Bruce	900	investments, Caxton Corp.
Kravis, Henry	900	Kravis, Kohlberg, Roberts (leveraged buyouts)
Peltz, Nelson	890	Triac Beverage (Snapple), leveraged buyouts
Abramson, Leonard	875	Aetna U.S. Healthcare
Lee, Thomas	875	leveraged buyouts, Snapple sale
Honickman, Harold	850	Pepsi bottler
Kohlberg, Jerome Jr.	850	Kravis, Kohlberg, Roberts (leveraged buyouts)
Taubman, Alfred	840	shopping centers
Shorenstein, Walter	800	San Francisco real estate
Solow, Sheldon	800	N.Y.C. real estate
Haas, Peter	775	Levi Strauss, inheritance
Adelson, Sheldon	750	COMDEX expositions (computer shows), casinos
Milken, Michael	750	Drexel Burnham Lambert, trading
Roberts, Brian	750	Comcast Communications
Geballe, Frances K.	725	Levi Strauss, inheritance
Haas, Josephine	725	Levi Strauss, inheritance

Katzenberg, Jeffrey	725	Dreamworks, Disney employment settlement
Haas, Evelyn	720	Levi Strauss, inheritance
Eisner, Michael	710	Disney CEO, employment options
Chernick, Aubrey	700	Candle Corp. (software)
Glazer, Guilford	700	real estate, shopping centers
Haas, Robert	700	Levi Strauss, inheritance
Levy, Leon	675	Odyssey Partners (leveraged buyouts)
Feld, Kenneth	650	Ringling Bros., Barnum & Bailey, Disney on Ice
Levine, Stuart	650	Cabletron Systems
Silverman, Henry	650	Cendant (HFS and CUC), Avis, Ramada, HoJo
Subotnick, Stuart	625	Metromedia

DROPPED FROM THE LIST IN 1999, WITH NET WORTH PUBLISHED IN 1998

Name	Millions $	Source
Pritzker, Jay	5,500	Hyatt Hotels, Marmon Group, investments, died in 1999
Fribourg, Michel	1,700	Continental Grain
Mandel family	1,300	Premier Industries (electronic and auto parts), Morton Mandel
Heyman, Samuel	800	GAF, investments
Hess, Leon	720	Amerada Hess, died in 1999
Milken, Lowell	700	Drexel Burnham Lambert, trading (Mike's brother)
Roberts, Ralph	680	Comcast, QVC, stake given to son Brian in 1999
Simon, Melvin	660	real estate, shopping centers
Illitch, Michael	600	Little Caesar's Pizza
Ansin, Edmund	600	TV stations
Werner, Tom	600	Carsey-Werner Co. (TV sitcom producer)
Koshland, Daniel Jr.	560	Levi Strauss, inheritance
Litwin, Leonard	550	N.Y.C. real estate
Nash, Jack	550	Odyssey Partners (leveraged buyouts)
Haas, Margaret	540	Levi Strauss, inheritance
Morris, William	530	J. & W. Seligman (money management)
Sommer, Viola	500	real estate, inheritance

| Wasserman, Lewis | 500 | MCA (music, movies) |
| Rennert, Ira | 500 | Renco Group (lead, coal, steel), investments |

DROPPED FROM THE LIST IN 1998, WITH NET WORTH PUBLISHED IN 1997

Name	Millions$	Source
Wynn, Stephen	780	Mirage Casino
Fireman, Paul	690	Reebok
Schwartz, Theodore	600	APAC Teleservices
Milstein, Monroe	530	Burlington Coat Factory

DROPPED FROM THE LIST IN 1997, WITH NET WORTH PUBLISHED IN 1996

Name	Millions $	Source
Friedman, Phyllis K.	490	Levi Strauss, inheritance
Gosman, Abraham	480	Mediplex Rehabilitation Centers
Weis, Robert	425	Weis Markets

PROFESSORS AND EDUCATORS

On the path to an advanced degree or after a short, unsatisfactory time in the business world, many Jews decide they like the academic life so much that they want to stay students for life. In Jewish society, scholars hold high social standing, even though their wealth may not be commensurate with their intellectual abilities. In old-world traditional Orthodox families, the young son-in-law was supported by his in-laws and his wife while he studied the Torah, the noblest of pursuits. In very Orthodox families the tradition continues today.

The wave of Jewish college academics is a relatively recent one. In 1940, only 2 percent of American professors were Jewish. By 1970 the number had increased fivefold, to 10 percent. Restrictive quotas from the first half of the century had ended, and a new generation of Jews was being educated in larger numbers. By the '90s, Jews made up 35 percent of professors at elite schools – and a Jew has now served as president of nearly every elite institution, including Harvard, Yale, Penn, Columbia, Princeton, MIT and the University of Chicago.

The actual time a professor is required to work is short, and the time for "self-directed" activity is great. *Money: Who Has How Much and Why* offers this look at professors' work schedules: "Courses are usually scheduled for thirty weeks, including examination periods. And most professors arrange their classes and office hours for two to three days on campus. In short, the basic work year for college faculties adds up to 90 days, not including sabbaticals, which allow them every seventh year off."[39] With so much time off, professors can have lucrative careers as consultants, board members and writers. In the field of economics, Paul Samuelson and Milton Friedman are Nobel Prize-winning professors who are also successful authors. Arthur Burns, Alan Greenspan and Paul Volcker are other notable Jewish economists who have all served as chairmen of the Federal Reserve over the past thirty years. Considered the second most influential person in government, the chairman of the Fed determines interest rates and in turn guides the financial markets in the U.S. and around the world.

Professors will say that they spend long hours out of class preparing for their classes and doing research. That is true for some. However, once they get a course developed, some professors spend little time revising and updating. As for research, there is a great deal of pressure to be published in scholarly journals in order to achieve academic success. But once a professor receives tenure, the pressure is off . . . for life! The only way to dislodge a tenured professor is to convict him or her of a serious crime.

Even with all the talk of making trade-offs for academia, professors' pay is well above the average American household income of forty thousand dollars. Because Jews in general attend more prestigious institutions and choose positions in the professional schools of law, medicine, science and business, their compensation is well above the average professor's. There are some superstars of academia – especially medical professors – earning more than $1 million a year, but that is extremely rare. However, figures are not available for professors' total income including outside earnings. These other incomes would substantially boost the average income figures, not to mention the value of the vacation and free time offered.

PROFESSORS' SALARY DISTRIBUTION
all ranks

More than $100,000	3%
$80,000 – $100,000	5%
$60,000 – $80,000	16%

$50,000 – $60,000	19%
$40,000 – $50,000	23%
Less than $40,000	34%

Medians

Full professors	$65,400
All ranks	$43,800

(Andrew Hacker, *Money: Who Has How Much and Why* [1997], p. 124)

AVERAGE FULL PROFESSOR COMPENSATION

Harvard	$107,000
Stanford	$103,100
Princeton	$101,400
Yale	$100,500
MIT	$96,900
NYU	$96,800
Chicago	$96,500
Columbia	$93,000
Northwestern	$92,000
Duke	$91,700
Georgetown	$91,200
New Jersey*	$90,800
Berkeley	$86,500
Michigan	$85,000
Dartmouth	$83,700
Cornell	$82,200
Virginia*	$81,400
Pennsylvania*	$77,600
Kansas*	$63,300
Wyoming*	$58,100
North Dakota*	$47,900

*Main state campuses
(Hacker, p. 139)

The problem with this idyllic scenario is that it is rapidly coming to an end. There is an entrenched professorial population and not many full-time positions are being created. In addition, many states, benefactors and students are pressuring colleges to keep their costs down. Consequently, the amount available after the senior professors have been paid leaves little resources for the new generation of aspiring assistant professors.

WHAT'S TO BE LEARNED?

1. Pursue a professional career, but be prepared to turn into an entrepreneur

2. Within your career, leave time for entrepreneurial pursuits

3. Pursue new opportunities or areas that are outside the mainstream

PURSUE A PROFESSIONAL CAREER, BUT BE PREPARED TO TURN INTO AN ENTREPRENEUR

Begin your career with a professional education, for three reasons. First, the skills are highly transferable to many pursuits. Second, a good career generates an above-average salary that can provide the initial capital you need to enter a business, invest or speculate. Third, professional careers put you in contact with other professionals who have money, knowledge, contacts and ideas. In addition, professional careers often provide intimate contact with the situations, opportunities and problems within an industry that serve as the sources of ideas for starting a new venture.

WITHIN YOUR CAREER, LEAVE TIME FOR ENTREPRENEURIAL PURSUITS

If you single-mindedly serve your employer without regard to your own interests, you display the same misplaced faith that many Jews had in the Germans back in 1939. Foolishly, the Jews believed that Nazis needed their skills and capital, and that there was no way they would exterminate them. In the corporate world today, with mergers, downsizing, abolition of pension plans and shareholder pressures, nobody is immune to the ax – regardless of their position or contribution to their employer. If you are not an owner, you are an "outsider." Therefore, employees have the obligation to educate themselves, maintain state-of-the-art skills, pursue new opportunities to enrich themselves and control their destinies. Management guru Tom Peters (not Jewish) in *The Tom Peters' Seminar* (1994) told the story about the layoff "of an 18-year veteran purchasing staffer from a company. 'It's a shame to lose all that experience,' one executive said to another. 'We didn't lose 18 years' experience,' replied the second, 'we lost one year's experience repeated 17 times over.' The joke is a little too cruel and cynical for me, but only a little. It's like that, as often as not."

The "Managing Your Career" column in the *Wall Street Journal* focused in February 1999 on the subject of independent employees. "Of course, there is a new ethic in the corporate world these days," wrote the columnist. "You can't ask for someone's total intellectual being to be with your company anymore." Jewish people have known that for years. Hal Lancaster went on to give some sound advice:

1. Make sure your boss is aware of your pursuits if they are significant. Talk about it beforehand and come to an understanding so that there are no conflicts with your full-time work. If your boss is not agreeable, you might have to reconsider whether your current job is right for you. When changing jobs, make sure that your outside pursuits are exempted from any non-compete clause in your employment contract or standard employment paperwork.

2. Make sure you have clear job objectives and goals. If you meet your objectives, your boss cannot say that your outside work is distracting you from your duties.

3. Convey to your boss your continued satisfaction and commitment to your job.

4. Demonstrate, if possible, that your outside activity contributes to your performance and benefits your company. You may be developing new contacts and be exposed to new ideas that can enhance your effectiveness.

My view is that you should be a "self-employed employee." It can be as simple as owning an investment property or writing books such as this one – or as complex as running an Internet business from your home. In the process, you actually become a more productive employee. Your entrepreneurial spirit, your quest for self-improvement and your business contacts will make you a valuable asset to your employer. If you are not totally dependent on your employer for your livelihood, you are apt to make more aggressive and creative decisions that may catapult the employer's business to new levels. Work for yourself . . . always!

PURSUE NEW OPPORTUNITIES OR AREAS
THAT ARE OUTSIDE THE MAINSTREAM

Within your profession, pursue areas that are new and emerging. Look for areas that others consider too complex or troublesome to pursue. These niches are exactly the places that can create wealth. This was the case for investment bankers and securities lawyers in the 1960s. Michael Milken pursued the sub-prime debt market. Computer geeks developed businesses on the Internet in the early 1990s. As late as 1993, the consensus was that the "information superhighway" was going to be five-hundred-station cable systems, not the crude and cumbersome Internet. Who knows? Cable modems may yet win out. New opportunities always exist!

CHAPTER 4

Develop Your Verbal Confidence

To succeed in business or just about any other pursuit, you've got to have chutzpah. Jews do. They even invented the word. Chutzpah – call it "verbal self-confidence" if you like – is the ability to speak up, say your piece, ask questions, make demands. *Chutzpah* is a Yiddish word that comes from the Hebrew word meaning "audacity." Alan Dershowitz, who wrote a book by the same name, defined *chutzpah* as "boldness, assertiveness, a willingness to demand what is due, to defy tradition, to challenge authority, to raise eyebrows."[1] Sometimes chutzpah can seem vulgar to a more-reserved Christian world, but that self-assertiveness in the competitive marketplace serves Jews well. In business passivity is not a virtue. The long list of Jewish members of the Forbes 400 attests to that fact. The higher level of education of Jewish people and the richer vocabulary derived from that education contribute to the verbal confidence that Jews display.

Rabbi Joseph Telushkin writes, "Verbal combativeness and aggression are well-known Jewish characteristics. 'Spare me from Gentile hands and Jewish tongues,' ran a nineteenth-century Yiddish proverb in Eastern Europe."[2] Televised debates in the Israeli Knesset (Congress) quickly demonstrate the relish with which Jews debate the important issues of the day. Again, when it comes to business, the law and the arts, this ability to express your will or opinion often serves as an advantage.

Sometimes words are not even needed if you know how to communicate. Marcel Marceau was Jewish. But that mime had chutzpah; he fought in the French resistance during World War II.

A prime example of Jewish straight talk is Dr. Ruth Westheimer, née Karola Ruth Siegel. Born in Germany, Dr. Ruth has lived in Poland, Switzerland, Israel, France and New York. After earning a degree in psychology and family counseling, she began her public career as a host of a radio talk show on which she counseled listeners about sexual problems. Dr. Ruth opened a new era of frank discussions about orgasm, masturbation, use of condoms and sexual responsibility – all during a period of the 1980s when the Religious Right preferred that such matters be kept strictly private. The spread of AIDS, however, required frank discussions of sexual issues. With her impish grandmotherly look and a thick European accent, she branched out to TV with the shows *Good Sex with Dr. Ruth* and *Sexually Speaking* and continues as the spokesperson for good, responsible sex. Is Dr. Ruth alone as a leading Jewish purveyor of self-help advice to America? Hardly. Dr. Joyce Brothers and Dr. Laura Schlessinger on the airwaves and Ann Landers (Esther Pauline Friedman Lederer) and her twin sister Abigail "Dear Abby" Van Buren (Pauline Esther Friedman Phillips) in print, all have made their living doing the same thing.

VERBAL CONFIDENCE IS PART OF JUDAISM

As noted earlier, Jews routinely study the Torah (Bible), the Talmud (the rabbinical commentaries) and the Mishna, books of codified Jewish laws for daily living. This study involves individual readings and then group discussions about the stories and the laws. It isn't about memorization and recitation; the discussions are critical reviews, with intensive questioning and debate. Even questions that might be considered heretical are dealt with analytically. The Christian approach to accepting one's fundamental religious doctrines without a great deal of critical debate is a major cultural departure from the Jewish tradition. Being able to ask a good question and debate all sides of an argument shows that one has a good grasp of the material.

Jews actively question and debate the Old Testament. Teachers encourage questions as a way to get closer to the faith. By overcoming objections and dealing with inconsistencies head on, young minds can learn. More importantly, if children are trained to question the Torah, the holiest of books, then their ability to analyze and question everyday things such as academic problems and business transactions becomes keener. To take an example from the Bible, Moses is said to have parted the Red Sea during the Exodus from slavery in Egypt. It is a fantastic story and made great cinematography. Could it be true? It is a legitimate question for Jewish kids to ask, and the question leads them to explore possible theories such as tidal movements that can be observed today at the Red Sea. Such discussions might expand to the "Ten Plagues" when the family reads the story of Exodus at the Seder dinner table. The same goes for the stories of Noah, Jonah and even Creation. A liberal reading of the story of Creation finds common ground with Darwin's Theory of Evolution: "The plants came before the animals, fish before fowl, fowl before animals, animals before man and woman." What is important here is not so much the subject matter, but that parents allow and encourage the children to investigate, read and critically examine any subject.

"CHILDREN ARE TO BE SEEN AND HEARD"

"Children are to be seen, not heard" is by no means a Jewish axiom. Children are not only included in the religious life of the Jewish family, they are an integral part of it. In one of the most sacred Jewish holidays, Passover, an important portion of the Seder dinner is called "The Four Questions." The youngest child able to read asks his or her father about the meaning of the holiday by chanting the four questions in Hebrew. Standing in front of guests, parents, grandparents and siblings, the child is under enormous pressure to perform well. To give you a flavor of it, the first two lines are:

(Hebrew transliteration)
Mah nishtanah ha-lailah hazeh mikol ha-laylot?

(English translation)
Why is this night different from all other nights?

(Hebrew transliteration)
She'b-khol ha-laylot anu okhlim hametz u'matzah,
ha-lailah hazeh kulo matzah.

(English translation)
All the other nights we may eat bread or matzah,
this night only matzah.

Later in the Passover ceremony, a passage in the Torah advises the father to answer the questions based on the intelligence of his children. "The Torah speaks about four sons: one who is wise and one who is rebellious; one who is simple and one who does not even know how to ask a question." The interesting example is the "rebellious son" because it gives an insight to the origins of Jewish legal training.

"The rebellious son asks, 'What is the meaning of this service to you?' Saying you, he excludes himself, and because he excludes himself from the group, he denies his heritage. The father should therefore tell him plainly, 'Because of what the Eternal did for me when I came forth from Egypt I do this, for me and not for you. Had you been there, you would not have been redeemed.'"

As the passage indicates, articulate speech is important to Jews. And for parents and children, being able to debate adequately is a critical skill.

The Bar Mitzvah for boys and the Bat Mitzvah for girls are the other Jewish ceremonial events in which Jewish children's verbal confidence is developed. At age thirteen, the Jewish child is recognized as an adult, able to make his or her religious choices and take responsibility for them. The boy or girl leads Sabbath's service by reading that week's passage from the Torah. As with the Passover ceremony, intensive preparation is required to read the Hebrew passages, and the young initiate is placed squarely in the spotlight. As Sherry Ellowitz Silver recalls, "I found out I could sing, be in front of a group and perform. I got a lot of pats on the back and later went on to get a B.A. in drama. My Bat Mitzvah was my first realization that I could be a performer, that I had talent." Later she became the religious school director at Temple Israel in Hollywood, California.[3]

The first reading of the Torah is a special event by the newly recognized adult, but only in recent history have Jews celebrated it with festivities and a special ceremony. The formal Bar Mitzvah ceremony goes back only four hundred to six hundred years, making it a modern custom. Technically, a Jewish child is considered an adult without the ceremony.[4] With the affluence of many Jews today, the reception after the Bar Mitzvah ceremony has been transformed into a lavish birthday party with entertainment. Indeed, it's now a competition, a matter of "keeping up with the Cohens."

A father was lecturing his Bar Mitzvah–age son on the advantages of thrift. "A fool and his money are soon parted," he said, quoting the old adage.

"I guess you're right, Dad," answered the boy. "But tell me, how did the fool and his money ever get together in the first place?"

JEWISH COMEDIANS

Jews' verbal confidence has often manifested itself in the entertainment industry – especially comedy. The ability to twist a phrase, the skill of timing and delivery, and the sheer bravery of facing an audience to make it laugh require all the chutzpah you can muster.

In the 1960s *Time* magazine estimated that 80 percent of the most popular comedians were Jewish. In their heyday in the '50s and '60s there were more than a thousand resorts in the Catskill Mountains of New York that served as the training ground for many newcomers. Called "the Borscht Belt" because of the beet soup called borscht that older European Jews enjoy, the area was filled with hotel resorts like Grossinger's, the Concord, Taminment, and The Nevele. Today, comedy is far more diverse, but Jews still make their mark with mirth.

Comedy is definitely not a profession with a high probability of a higher income. In fact most comics earn little and give up. However, it's possible to hit it really big. At the top of the list is Jerry Seinfeld, whose show was "the most profitable piece of entertainment of all time," said *Forbes* in 1998. *Seinfeld* earned almost $200 million in annual advertising revenue in its later years. Even though the show's last episode was only in 1998, up-front syndication sales had already totaled $1.7 billion by September of that year. The show's profitability is nothing to laugh at, with $400 million for NBC, $600 million for Castle Rock Entertainment and $250 million for Columbia Tristar. As for the Jews, Jerry earned $300 million and his producer buddy Larry David earned $270 million. "George," Jason Alexander (Jay Scott Greenspan), and "Elaine," Julie Louis-Dreyfus, made $15 million each.

On his own show Tim Allen, America's funny handyman, earned $77 million in 1998. Paul Reiser, star of the prime-time sitcom *Mad About You*, earned $48 million in 1998. In fact, five of the top ten of *Forbes'* Top 40 Entertainers in 1998 were Jewish: three comedians, a producer and an actor: Jerry Seinfeld, $225 million; Larry David, $200 million; Steven Spielberg, $175 million; Tim Allen, $77 million[5]; and Harrison Ford, $58 million. Yes, Harrison Ford is Jewish. His mom was a Jewish girl from Brooklyn, and his grandmother came from Russia and kept a kosher home.[6]

In the past, many Jewish comedians kept their Jewishness either a secret or just below the surface, except when performing in the Catskills. Most changed their names to something more "acceptable" for the general stage. Today's comedians are more forthright about their Judaism and most keep their given names.[7]

OLDER-GENERATION JEWISH COMEDIANS

Stage Names	Given Names If Different
Woody Allen	Allan Konigsberg
Jack Benny	Benjamin Kubelski
Milton Berle	Milton Berlinger
Joey Bishop	Joseph Gottlieb
Victor Borge	Borg Rosenbaum
Mel Brooks	Melvyn Kaminsky
Lenny Bruce	Lenny Schneider
George Burns	Nathan Birnbaum
Sid Caesar	
Eddie Cantor	Isador Iskowitch
Norm Crosby	
Rodney Dangerfield	Jacob Cohen
Phyliss Diller	
Shecky Greene	Sheldon Greenfield
Buddy Hackett	Leonard Hacker
Buck Henry	Buck Zuckerman
Al Jolson	Asa Yoelson
Danny Kaye	David Kominsky
Alan King	Irwin Knilberg
Harvey Korman	
Al Lewis	

Jerry Lewis. . . . . Joseph Levitch
Marx Brothers:
    Chico Marx . . . . Leonard Marx
    Groucho Marx . . . . Julius Marx
    Harpo Marx . . . . Adolph Marx
Jackie Mason . . . . Yacov Maza
Molly Picon
Carl Reiner
Don Rickles
Ritz Brothers:
  Al Ritz
  Harry Ritz
  Jimmy Ritz
Joan Rivers . . . . Joan Molinsky
Mort Sahl
Soupy Sales . . . . Milton Supman
Peter Sellers
Phil Silvers. . . . . Philip Silversmith
Three Stooges:
    Larry Fine . . . . Louis Fineberg
    Curly Howard . . . . Jerome Horwitz
    Mo Howard . . . . Moses Horwitz
    Shemp Howard. . . . . . . Samuel Horwitz
Sophie Tucker . . . . Sonia Kalisn
Henny Youngman

NEWER-GENERATION JEWISH COMEDIANS

Stage Names	Given Names If Different
Tim Allen	
Richard Belzer	
Sandra Bernhard	
Elayne Boosler	
David Brenner	
Albert Brooks	Albert Einstein
Andrew "Dice" Clay	Andrew Silverstein
Billy Crystal	
Fran Drescher	
Al Franken	

Gilbert Gotfried

Gabe Kaplan

Andy Kaufman

Robert Klein

Krusty the Clown . . . . Hershel Krustofsky

Richard Lewis

Jon Lovitz

Howie Mandel

Rick Moranis

Pee-Wee Herman . . . . Paul Reubens

Gilda Radner

Paul Reiser

Roseanne (Barr)

Bob Saget

Adam Sandler

Jerry Seinfeld

Garry Shandling

Harry Shearer

Pauly Shore

Ben Stein

Howard Stern . . . . (Jewish father)

In a bit of a switch of the name game, Caryn Johnson took the name Whoopi Goldberg. She made the change, according to a 1997 *Philadelphia Inquirer* interview, to honor her Jewish ancestors.

Is Jewish humor different from other people's comedy? There are many theories. Some see it as the Jewish love of words and argument. Others see a tendency for drama and exaggeration:

Customer: "Oh, waiter!"

Waiter: "Yes, what's the matter?"

Customer: "Taste the soup."

Waiter: "You always have this soup. Today, you don't like it? Look, mister, you don't like the soup, I'll bring you another soup."

Customer: "Taste the soup."

Waiter: "You don't want the barley soup, OK, I'll bring you some matzah-ball soup."

Customer: "Taste the soup."

Waiter: "All right! All right already! I'll taste the soup. Where's the spoon?"

Customer: "AH-HA!!!"

Jewish humor also tends to be more self-critical, sometimes directed at Jews as a whole, or at certain personality types within the community. If the joke involves sex, so much the better:

Father Flaherty is sitting in the confessional booth when he hears an unfamiliar voice with a heavy Jewish accent.

"Father, my name is Morris Lipsky. I am 79 years old. I am currently involved with a 24-year-old girl and also, on the side, with her 19-year-old sister. We engage in all manner of sexual pleasure, and in my whole life I never felt better!"

"My good man," asks the priest, "are you a Catholic?"

Lipsky replied, "No, Father, I'm not."

"Then why are you telling me?"

Lipsky replied proudly, "I'm telling everybody!"

And of course, the quest for material success is an inexhaustible well for humorous material:

A poor Jew walking in the forest feels close enough to God to ask, "God, what is a million years to you?'

God replies, "My son, a million years to you is like a second to me."

The man asks, "God, what is a million dollars to you?"

God replies, "My son, a million dollars to you is less than a penny to me. It means almost nothing to me."

The man asks, "So, God, can I have a million dollars?"

And God replies, "In a second."

THE ENTERTAINMENT INDUSTRY

MOTION PICTURES

Another area of the performing arts in which Jewish people have excelled
is the motion picture industry. In fact, Jews were the creators of Hollywood
and the large studios that defined it. The Jewish involvement in motion pictures is more than a success story; it is the basis of the disproportionate
influence that Jews have had in shaping American popular culture. And it
does not end with movies, since the film industry, in effect, gave birth to
the television industry.

The movie industry began rather modestly with the installation of nick-
elodeons in saloons and other working-class haunts, where people would
pay a nickel to see these "peep shows" that exhibited short scenes of comedy or mayhem. By the beginning of the century the purveyors of this
entertainment realized that movies would not be embraced by the masses
unless they moved out of the bars and into respectable theaters. Adolph
Zukor, a New York furrier, and Carl Laemmle, a Chicago clothing-store
manager, independently realized that if they created the right environment,
the masses would come to see a movie. At the age of nineteen, Louis B.
Mayer, the son of a scrap-metal dealer, took over a seedy burlesque house
in Boston and renovated it – the first of his several theater palaces. The
problem with the business was that there were few worthwhile movies to
show. The movies that came from Europe were not well suited for
Americans, so out of necessity these Jewish theater owners moved from
exhibition to distribution and finally to production. Mayer and Samuel
Goldwyn went on to form MGM. Zukor founded Paramount Pictures.
Laemmle started Universal Studios.

Their stories read just like a classic movie. Goldwyn, born in Warsaw
as Schmuel Gelbfisz, started out as a telegraph delivery boy in New York,
and his chutzpah and his newly acquired confidence in the English language took him far. While attending night school to learn English, he read
newspapers that he had fished out of the garbage. By accident he saw an
ad for glove factory workers in nearby Gloversville. He moved to take the
job, but quickly tiring of it, talked his way into a salesman's job and got
the boss to advance him a small inventory to peddle. He became a fast-
talking sales machine and had soon saved about $10,000 from his com-
missions, a small fortune at that time. On his regular selling route in
1912 he met his wife-to-be, Blanche Lasky, who with her brother Jesse

Lasky were minor performers at Catskills hotels.

By pure accident Goldwyn and the Lasky siblings went to see a movie in New York, and Goldwyn became immediately enamored by the spectacle of Mary Pickford on the screen. The plots were simple, and the production looked simple to Goldwyn. He decided that very evening that he would go into the motion picture business. According to Stephen Birmingham, it was Blanche, a native of southern California, who pointed out that more and more movies were being made on the West Coast because of the cleaner air and longer hours of sunshine. She also noted the cost consideration of not having to heat a studio in winter.[8]

Goldwyn used his savings to back the venture, but he and the Laskys still needed a director. They happened to know a young playwright-actor, Cecil Blunt DeMille (not Jewish), who they thought might be able to direct. DeMille had never directed before, but he was game. In fact, he wanted to change the game. Instead of the simple, short film that was the standard fare at the time, he wanted to make the first full-length film that told a story. After sneaking around to observe the shooting of a film in upstate New York, DeMille decided there was nothing to it. After raising an additional $15,000, they were in business with a budget of $25,000. In 1914 they chose *The Squaw Man* as their subject and filmed it in a barn in Santa Monica. Although the film was not artistically up to the standards of his films to come, it was popular, and Goldwyn, Lasky and DeMille were in business.

A year later, in 1915, the blockbuster *Birth of a Nation* proved once and for all that people were ready to go to the movies. The fortunes of the fledgling Jewish studios began to grow. Goldwyn's company, the Jesse Lasky Feature Play Company merged with Adolph Zukor's Famous Players Company to form the Famous Players–Lasky Corporation. Goldwyn could not get along with his partners and formed the Goldwyn Picture Corp., which became MGM. Famous Players–Lasky eventually became Paramount Pictures.

By 1918 there were more than seventy production companies in Los Angeles and more than 80 percent of the world's movies were being made there. In 1925, Bell Labs invented the process of synchronizing sound with pictures and called the process Vitaphone. Sam and Jack Warner saw its promise and produced the first big-screen musical, *The Jazz Singer* with Al Jolson. The movie is about an Orthodox Jewish boy who rejects his father's wish that he succeed him as cantor in his synagogue and instead runs off to become an entertainer. It is amazing that in a time when anti-Semitism was so high, that story played in Peoria.

Other notable Jewish media moguls of early Hollywood include: William Fox who founded Twentieth Century Fox, Marcus Loew who started Metro Pictures of MGM and the Loew's theaters, and Harry Cohn who began Columbia Pictures.

The business was in its infancy and all of these men ran the day-to-day operations of their studios with an iron hand. They selected the scripts, the directors, the sets, the actors and the actresses. Often called boorish and tyrannical, they controlled by their forceful wills the lives of thousands of Hollywood employees.

Many actors, like comedians, changed their names to conceal their Jewish identity. While some touch of Jewishness was tolerated in comedy, dramatic actors were expected to be totally assimilated. Their lives mirrored the lives of the studio chiefs who were themselves trying to enter mainstream society and gain acceptance by keeping their Jewishness secret. As Birmingham observes, "It was joked that the movie tycoons went from Poland to polo in one generation."[9]

The rise of the comic actor Danny Kaye (David Kominsky) is a case in point. Kaye developed his material in the Catskills and then became a success in a New York City nightclub in 1940. Sam Goldwyn caught his act, loved his performances and signed him for a movie without a screen test. When Kaye was tested in California, Goldwyn was disturbed that his nose and look were "too, too Jewish." Kaye refused to fix his nose, and lighting and makeup could not solve the problem. Goldwyn had discovered Danny Kaye, and he was not about to give up. Then it hit him, "I've got it! He'll be having his hair dyed blond." With Kaye's wavy mane of blond hair instead of brown, the camera and the audience would be drawn away from his telltale nose and he would have a Nordic look. Danny Kaye, the Jew, had disappeared.[10] Other notable Jewish actors who became Gentiles on screen were Kirk Douglas (Issur Danielovich), Edward G. Robinson (Emanuel Goldenberg), Lauren Bacall (Betty Joan Perske) and Tony Curtis (Bernard Schwartz).

The day of the big studios has passed, but the Jewish influence on Hollywood remains. Dreamworks owners Steven Spielberg, David Geffen and Jeffrey Katzenberg together have a $5 billion nest egg to back them. Sumner Redstone, who owns Paramount Pictures through his Viacom, once owned a large percentage of Columbia Pictures and Twentieth

Century Fox. Michael Eisner leads the Disney studio, which in Walt's day, ironically, excluded Jews. Edgar Bronfman's Seagram owns Universal Studios. Michael Ovitz manages major celebrity careers.

Bob and Harvey Weinstein got their start by holding concerts and playing B movies at a dilapidated movie house in Buffalo, New York. With a trip to Cannes in 1979 they entered into movie distribution and began to build Miramax. Ten years later they hit their stride with *Cinema Paradiso*, *My Left Foot*, and *Sex, Lies and Videotape*. They hit again with *The Crying Game* in 1992 and *The Piano* in 1993. Eisner's Disney bought their company for a reported $60 million to $80 million that year, and the next year Miramax released *Pulp Fiction*, which grossed more than $100 million.

In addition to the corporate chieftains, a huge number of Jewish people participate in the entertainment industry. It has not been part of a grand scheme, but when an ethnic group becomes as heavily involved, and as successful, in a particular industry as Jewish people have been in movies, the group's influence, connections and power produce a vast ripple effect, and other Jewish actors, writers, editors, technicians, directors and producers follow in their footsteps.

Producers and directors require especially strong interpersonal skills and force of will to lead a group of egocentric creative people through the daunting task of producing a film. Steven Spielberg has been the most successful producer/director of all time, with a net worth of $2 billion in 1999. His list of credits and Oscars is legendary as he has produced or directed seven of the top-ten-grossing films. His credits include *Jaws* (1975), *Close Encounters of the Third Kind* (1977), *Raiders of the Lost Ark* (1981), *E.T.* (1982), *Back to the Future* (1985), *The Color Purple* (1985), *Schindler's List* (1993), *Jurassic Park* (1993), *Men in Black* (1997) and *Saving Private Ryan* (1998).

Spielberg has a lot of Jewish company in the exclusive ranks of successful Hollywood producers and directors. A short list includes: Erich von Stroheim (*Greed*, 1924), David O. Selznick (*Gone With the Wind*, 1939), Otto Preminger (*Laura*, 1944), Billy Wilder (*Sunset Boulevard*, 1950), Stanley Kramer (*The Caine Mutiny*, 1954), Stanley Kubrick (*2001: A Space Odyssey*, 1968), Mike Nichols (*The Graduate*, 1968), Sydney Pollack (*Out of Africa*, 1985), Oliver Stone (*Platoon*, 1986), Rob Reiner (*Stand by Me*, 1986) and Nora Ephron (*Sleepless in Seattle*, 1993). Surprisingly, Norman Jewison, who directed *Fiddler on the Roof* (1971), is not Jewish.

TELEVISION NETWORKS

The Jewish influence is just as pronounced in television as it is in the movies. After graduating from the University of Pennsylvania's Wharton School of Business in 1922, William Paley went to work for his father's Congress Cigar Co. When the company advertised on the radio and saw its sales take off, Paley saw the potential of radio and changed careers. He invested in a small radio network called the Columbia Phonographic Broadcasting System in 1927 and built it into what we know as CBS today.[11] As head of the CBS television network, where he reigned until his death in 1990, Paley personally controlled the programming. Under his leadership, *I Love Lucy, Gunsmoke, The Ed Sullivan Show,* and Edward R. Murrow came to the airwaves (Lucy, Sullivan and Murrow were not Jewish).

Mel Karmazin currently runs CBS and in September 1999 he also became the operating chief of Viacom after the merger of the companies. At the time he told the *Wall Street Journal,* "This is a deal I wanted to make I think from the time I was bar-mitzvahed."

David Sarnoff founded the NBC radio network and started NBC television. In the 1950s under the chairmanship of Leonard Goldenson, a group of NBC stations broke away from the network and formed ABC. Disney's Michael Eisner bought ABC in 1993, and in March 1999 he hired Steve Bornstein as president of the ABC Group, which includes the network, radio and TV stations, ESPN and the Disney Channel. Bornstein had been the president of ESPN, where he programmed the network's 24-hour format from its beginning in 1980.

JEWISH TV PROGRAMMING

Television in the early years, from the late 1940s to early 1950s, openly portrayed Jewish characters. *The Goldbergs,* for example, was a popular show from 1949 to 1955. The Yiddish theater actress Molly Picon starred in *The Molly Picon Show* in 1949. But times changed. According to a 1996 article in the Jewish magazine *Inside,* "By the late 1950s and early '60s, while marginally Jewish performers could still host variety shows such as *The Eddie Fisher Show* (1957–59), *The Gypsy Rose Lee Show* (1958), *The Danny Kaye Show* (1963–67) and several programs starring Milton Berle (1948–67), television's fictional heroes were growing less and less ethnic." The network heads became just as focused upon downplaying Jewishness as the studio heads had been in the movies. "Urban sitcoms were replaced by homogeneous settings. The family shows were all-American, which meant vaguely northern European and carefully noncontroversial. Just one character in 700 was Jewish."[12]

In 1960 Carl Reiner presented CBS with a pilot for a sitcom starring himself about a New York comedy writer. CBS only bought the show when Reiner agreed to make it "accessible to the public." Dick Van Dyke, definitely a non-Jew, was chosen to star as writer Rob Petrie, and Reiner appeared occasionally as Alan Brady, the fictitious star of the show within a show. Buddy Sorrell, played by Morey Amsterdam, was not openly Jewish until its final seasons, when he belatedly celebrated his own Bar Mitzvah as a grown-up as a present to his mother. In a bit of a twist, Werner Klemperer reveled in his role parodying the Nazis as Colonel Wilhelm Klink on *Hogan's Heroes*.

In the 1970s the self-imposed freeze began to thaw just a bit. Because of its talented producer Norman Lear, *All in the Family* became a groundbreaking sitcom in which the issues of prejudice and civil rights became not only the topics for on-air comedy and but also the subject of conversations of American households. Valerie Harper as Rhoda Morgenstern appeared as an openly Jewish woman in *The Mary Tyler Moore Show* (1970–77) and even had her own spinoff, *Rhoda*, in 1974. With Beatrice Arthur as Maude, Lear was told to write Jewish but to think of her as a Gentile. Lear also produced *Sanford and Son, The Jeffersons, Good Times, One Day at a Time, Diff'rent Strokes, Soap*, and *Mary Hartman, Mary Hartman*.

In other roles both Tony Randall (born Leonard Rosenberg) and Jack Klugman had played Jews, but their TV characters on *The Odd Couple* were not. Peter Falk was not overtly Jewish in *Columbo* from 1971 to 1990. Dinah Shore (born Fanny Rose Shore) had a daytime talk show for years, and her Jewishness rarely became a topic of conversation. *Welcome Back Kotter* with Gabe Kaplan was successful from 1975 to 1979, but his religion was not made an issue. For Hal Linden (born Harold Lipshitz), *Barney Miller* was written to keep his Jewishness "just below the surface." According to writer-producer Danny Arnold, "They were very supersensitive at the time (1974) to anything ethnic. So we kept it very quiet once the show started. When people asked me if he was Jewish, I'd say, 'You don't have to think he is, but don't tell me he isn't.'"[13] Later in the 1970s Lear returned and Archie Bunker took on a Jewish business partner in the last incarnation of *All in the Family*, called *Archie Bunker's Place* (1979–83).

Maybe not as controversial, but just as entertaining, were producer

Aaron Spelling and his lesser-known partner, Leonard Goldberg. Spelling made his first mark on the face of television in the late 1960s with *Mod Squad* and hit the mainstream – with no references to Jews at all – in the 1970s, right alongside Norman Lear's ethnic sitcoms. Spelling and Goldberg succeeded by understanding what Americans wanted to watch: light, escapist dramas – *Charlie's Angels* (1976–81), *Fantasy Island* (1978–81), *The Rookies, Starsky and Hutch, Dynasty* (1981–89), *Hart to Hart* (1979–84) and *Family*. On his own, Spelling created *Love Boat, Vegas, Hotel* and, even more recently, *Beverly Hills 90210* and *Melrose Place*.

In the 1980s there was a conspicuous absence of Jews on prime-time. Perhaps it was because of the Reagan revolution, the rise of conservatism or the Yuppie culture; for whatever reason, Jews were invisible. Michael Landon (Eugene Orowitz), the most prominent Jewish actor in prime time, portrayed an angel on *Highway to Heaven*. Judd Hirsch of *Taxi* remembers that it took a few seasons before "they eventually, finally let me refer to being Jewish."[14] Not until *Anything but Love*, starring Richard Lewis (1989) as the neurotic Jewish boyfriend of Jamie Lee Curtis, reached No. 10 in the ratings did openly Jewish characters reappear. Dr. Joel Fleischman was the "fish out of water" Jew in Alaska in *Northern Exposure*. *Murphy Brown's* Miles Silverberg played a Jewish TV producer. With urban Jewish characters coming back into vogue, Jerry Seinfeld in *Seinfeld*, Paul Reiser in *Mad About You* and Fran Drescher in *The Nanny* followed in the 1990s.

Following Norman Lear's success with sitcoms in the 1970s, Tom Werner and his Gentile partner Marcy Carsey made it even bigger in the 1980s and 1990s.[15] Werner graduated from Harvard and went on to make documentary films. Carsey went to the University of New Hampshire and started as a page at NBC. In 1976 Werner became Carsey's assistant as a manager of comedy development at ABC, for which Carsey became the senior vice president in charge of prime-time series.

Under their leadership ABC developed the huge prime-time hits *Happy Days, Mork & Mindy* and *Three's Company*. In 1980 Carsey left to form her own production company, and Werner took her job at ABC. He rejoined Carsey a year later in a one-room office above a 7-Eleven Store in Westwood, California. By 1983, with their initial projects all failures, they were at the end of their rope. They were heavily in debt and barely able to pay the phone bill. Then in 1984, NBC asked them to develop a sitcom featuring Bill Cosby. With one-third ownership of the show, they spent all their remaining assets paying for the expenses that were not covered by NBC in the first season. The rest is history. *Cosby* was the smash hit that began NBC's dominance on Thursday nights. *Cosby* in syndication has generated more than $1 billion. In 1998 *Forbes* estimated each of the partners' net worth at $600 million. The two went on to create *A Different World, Roseanne, Cybill* and *Grace Under Fire*. On *Roseanne*, Roseanne's character is not Jewish, although the actress is Jewish. Interestingly, in Werner's and Carsey's only sitcom with a Jewish flavor, Jackie Mason starred in *Chicken Soup* in 1989, but the series failed to make it past its first shows.[16]

In 1996, on another successful Carsey-Werner production, aliens on *3rd Rock from the Sun* had assumed human shapes, human names and human jobs. The only thing left for them was to pick an ethnicity. After an episode of deliberation, during which they tried being Italian and African American, they decided to be Jewish.

TV GAME SHOWS

Another aspect of television programming that has a strong Jewish connection is the TV game show. Mark Goodson began building his game show empire at the very infancy of television. His parents were Russian immigrants and opened the first health-food store in Berkeley, California. Goodson started as a radio DJ and eventually became a radio producer. In 1939 he created his first radio game show, *Pop the Question*, in which contestants threw darts at balloons containing questions. In 1950, he and a partner Bill Todman, a radio writer, took their already-successful radio game shows *Stop the Music* and *Beat the Clock* and transferred them to the TV format. They worked even better on TV, as the shows were inexpensive to produce and the drama of their games played well on TV.

Game shows became a national obsession in the 1950s, and Goodson–Todman created an unparalleled string of game show hits that included 42,000 half-hours of TV. Fortunately the two men were not caught up in the game-show scandals that rocked *Twenty-One* and *The $64,000 Question*, and they went on to make shows for four more decades. *What's My Line?* (1950), *I've Got a Secret* (1952), *The Price Is Right* (1953), *To Tell the Truth* (1956), *Concentration* (1958), *Password* (1961) and *The Match Game* (1962) were among their hugely popular creations. Their last smash hit was *Family Feud* in 1976. At the time of his death in 1992,

Goodson's wealth was estimated at a minimum of $450 million.[17]

Merv Griffin, a Catholic, worked for Goodson–Todman for a time and learned the trade well from the masters. Merv is a shining example how somebody who is not Jewish can benefit from Jewish wealth wisdom. Merv Griffin's first TV job was hosting a talk show called *Look Up and Live* that focused on Jewish issues. He proved to be such a good host that everyone assumed he was also Jewish. He wasn't, but when he entered the game-show industry, he was such an eager learner that he might well have been. Griffin invented *Jeopardy!* (1959) and *Wheel of Fortune* (1975), which became the most profitable game shows in history. Retaining a 30-percent stake of the show's future profits, Griffin sold his production company in 1986 to Coca-Cola for $250 million.[18]

TELEVISION NEWS AND JEWS

On the TV news desk, Jews have been very visible in front of the camera. As journalists, their personal religious and cultural beliefs are not made an issue in their reporting, but their power is significant because they influence how we as Americans view the world and shape our opinions. Ted Koppel, Matt Lauer, Leslie Stahl, Larry King (Zeigler), Lynn Sherr, Bettina Gregory, Barbara Walters, Giselle Fernandez (Jewish mother) and Geraldo Rivera (Jewish mother) are on the air every day. Bob Simon, Morton Dean, Morley Safer, Mike Wallace, Jeff Greenfield, Marvin and Bernard Kalb, Irving R. Levine, Edwin Newman, Maury Povich and Daniel Schorr are on TV at least once a week. Geraldo Rivera was the highest-paid TV journalist with $10 million total earnings in 1998.

Jews seem to have a talent for movie criticism as well. Gene Shalit, Joel Siegel, Leonard Maltin, Jeffrey Lyons, Michael Medved and the late Gene Siskel are all Jewish. On the sports beat, Howard Cosell made his mark with Muhammad Ali in the 1970s, and Marv Albert made his mark as a broadcaster and in the courtroom in 1997.

Needless to say, these TV journalists have chutzpah. As Barbara Walters puts it, "You can be the nice girl reporter who doesn't offend, or you do what you have to do."[19] Walters of ABC News was the first network anchorwoman and the first to have a million-dollar contract; she earned $8.5 million in 1998. Larry King voiced a similar sentiment: "I always knew I was different. I thought about things and looked at things differently. The world was a little crazy to me. I was always questioning. I drove the rabbis crazy."[20]

Even more influential than reporters are the television news producers, since they decide which stories will go on air, in which order and how long they will run. A disproportionate number of these are Jewish as well. Today both of the major newsmagazines have Jewish producers, Don Hewitt of *60 Minutes* and Victor Neufeld of *20/20*. *60 Minutes*, in particular, started in 1968 and has become the longest-running newsmagazine show. It maintains its top-ten ratings year after year. With Mike Wallace, Morley Safer and Leslie Stahl reporting (all Jewish), the show has a history of creating news through its unique form of investigative TV journalism.[21] This show more than any other has moved Washington and the world to action on issues ranging from consumer fraud and government waste to human rights atrocities. Av Weston, former vice president of program development at ABC says, "Don Hewitt, who took charge of *CBS Evening News* in 1950 at the age of twenty-five, developed many of the techniques that turned television news into a distinctive journalistic form; before Hewitt's innovations, TV newscasts resembled the old movie newsreels."[22]

At one point in the 1980s, the executive producers of all three evening news shows were Jewish. Furthermore, as *Jewish Power* points out, while Jews make up "5% of the working press nationwide – hardly more than their share of the population – they make up one-fourth of the writers, editors and producers in America's 'elite media,' including network news divisions, the top newsweeklies and the four leading papers."[23]

The remarkably high percentage of Jewish people in television has lasted for generations, perhaps because it is a relatively small and close-knit community. In a poll of TV's creative leaders, 59 percent said they were raised in the Jewish faith, while 38 percent still identified themselves as Jews.[24]

VERBAL CONFIDENCE: LINKS TO THE OTHER KEYS

Verbal confidence is a crucial key in unlocking the other secrets of Jewish wealth wisdom. Doctors, lawyers, real estate brokers, securities traders and retailers are but of a few of the professional people for whom a quick wit and eloquent tongue are critical. And as for "taking care of your own," the Jewish support of civil rights, women's rights in particular, and the heavy Jewish involvement in politics require the well-developed skills of confident speech. Even academic success often hinges upon one's ability to speak up and participate in class.

HOW CAN OTHER GROUPS DEVELOP THEIR VERBAL CONFIDENCE?

1. Encourage your children to ask questions

2. Proactively explain new ideas to your children

3. Have "active" dinners together as a family

4. Encourage participation in the performing arts and sports

5. Consider joining Toastmasters as an adult

ENCOURAGE YOUR CHILDREN TO ASK QUESTIONS

Learning to speak up begins early. Make it clear to your children that it's alright to ask questions. An open line of communication between a parent and child is the child's first social interaction, and it is very important. If a child's questions are greeted with enthusiasm and understandable answers, they will continue, which is the basis for good verbal skills. If questions are treated as a nuisance, communication will diminish. Verbal confidence will give your child an incredible advantage.

PROACTIVELY EXPLAIN NEW IDEAS TO YOUR CHILDREN

The world is a new and exciting place to children. What adults consider ordinary, children see as an adventure. Explaining new things to children gives them both confidence and a sense of the world's wonder. At the park, explain the natural phenomena around you: the sun, the seasons, the plants, gravity. When at home, explain how water gets to your bathtub. How about describing how the parent or parents earn money to pay for the things that the family needs? When children begin to understand the rules of the world, they see how they fit in and start to participate. The more they want to get involved, the more they will develop their verbal skills.

HAVE "ACTIVE" DINNERS TOGETHER AS A FAMILY

One of the best forums for early verbal education and communication is at the dinner table. Expressing themselves clearly for their parents and siblings is an important proving ground for children. As a parent, ask your children what they did during the day. And most importantly, give them time to talk and really listen to what they say. As your children grow, politics, current events and social issues will become endless sources for lively table conversation and debate. When your child offers an opinion, ask him why he thinks that way, thus encouraging him to understand that good opinions must be well reasoned. In the Jewish household, such lively debate is par for the course and provides Jewish children with a competitive advantage in their educational and professional endeavors.

ENCOURAGE PARTICIPATION
IN THE PERFORMING ARTS AND SPORTS

Not every child has the talent to be a great singer, actor or varsity letterman, but there are many opportunities for children to participate. What is important is that children get the experience of appearing before other people. Public speaking, singing, playing an instrument and athletic performances are character-building and confidence-building experiences. Appearing publicly requires preparation and practice. And when it is game day or show time, the pressure to perform is real and immediate, just as it is in adult life.

CONSIDER JOINING TOASTMASTERS AS AN ADULT

If I have children, I can help them develop their verbal confidence, but how about if I am a shy adult? The nonprofit organization Toastmasters International has more than 8,000 chapters worldwide. This group's goal is to build the verbal confidence of its members. Public speaking and confident conversation are what Toastmasters works on. Toastmasters groups meet in most cities in the United States. Check it out at *www.toastmasters.org*. It is a good way to overcome shyness and build up your own verbal confidence.

CHAPTER 5

Be Selectively Extravagant
but Prudently Frugal

Plenty has been written about successful Jews and how much money they have made. Accumulating wealth and keeping it, though, are two different stories. Not all Jews have rags-to-riches stories in spite of their education and better-paying jobs. That is why the "spending" part of the story is so important. To accumulate wealth, you have to learn how to save and how to spend wisely. So, how do Jews spend? Jewish spending habits can be described as a balance of selective extravagance and prudent frugality. The basis for the anti-Semitic perception of Jewish miserliness stems from the fact that Jews have had extraordinary success in accumulating wealth in their professional pursuits, and that for many people the "hateful miser" theory is easier to accept than the fact that hard work, a better education and successful commerce have made them wealthy.

According to a *Forbes* article entitled "Titans of the Tightwads," the most notorious misers are not Jewish. Calvin Coolidge owned only two suits at a time. J. Paul Getty installed a pay phone in his house saying, "You get some fellow talking for ten or fifteen minutes, well, it adds up!" When out of town, he had porters re-address and forward his mail, rather than splurge for new postage stamps. Clark Gable used to argue with his grocer in Encino, California, over a few cents' difference in what jelly beans cost compared to the year before. Cary Grant marked all the milk bottles in the refrigerator with a red pen to keep the household staff from pilfering. And as for Lee Iacocca, "If you have lunch with someone who looks like Iacocca and sounds like Iacocca," the saying went among Chrysler executives, "rest assured – if he offers to pick up the check, it's not Iacocca."[1]

Being frugal with your money does not mean being a miser. It's fair to define "miserly" as going far out of your way to save very little money. For example, if you are at a fast-food restaurant and order a small drink, knowing that refills are free, that's frugal. It's easy to save money, and it takes very little effort to get a refill. On the other hand, bathing only weekly to save water, soap and laundry expenses for towels is miserly. You are subjecting yourself and others to needless unpleasantness for a very minor reward. There are no studies that demonstrate a higher occurrence of misers in the Jewish population than in others. Jewish people have productively stewarded their finances to create an unparalleled amount of capital.

For sure, the stereotype of the Jewish miser exists even in the Jewish community, but Jews protest when anti-Semitic people try to perpetuate this image. In France in November 1995, the respected *Robert Dictionary of Synonyms* listed the French word for "Jew" as equivalent to "miser." As you might expect, the publisher, facing a torrent of protests from the Jewish community, withdrew the book from the shelves. Even Shakespeare's character Shylock in *The Merchant of Venice* still brings rounds of protest in the United States when the play is performed. Shylock, the villain in the play, is portrayed as a foolish miser who loses his daughter and his wealth. According to an article in the newspaper *Globe & Mail*, "The thing that provokes more outrage beyond the stereotyping was that Shylock was forced to convert to Christianity, and that was meant to constitute a happy ending."[2]

Today, however, defaming Jews as misers can be an expensive proposition. When Jeffrey Graber, a 41-year-old senior equipment operator, did not contribute to a pool to buy the boss a Christmas gift, his immediate supervisor called him a "cheap Jew." The same supervisor had made other ethnically disparaging remarks, but this final incident prompted Graber to sue. "I was raised as a Jew, and I'm proud of my heritage," Graber said. "They messed with the wrong person." In August 1998, in the largest such award for an anti-Semitic case, the court made Graber's three supervisors pay him $10,000 each for the offenses. In addition, the court awarded Graber an additional $2.2 million from his employer, Litton Guidance and Control Systems, a major U.S. defense contractor, because it did not monitor its supervisors and because it allowed an openly hostile environment toward minorities to continue.[3]

While I researched this book, I discovered a common sentiment about Jewish spending habits: "I do not like to throw my money away, but when something is important to me I want the best." In the second chapter, we found that Jews give twice the national average to charity. When it comes to education, Jewish students attend the expensive, elite institutions in greater numbers. With higher incomes, an understandable desire to live well and a need for the best schools for their college-bound children, Jewish people spend their money and move into more expensive neighborhoods. At the delicatessen, Jews pay a stunning twenty dollars a pound for lox (smoked salmon) for their bagels. On the other hand, the "verbal confidence" can especially manifest itself when they feel there is room for negotiation or they are not treated fairly at the cash register. Mismarked items and improper applications of discounts are not likely to be overlooked. "Prudent with money" may be a better way to describe Jewish spending habits.

"Why are Jews so smart with their money?" This question was addressed by a Frenchman to the proprietor of a Jewish delicatessen in a Paris neighborhood.

"The answer is very simple," replied the owner. "It is because Jews eat herring."

The Frenchman thereafter became a daily visitor at the deli and consumed herring voraciously.

A few days later the Frenchman entered the deli with a sour look on his face. "You have a lot of nerve to charge me five francs for herring when I can get it down the street for three," bellowed the Frenchman.

"Aha," said the Jew, "I see that you've become smart already."

HISTORIC SPENDING, SAVING AND WEALTH CREATION

During the waves of Eastern European immigration at the turn of the century, Jews were indeed tight with their money, which may have inspired their miserly reputation, particularly in the United States. These immigrants had low-paying jobs in the garment industry, and to save money in order to improve their dismal situation required extreme measures. The average Jewish immigrant arrived with the sum of nine dollars, even less than the average fifteen dollars of other immigrants.[4] The Jewish immigrants' remarkable thrift often brought disapproval. In *How the Other Half Lives* (1893) Jacob Riis wrote that their frugality was "becoming an overmastering passion with these people who come here in droves from Eastern Europe to escape persecution. Saving has enslaved them in bondage worse than that from which they fled. Over and over again I have met Polish or Russian Jews deliberately starving themselves to the point of physical exhaustion while working night and day at tremendous pressure to save a little money." Riis's observations were accurate enough, but he failed to grasp the meaning and implications for the future of what he saw. As Silberman notes in *A Certain People*, "Saving was not an end in itself; it was, rather, a means to another end: to go into business for oneself, or to enable one's children to go into business or to spend the long years of study needed to enter a profession."[5]

Such severe habits had their place in Jewish immigrant history and have affected the saving and spending habits of these immigrants' children and to a lesser degree their grandchildren and great-grandchildren today. This propensity to save has had a profound impact on the relative wealth of Jewish people. Similar spending behavior is found in people who lived through the Depression of the 1930s, and it became the basis for many great fortunes, both Jewish and non-Jewish. Everyday frugality can have a profound long-term impact. The magic of compounding interest will turn a savings of only $175 a month from ages twenty-one to sixty-seven into $1,000,000 at retirement if it is invested at a conservative 8 percent return. Multiply the savings and investing patterns of thousands of ordinary Jews, and you see how a huge pool of Jewish capital has been created.

JEWISH SPENDING HABITS

A 1993 survey of subscribers of the *Exponent*, the Philadelphia weekly Jewish newspaper, gave a clear picture of Jewish wealth and also of Jewish spending. Such surveys are decidedly unscientific, but the results show that Jews are conservative, yet they spend for things that they value.

◻ 26.1 percent owned a second home.

◻ 34.7 percent had traveled outside the United States in the past twelve months.

◻ 49.2 percent had dined out ten or more times in the last thirty days.

◻ 21 percent belonged to a health club.

AUTOMOBILES

The *Exponent* survey surprisingly did not turn up a high percentage of Jews with expensive cars. Chevrolet was the most popular make: 22 percent of readers owned a Chevy versus 24 percent for the general population. An unusually high percentage owned an Oldsmobile, 18 percent versus 9 percent for the general population, but Jewish people really disliked Fords, with 7 percent versus 20 percent. Cadillacs did not rank highly – 5 percent – nor did Mercedes with 2 percent. Japanese cars were especially favored, at over twice the percentage of the general population. It goes without saying that these cars are often reliable and present good value. Forty-nine percent paid cash for their cars, demonstrating a determination to live within their means.

DOMESTIC MAKE

	% owned	Natl. Avg.	Index / 1 = Natl. Avg.
Chevrolet	22.0	24.1	0.9
Oldsmobile	18.1	9.8	1.8
Buick	12.0	9.1	1.2
Chrysler-Plymouth	10.2	8.4	1.2
Ford	7.5	20.1	0.4
Cadillac	5.3	2.9	1.8
Lincoln-Mercury	4.6	6.1	0.7
Dodge	3.0	6.0	0.5
Pontiac	5.1	7.2	0.7

FOREIGN MAKE

	% owned	Natl. Avg.	Index / 1 = Natl. Avg.
Toyota	8.5	4.9	1.7
Nissan	6.1	2.7	2.3

Honda	6.1	2.7	2.3
Subaru	3.7	1.0	3.7
Audi	2.0	0.4	5.0
Mazda	2.0	1.0	2.0
BMW	1.6	0.8	2.0
Mercedes	1.6	0.5	3.2
VW	1.4	4.0	0.4

BOOK PURCHASES

In the publishing industry, it is acknowledged that Jewish people are "the people of the book." An article on Jewish book buying reported that Jews "celebrate and promote books and reading like no other segment of society."[6] Jews are the cornerstone of hardcover book sales, "accounting for between 50 and 75 percent of non-institutional hardcover sales in the United States." Even 25 percent would represent an amazingly disproportionate share of total sales. Hardbacks are the more expensive editions that precede the cheaper paperbacks and provide publishers with their greatest margins. Jewish-American buyers, then, are extremely important to the publishing industry. Any trip to a large bookstore will reveal an entire section of books on Jewish subjects, far exceeding the shelf space devoted to any other ethnic group. In fact, publishers annually release more than five hundred titles exclusively on Jewish subjects. In a study of buying habits of the readers of *Reform Judaism* magazine, 70 percent reported having bought a hardcover book in the past twelve months, compared with 19 percent of the general population.

HARDCOVER PURCHASES

	Natl. Avg.	Jewish Readers	Index / 1 = Avg.
Bought a book in past 12 months	19%	70%	3.8
1 – 5 books	13%	39%	3.0
6 – 9 books	3%	9%	3.0
10 or more	3%	17%	6.2

(*Simmons Study of Media and Markets 1989*, Simmons Market Research Bureau, 1990)

This buying preference is not lost on Jewish charities and institutions. Jewish book fairs are held across the country as lucrative fundraisers during Jewish Book Month. The month-long celebration takes place during the thirty-day period before Hanukah, in November and December. These popular events reconfirm two of our eight fundamental principles: the importance of education and caring for one's own. The fairs are a celebration of being Jewish, but they are also raise thousands of dollars for community events and services.

Besides being avid book purchasers, Jews have been active participants in the book publishing industry. Alfred Abraham Knopf founded the publishing company by that name in 1915 and later sold it to Random House, which had been founded by Bennett Alfred Cerf in 1927. In 1965, Cerf sold his company to David Sarnoff's RCA for $40 million worth of RCA stock. More recently, in 1998, Si and Donald Newhouse's Advance Publications sold Random House to Bertelsmann A.G. for $1.4 billion. Richard Leo Simon and Max Lincoln Schuster founded Simon and Schuster in 1924. Their first published book was a collection of crossword puzzles, complete with a bound-in pencil. Later they started Pocket Books and Golden Books. Simon and Schuster was eventually acquired by Paramount Communications. Sumner Redstone bought Paramount for $10 billion in 1994 and in 1998 sold S&S for $4.6 billion. Viking and Bantam were also founded by Jewish people; like the other houses, they were acquired by conglomerates and are owned today by Penguin and Bantam Doubleday Dell, respectively. Warner Books and Little, Brown are the children of Time Warner Communications, whose chairman is Gerald Levin. In 1961 Warner Books was created as a subsidiary of the Warner Brothers movie studio founded by Harry, Abe, Jack and Samuel Warner in 1923. Harry Scherman joined Maxwell Sackheim and Robert Haas in 1926 and created the Book of the Month Club.[7]

ACADEMIC RESEARCH: AMERICAN JEWISH ETHNICITY AND ITS RELATIONSHIP TO CONSUMER BEHAVIOR

In one of the few published studies of Jewish consumer behavior, Elizabeth Hirschman, associate director of the Institute of Retail Management and assistant professor of marketing at NYU, conducted controlled scientific studies in 1981 to test several hypotheses about American Jewish consumer behavior.[8] Indeed, Jews are savvy consumers: armed with extensive product knowledge, selectively extravagant on a few important items and pervasively frugal on the rest. Hirschman points out that ethnicity is infrequently considered when developing "hypotheses regarding the ways a group may be expected to differ from the surrounding society." She found that Jewish ethnicity exerted a relatively stronger effect on the individual's behavior because it is multidimensional. "When one is born a Jew, he or she is born into a culture and a religion simultaneously. One set of values is developed both by informal social interaction and religious instruction; therefore, the Jewish individual experiences a much more similar upbringing than many other groups. Irish ethnicity, for example, may be exhibited quite differently, depending whether one is Irish Protestant or Irish Catholic."

Hirschman performed two controlled studies. One group involved college students at four colleges in different regions of the country. Of the 298 students studied, 98 came from New York University, 40 from the University of Michigan, 145 from Georgia State, and 25 from UCLA. All were 20 to 29 years old and majored in business administration. There were no significant differences in employment status, marital status or educational attainment among the student subjects. In addition, both Jews and non-Jews had a similar strength of affiliation to their racial/ethnic group.

Hirschman conducted the other study with older adults. All were of similar economic status to compensate for the influence of higher Jewish incomes, but included other religious and ethnic groups. Of the 363 adults studied in the New York City area, 120 were Jews, 114 were Protestant and 98 were Catholic. The other 31 were Greek Orthodox, Hindu, Muslim and those with no affiliation. As with the students, both Jews and non-Jews had a similar strength of their affiliation to their racial/ethnic group. There were also no significant differences between the Jews and non-Jews for any demographic features examined, such as age, marital status, income, education and occupational status.

Her research confirmed four exploratory propositions as outlined below:

Proposition 1: Jewish ethnicity is positively related to childhood information exposure. Specifically, Jewish children receive more exposure to reading material, special training and instruction, and group participation.

Proposition 2: Jewish ethnicity is positively related to seeking information as adults. Specifically, Jewish consumers expose themselves to a greater quantity of information sources. Adult subjects were asked about their recent media exposure, including radio, television, magazines and newspapers.

Proposition 3: Jewish ethnicity is positively related to the willingness to innovate and be early adopters of new product. Jewish consumers are more willing to adopt new products independent of the judgment of others. To measure this, subjects were asked to indicate their willingness to adopt new products in a variety of consumption domains, independent of the judgment of other people who had purchased the products. Fifteen consumption domains were explored, ranging from specific personal items (a new hairstyle) to general ideologies (religious and political ideas).

Proposition 4: Jewish ethnicity is positively related to the transfer of product information to others. Jewish consumers talk more about what they buy and pass their experiences to others. Using the same consumption domains used to investigate the third proposition, researchers asked the groups about their frequency of providing information to others in particular product domains.

Hirschman found that Jewish subjects in the two survey groups "differed significantly from non-Jewish subjects" in all four areas. "Significantly," as used by Hirschman, means that the results had statistical validity.

Hirschman's findings support our picture of Jews as selectively extravagant and prudently frugal. The research suggests in general that when it comes to everyday purchases, Jews possess and pursue a higher level of product knowledge to get the best price, quality, features and durability. These habits contribute to their ability to save and to create the capital required for investment. In addition, the research suggests that once Jews find a good buy, they share that information freely with their friends, so the community also benefits. This has broader implications for marketers who wish to introduce new products using the aid of opinion leaders.

JEWISH CONSUMERS IDENTIFIED

In the age of computers it's easy to target a specific audience, and marketers have been quick to compile Jewish names for direct mail and phone solicitations. A. B. Data of Milwaukee publishes the *Direct Marketing Guide to the*

Jewish Community and offers to rent the names on the more than 300 lists
that it has either compiled itself or represents. The guide claims to be "the
most comprehensive list of Jewish data compiled anywhere." Using A. B.
Data's proprietary software, called the Jewish Ethnic Surname Identification
Program (JESIP), the company can provide a 95 percent confidence level that
those on a list are Jewish. "Each and every known Jewish name was individ-
ually researched in consultation with sociologists, historians, genealogists
and other scholars," the company claims. "Using over 85,000 Jewish surnames, a statistical model was developed that could be used to predict the
probability that any given surname was Jewish."

The data help flesh out our portrait of the frugal, yet sometimes extravagant Jewish consumer. There are 57,000 Jews on the bargain-seekers lists
of the Fingerhut catalog and 243,000 on the list of contributors to the U.S.
Holocaust Memorial Museum in Washington, D.C., which raised $168 mil-
lion. Since Jews buy a lot of books, there are nineteen book-related lists
available with more than 478,000 names on them, ranging from "Jewish
Baseball Buffs" (1,900) to purchasers of the *Encyclopedia Judaica* (14,000).
There are also 23,000 names on a list of Jewish chocolate buyers. There are
35,000 Jewish mail-order buyers who can't live without the authentic New
York delicacies of the world-famous Second Avenue Deli. Jewish political
cartoon collectors number 4,300. Want to send a Rosh Hashanah (Jewish
New Year) card to all the Jewish diamond dealers on New York's 47th
Street? Then you'll have to buy 1,700 cards. There is a list of Jewish people
buying, supporting and belonging to just about everything.

For social action there are more than seventy Jewish donor lists. A sam-
pling includes Amnesty International (29,000), Greenpeace (24,000), Sierra
Club (12,000), ACLU (26,000), Common Cause (20,000), Planned
Parenthood (29,000), Handgun Control (30,000) and even the conservative
Heritage Foundation (23,000).

The granddaddy of the lists is the National Directory of Jewish
Households. It has 2.5 million entries. With the aid of computer overlays
you can sort names by income, age, occupation, education, credit card use
and many other criteria.

MONEY MEANS POWER AND SECURITY TO JEWS

Jewish households with higher incomes and controlled spending habits
have created a great deal of personal wealth for the Jewish community to
draw upon. As *The Millionaire Next Door* demonstrated, living below

their means is one of the factors common among millionaires. For Jews, wealth is a tool for survival. Without money, Jews view themselves as "naked to their enemies." In Old World Europe, Jews were segregated, restricted and exploited with taxes of all kinds. Jews had to pay special taxes for praying, traveling, marrying and even burying their dead. However, as I mentioned in chapter 1, Jews have priorities. First comes education, then the money and then the material things. Money is a source of power, and to acquire it without education will create a household with many things, but with little security to maintain and support itself.

In a readers' survey in *Reform Judaism*, Jews were shown to hold a high quantity of liquid assets. For example, 27 percent of the general public directly own stocks and bonds, yet 73 percent of Reform Jews did. When the dollar amounts are viewed in detail, the differences were more striking.

SECURITIES AND INVESTMENTS OWNED

VALUE OF SECURITIES OWNED

	Natl. Avg.	Jewish Readers	Index / 1 = Avg.
Own any securities	27%	73%	2.8
$50,000 – $99,999	2.1%	12%	5.6
$100,000 or more	1.8%	38%	21.1
$100,000 – $499,999	NA	24%	
$500,000 – $999,999	NA	7%	
$1 million or more	NA	7%	
Average value owned	$254,000		
Median value owned	$110,400		

(*Simmons Study of Media and Markets 1989*, Simmons Market Research Bureau, 1990)

For Jews, wealth is more than the power to buy things; it is power itself. Money can overcome the prejudices of most bigots, especially in America. In Great Britain, ancestry still creates a classed society that new wealth cannot penetrate. In the United States, money breaks down the barriers faster than any pleadings for help. Wealth speaks loud and clear. Some do not like Jews, but most will accept their money. And in response to the places where their money was no good, Jews built their own. "Can't join your country club? We'll build our own." "Can't practice at your hospital? We'll build our own."

Money also meant physical safety and survival. Jews over the centuries had used their financial clout to buy special protection from the local power broker, such as the police or king, to protect themselves from the wrath of anti-Semitic hoodlums. The Nazi experience was a glaring exception. Jews were unable to buy their freedom and their lives because Nazis' anti-Semitism overpowered their greed. That makes the support of Israel, as well as the civil freedoms of the United States, a priority for Jews today.

On the microeconomic level of the family, Jews' view of money surfaces at wedding time. At traditional Gentile weddings the bride and groom are showered with gifts ranging from crystal to sterling. To Jews, it seems odd for young couples to have all these luxuries with no money in the bank; consequently the most traditional wedding gift to a Jewish couple is cash. A gift of money seems impersonal to non-Jews, but in fact it is a very personal gift. It says, in essence, "We care about you enough to give you the option to allocate our gift to your most pressing needs." The couple may need seed money to establish their new household: put together a down payment on a house, buy furniture, pay off accumulated debts. The couple may be starting a new business. They may want to bank it and add to their own nest egg. How many toasters or food processors do you need? It is a matter of priorities.

PAINLESS FRUGALITY OFFERS BIG PAYOFFS

The following suggestions for frugality are easy to follow and have the potential for huge capital accumulation over time. The general population saves virtually nothing, with their home equity being the bulk of most families' accumulated wealth. The median net worth of the average household in the U.S. is only $56,000. In contrast, informed, prudent spending and saving have played a major role in the financial success of Jewish people.

Our seniors as a whole finish their working careers with little accumulated wealth. The median net worth of the average household older than 65 is only $106,000. Adding a senior's Social Security benefits and the income from such a small nest egg, annual income would be less than $20,000 per year.

Before considering these savings tips, however, remember, the proverb: "Don't step on the dollars to pick up the pennies." *Built from Scratch* (1999), a book about the Jewish founders of The Home Depot, Bernard Marcus and Arthur Blank, recounts the most costly "attempted" savings in history.

In 1978 Marcus and Blank had just been fired from Handy Dan Hardware and were looking for investors to back their idea of hardware superstores. They figured that if they bought directly from manufacturers, passed the savings on to customers and kept a wide inventory, the complacent hardware industry would, as they put it, "choke on our sawdust." They met with billionaire Ross Perot of Electronic Data Systems (definitely not Jewish), who was intrigued by their plan. However, one detail disturbed him. Marcus wanted The Home Depot to assume the lease payments on his used Cadillac. Perot's response, according to the book, was firm: "My people don't drive Cadillacs: My guys at EDS drive Chevrolets."

Marcus recalls his comeback: "Look, this is a four-year-old car, and I'm a big guy. It is cheaper to have an old Cadillac than it is to go out and get a new Chevrolet." Perot was unmoved, and the deal fell through. Perot's $2 million would have bought a 70 percent interest in the company – a stake that would be valued at more than $60 billion at today's stock price.[9] Although Perot is not hurting, with a fortune estimated at $3.8 billion in 1999, that "Cadillac thing" prevented him from challenging Bill Gates at the head of the list of the world's wealthiest people.

Here are some productive suggestions that can easily turn "minor" savings into substantial assets over your lifetime. If you take the following suggestions, adopt them at age twenty-one, follow them until retirement at age sixty-seven, and invest the annual savings in a conservative balanced stock-and-bond mutual fund that yields 8 percent, you would create the following results at retirement:

1. Buy a moderately priced car and drive it for a long time: $1,046,065

2. Brown-bag a lunch once a week: $174,065

3. Use $5 of coupons a week: $108,790

4. Eat at home more frequently: $125,527

5. Skip daily junk food and expensive coffees at work: $217,581

6. Smoking is hazardous to your wealth: $456,176

7. Buy term life insurance via Web agencies: $209,213

BUY A MODERATELY PRICED CAR AND DRIVE IT FOR A LONG TIME
Other than the purchase of a house, car purchases are first on the list of importance. The big difference is that cars depreciate in value. Although many people consider their cars an extension of themselves, their personality, and

their social position, automobile expenses pose a serious threat to their net worth. Conversely, saving on auto expenses can be a huge capital-building opportunity. If you purchase a moderately priced, low-maintenance, slightly used car and keep it for more than 100,000 miles, the savings over a lifetime are compelling. You save on the initial purchase, save on insurance in later years and save on maintenance costs if you buy the low-maintenance cars indicated by *Consumer Reports*. And best of all, after you pay off the auto loan, you will have many years without car payments. (My car has been payment-free for a decade!)

When the salesperson offers you rustproofing, forget it. In most later-model cars the factory has already done it. In addition, excess rustproofing compound may clog the drain holes in the doors and elsewhere and actually cause rust to occur. Another potential hazard is the extended warranty. Salespeople make big commissions on extended warranties because there is so much profit in them. Most of the car's major components today are covered by long original warranties. In the case of used cars, warranties transfer to new owners when they are sold. Try to determine if the coverage is a duplication of the original warranty or is very expensive in relation to the possible repairs not covered. Plus, if you buy a reliable car, repair costs should be low anyway.

When negotiating your car's purchase price, consult a Web shopping service such as *autobytel.com*. Such sites provide the vital information on the dealer's invoice and cost of options that help you to negotiate the best price. If you use a Web service, it will put your automobile specifications up for competitive bid and you are assured a good deal.

Leasing an automobile is foolish. The whole leasing phenomenon began in the 1980s when cars became unaffordable for many people who wanted to drive cars above their means. At the end of the term you own nothing, and you often owe penalties for excess wear and mileage. Only in cases in which the car is leased for a business and it is important to create an upscale image does a lease make sense.

On average you can save more than $2,500 a year by buying a car and driving it for years. If you follow this strategy throughout your adult life and invest that money in an ordinary, balanced-portfolio mutual fund with a return of 8 percent, your savings would grow to $1,046,065 by retirement age.

Also you can find savings on your car insurance on the Internet. By avoiding the expensive broker network, you can save a lot of money each year. Geico (*geico.com*) and Reliance Direct (*reliancedirect.com*) are two of the largest reputable direct-marketing companies selling automobile insurance at very competitive rates.

By the way, if you rent a car on vacation or on business, the counter salespeople will try to sell you their most profitable product, extra car insurance. Check your own car insurance coverage or your company's; in most cases you are already covered by your own plan.

BROWN-BAG A LUNCH ONCE A WEEK

An average lunch out costs about ten dollars with a tip. If you decide to brown bag a lunch from home once a week with a cost of two dollars, you can save $416 a year. That would create a benefit of $174,065 at retirement if you began at age twenty-one.

USE $5 OF COUPONS A WEEK

Coupons are great if you use them for things that you normally buy, like paper products, cereal, canned goods, toiletries, soaps and detergents. The $260 saved each year if invested would swell to $108,790 at retirement.

EAT AT HOME MORE FREQUENTLY

If you avoid a single meal out each month and cook a special meal at home instead, the savings can be very appetizing! Assume you would spend fifty dollars for a good meal out. The ingredients for an elaborate home meal may cost twenty-five dollars. The annual savings of $300 would grow to $125,527 at retirement. Even considering inflation, that would buy quite a feast.

If you do eat out, the portions served at most restaurants are enough for two. Splitting an entree is really a good way to avoid overeating and to save money. If you are dining alone, you have a second meal for tomorrow. If you are with a companion and there is not enough food, also share an appetizer. Depending on where you are dining, you can save five dollars to twenty-five dollars off your check.

SKIP DAILY JUNK FOOD AND EXPENSIVE COFFEES AT WORK

This may be a bit more difficult for snackaholics. However, in addition to the benefits of lowering your weight and improving your health, the potential monetary rewards are considerable. If you save just one dollar each working day starting at age twenty-one, that grows to $108,790. If you are big snacker with a yen for mocha latte and a sweet, a two-dollar-a-day saving grows to $217,581.

SMOKING IS HAZARDOUS TO YOUR WEALTH

Smoking is hazardous not only to your physical health but also to your financial health. Just as the diseases from smoking take their toll over time, the benefits of not smoking can have equally as dramatic positive effects over time.

Suppose you are a light smoker with a pack-a-day habit. The average price per pack in 1999 with all the new taxes applied was about three dollars. Assuming that the price will go up only 5 percent a year in the future and you give up the habit at age twenty-one and invest the savings, the cumulative effect would be $458,176 at retirement. If you quit at age twenty-five, $333,146. At age thirty, $222,362. At age thirty-five, $146,963. At age forty, $95,649. These figures are very conservative since they do not include any nonsmoker discounts on health insurance or life insurance, cleaning bills, and lost wages or medical bills due to smoking-related illnesses.

BUY TERM LIFE INSURANCE VIA WEB AGENCIES

The insurance business is undergoing a revolution that will be a boon for consumers. The old agent network is crumbling under the competition from no-frills Internet companies. By answering a short questionnaire about your needs, their databases find you the best policy at the lowest prices. The competition is so fierce that prices are at an all-time low. For only $500 a year, if you are a non-smoker in good health, thirty-five years old, you can purchase $400,000 worth of term life insurance.

Experts recommend buying a policy that is at least five times your annual salary if you have dependents. A $400,000 policy is therefore appropriate for a family with an income of $80,000. Suppose that you buy a policy from your local broker for $1,000 or buy a whole-life policy for even more. If you want the savings-account feature of a whole-life policy, it is more advantageous to invest the money yourself and buy the insurance separately. If the minimum savings are $500 a year and you invest the savings each year from ages twenty-one to sixty-seven, you would have $209,213 at retirement. Want to check it out? There are many Web sites available, including Selectquote, Quotesmith, Termquote, Primequote, Masterquote, Insuremarket and Iquote.

And while we're saving, here are a few additional common-sense suggestions:

TAKE FULL ADVANTAGE OF 401(K) PLANS AND IRAS

IRA accounts and 401(k) plans are among the best investment vehicles that you can have. By investing money before federal income taxes are taken out, you have an immediate boost of 15 percent to 40 percent (depending on your tax bracket) to your investment portfolio because of the tax savings. In addition, with a 401(k), the employer may match your contributions as a bonus. Once invested, the money grows tax-free until taxes are paid on earnings when withdrawn at retirement. In a Roth IRA, there are no immediate tax savings, but the earnings are tax-free. In any case, the first avenue for your savings should be to max out your tax-advantaged investment possibilities. In a survey of readers of the *Jewish Exponent* completed in 1998, 69 percent had IRA accounts versus 27.8 percent of all U.S. adults.

When buying mutual funds for your retirement plans, be careful not to buy funds with "front-loaded" fees unless you really know what you're doing. Even if a fund is a "no-load" fund, you need to check whether there are hidden fees. An additional percentage-point drag on your investment earnings makes a huge difference on your return over your lifetime. The low-fee fund group called the Vanguard Group is an excellent place to put your money (*vanguard.com*). Morningstar provides reliable ratings on all funds (*morningstar.com*) and offers a wide variety of index funds to diversify your portfolio. With more than 80 percent of the mutual fund industry unable to beat the benchmark indexes, a portfolio with a portion invested in a low-fee index fund is a wise idea.

If you trade individual stocks and bonds, a low-cost Internet broker can save you money. Compared with full-service brokers who provide little advice, slower executions and often unwanted solicitations, Internet brokers offer comparable service for a fraction of the cost. Even if you make only five to ten trades a year, saving fifty dollars to two hundred dollars per trade adds up. E*Trade and Schwab are just two of the low-cost on-line brokerage services. If your full-service broker has provided you with the opportunity to participate in lucrative Internet IPOs, then by all means maintain your loyalty, because your broker has earned it.

AVOID STOCKPILING AT BUYING CLUBS

People who shop at one of those wholesale buying clubs often fall into the spend-money-to-save-money trap. You have to pay an annual fee of about thirty dollars, and then you are forced to stock up on items to receive any substantial discounts. With the extremely competitive retailing marketplace today, the clubs' pricing advantage has eroded considerably. The clubs don't accept coupons, and for many consumable items such as cereal and tissue, coupons make up for the clubs' discounts. Plus, if you buy a large quantity of product, it is human nature to use it indiscriminately. And if it's a food item, of course, it might go bad before you get to use it.

STAY MARRIED IF YOU CAN; DIVORCE IS VERY EXPENSIVE

About 50 percent of marriages in the U.S. end in divorce – not only an unfortunate statistic for our nation's families' emotional and mental well-being, but also a frightening danger to the financial health of the household. Alimony and lawyers' fees can be expensive, and in addition to these costs, the economies of shared housing and expenses evaporate. Also the cost of all those extravagant "feel-good" expenditures that both spouses incur when they become single again can be substantial.

Jewish families have a divorce rate of 12 percent, one quarter of the national average. That has given a big boost to the relative household wealth of Jewish families when compared to the general population. The reasons for this disparity in divorce rates have not been scientifically explored; however, there are some obvious Jewish reasons that come to mind. A lower divorce rate in the community increases the social pressure to keep the family together. Also higher household income levels provide opportunities for unhappy spouses to divert their attention away from their relationship and to pursue other material and social goals. Even in unhappy marriages, spouses tend to stick it out, as Moses did for forty years in the desert. Perhaps the Jewish people's long history of suffering extends to marriage.

Sadie and Morris were extremely unhappy in their marriage. They fought, bickered and generally were hostile to each other. After sixty-three years of marriage, Sadie decided that she would petition for a divorce. Sadie went before the judge to list Morty's bad habits, which made it impossible for her to live with him anymore. The judge listened intently and said, "I can't believe it, after sixty-three years of marriage, why ask for a divorce after so many years?"

Sadie said, "Enough is enough!!"

Along with a civil divorce, Jewish couples also must go to the trouble and expense of obtaining a religious divorce in order to remarry. According to biblical law outlined in the book of Deuteronomy, a man must present a document called a "get" to his wife after efforts to save the marriage have failed. The wife in turn must accept the "get" before the divorce becomes valid. Without the "get," any children born during a second marriage would be considered illegitimate in the Jewish religion. Problems occur when a man refuses to grant a "get." Under Jewish law, a man can remarry without a "get" if he gathers the signatures of one hundred rabbis. As with many other Jewish laws, the rules are not equally applied to both sexes. The wife is not eligible for a similar exemption. She is often at the mercy of the husband to grant the "get" so she can move on with her life. In any case, both civil and religious divorces can become ugly and expensive.[10]

MOVE YOUR MONEY-MARKET SAVINGS AWAY FROM COMMERCIAL BANKS

Many of us wisely keep some cash available to pay sudden expenses and to serve as an emergency fund. However, if you are keeping that cash in a money-market account or savings account at a traditional bank, you are literally making a charitable contribution to these institutions. If you would like to make a charitable contribution of a few hundred dollars a year, at least pick a charity that supports a good cause and get a tax deduction.

Money-market rates at commercial banks range from 2 to 3 percentage points lower than those available at a brokerage house. That's approximately 50 percent lower. In 1999, rates in a Charles Schwab One money-market account were 4.18 percent and Schwab's Value Advantage Fund paid even more (*schwab.com*). First Union and other major banks were paying 1.8 percent or less. If you need easily accessible cash, you can write a check on a brokerage account just like a checking account. Other brokerages have equally attractive money-market rates.

AVOID CREDIT-CARD DEBT AND MAKE CREDIT CARDS A SOURCE OF INCOME

Credit cards are meant to be used and abused. By "abuse," I do not mean the credit-card company's high interest rates, but rather to how you can take advantage of the credit-card company. The first rule is to never use a credit card for an expense that you do not intend to pay off in the next month's statement. If your income or cash fund cannot cover the expense, you are living beyond your means. Credit-card debt is one of the most expensive ways to borrow money and should be avoided like the Ten

Plagues that God visited upon the Egyptians in the Passover story. If you do accumulate a credit-card debt, refinance it with lower-rate cards, a lower-rate home equity loan, or with other savings.

On the other hand, credit cards are a great way to get the use of money interest-free. The grace period between the time you spend the money and you pay your credit-card bill amounts to an interest-free loan. In addition, if you want to take advantage of Discover's family of credit cards, you can get a 1 percent rebate on your charges. To take full advantage of the opportunity you will need to charge many of the expenses for which you would normally use other credit cards, store cards and gas cards. It also makes balancing your checkbook easier because you write fewer checks.

If the credit card addiction is too strong and you must run a balance, shop for the card with the lowest interest rate. If you want to keep the same card or don't have time to search for the lowest rate card, call and ask the card company to lower your interest rate. Tell the company that you want a lower rate or else you will move your account. Companies really want to keep your account because getting a new customer is very expensive. You have a high probability that they will lower your rate over the phone if you have been paying your bills. If you occasionally send your payment in late and incur a penalty, you have the same leverage. Just call your credit-card company and ask; in most cases it will cancel the late fees, interest and penalties in order to keep you as a customer.

OWN YOUR HOME; DON'T RENT

As recently as the turn of the 20th century, most European Jews were prevented from owning property or land. This is one reason so few Jews have been in involved in agriculture. In the United States, however, Jewish people own their own homes in a larger percentage than the general population, greatly contributing to their wealth and security. Unless you plan to move every few years or live in a declining area, renting an apartment or home is like leasing a car – you shouldn't do it. Home ownership can have a profoundly positive effect on your financial situation. A cornerstone of our federal tax system is the subsidy of home ownership with its deductions for mortgage interest and property taxes. Especially in the first years of a mortgage, most of the payment is deductible. Depending on your marginal tax rate, it is like getting a 15 to 40 percent discount on your housing expenses. If you are not taking advantage of the subsidy, you are subsidizing everyone else.

In addition to the tax break, you build equity in your house that renting never does. Recently housing costs have been stable, unlike the inflationary '70s and '80s. In the long run, however, the cost of housing will increase. As a renter you are guaranteed a rent increase. By owning you are in effect locking in your rent payments for fifteen to thirty years. In many cases payments for ownership are nearly equal to the cost of rent, especially with the historically low mortgage rates in the '90s. The largest single investment of retirees is their home equity. In many cases it is their only equity.

If you do choose to own, don't be lazy when you shop for a mortgage. A quarter of one percentage point of interest will cost you thousands of dollars over the life of the mortgage. It pays to negotiate. The competition for your mortgage business is fierce, and you have the leverage to get a good deal.

The other two issues related to mortgage that provide additional opportunities for savings are the down payment and the length of the mortgage. If you put less than 20 percent down, you will have to pay for PMI, purchase mortgage insurance. If you can put down 20 percent, you can avoid hundreds of dollars each year. If you must pay PMI, make sure that you petition to stop such payments when the equity in the house eventually exceeds 20 percent of the house's current value. Most people simply overlook this option and keep on paying. Because many mortgage servicers resist PMI cancellations, the Congress passed the Homeowners Protection Act of 1998 to compel lenders to facilitate the process.

The choice of a fifteen- or thirty-year mortgage also has a great deal of impact on your equity position. By taking a fifteen-year mortgage you get the advantage of a perhaps a half percentage point lower interest rate, lower interest expenses and a quicker payoff of loan principal. If you pay PMI, it will cease that much sooner. Remember, after fifteen years, your payment will not only be less than a thirty-year mortgage, it will be zero.

As a homeowner, you can borrow on the equity of your home. In the case of a car purchase, a home equity loan versus a conventional car loan can make the interest cost of owning a home a bit lighter because you can deduct the interest expense. Equity loan interest, like mortgage interest, provides you with a 15 to 40 percent government-sponsored subsidy. But if your car manufacturer is offering a special ultra-low interest rate special, his deal might be better.

TAKE CARE OF YOUR HEALTH

Your health and wealth are very closely related. Your physical and mental health directly affects your earning capacity. It goes without saying that regular checkups to prevent disease and tooth decay are far more cost-effective than addressing an advanced condition.

Jews have an above-average knowledge of medicine. Not only are Jews better educated, but 15 percent of the nation's doctors are Jewish. It is a pretty sure bet that a majority of Jewish families have a doctor in their extended family. As a "verbally confident" people, they ask questions, seek second opinions and do their own research. There is so much going on in the medical field that it is impossible for any single physician to be an expert on everything.

In *Mental Health in the Metropolis*, Leo Srole, the director of the largest study on the subject of ethnic usage of health care services, concluded that "there must be a survival insurance process rooted in the Jewish family and religious tradition. . . . The Jewish group historically can be viewed as a culture mobilized for prevention and, that failing, for the healing of ailments of the body and mind. One consequence is that Jews consult psychiatrists as well as physicians, far more often than Protestants or Catholics do."[11]

Also critical to your financial security is the high cost of long-term health care. Many long-term care policies have lifetime limits on coverage and also limits on reimbursements on nursing home care. The older you get the more expensive the coverage becomes, but if you are so unfortunate as to need the services, it can bankrupt you and your family. Consider long-term health care coverage if you are middle-aged, when the coverage is still affordable. If you are younger, make sure that your parents have the coverage, not only for their benefit, but also for your peace of mind, as you are their ultimate guardian.

LOWER YOUR LONG-DISTANCE PHONE BILLS

People are as lazy about their phone bill as they are about keeping money in commercial banks. Millions of people are continuing to pay the highest phone rates allowed by stubbornly sticking with standard AT&T long-distance service. AT&T still has over 50 percent of the long-distance business because people just don't want to shop. With a minimum of effort you cut out a large percentage of your monthly phone bill. AT&T charges less to those savvy users who ask for a discounted plan and charges more to those who do nothing and just want to make a contribution to AT&T's earnings. Depending on your monthly long-distance usage, it could mean savings of hundreds of dollars each year.

There are MCI Worldcom, Sprint and a legion of other carriers. Each company offers many different programs simultaneously. You need to ask what is available. MCI Worldcom, AT&T and Sprint are continually driving the per-minute rate well below 10 cents with special plans. With each plan there is a monthly fee, so calculate if the lower minute rate more than compensates for the monthly fee. You have to make only a modest effort to get big savings.

CONSULT *CONSUMER REPORTS* FOR MAJOR PURCHASES

Over your lifetime, you will purchase hundreds of thousands of dollars worth of cars, appliances and electronics. Since you can't be an expert in all the latest products, you need to educate yourself on the best features and benefits of the products you plan to purchase. The research shows that Jewish people seek out more product information than the general public. It makes great economic sense to find the best-made product, because fixing things is both expensive and a hassle. For some items there is no service at all. Check out the reliability studies that *Consumer Reports* conducts before making product decisions. Even if you are not a subscriber to the magazine, it is readily available at your local library.

Once you decide exactly what model you want, you can harness the shopping power of the Web by using one of the popular shopping tools. These sites scour the Web for the best prices for specific items in all types of goods available on the Web. Independent Internet price-searching tools can be found at *bottomdollar.com* and *shopper.com*.

CHAPTER 6

Celebrate Individuality:
Encourage Creativity

One might mistakenly surmise that because Judaism emphasizes its history and religious writings, it is a conservative culture that does not encourage individuality and creativity. On the contrary, these qualities have been integral to the Jewish character. The precedent was set by the Jewish patriarch, Abraham. Abraham broke with tradition by proclaiming a single God in a time when everyone else prayed to idols. In fact, his father, Terah, owned a shop that sold idols. Abraham could not accept the idea that these idols possessed any powers and so he destroyed them. Then and there Abraham stood alone, an individual, and the first Jew. What a battle that must have been!

There are several stories about Abraham that do not come from the Bible but have been repeated for centuries. As a boy, Abraham once waited on an elderly customer who wanted the perfect idol. Abraham asked the man how old he was, and he answered he was seventy. "What a fool you must be," said Abraham. "How can you worship an idol that is so much younger than you are? This idol was made only yesterday!"

In another story, Abraham took an ax to his father's idols and chopped them all to bits except the largest one. He then put the ax in the hands of the remaining idol. When his father came back, he was angry and confronted Abraham. Abraham said that the largest idol had done the damage.

Terah insisted that was impossible because "Idols can't do anything!" Abraham retorted: "Listen to what you have just said."

In yet another story, Terah ordered Abraham to place food and wine before the idols. When the idols did not partake of the food, Abraham observed: "They have mouths but they do not speak. They have ears but do not hear. They have noses but do not smell. They have hands but do not handle. They have feet but they do not walk." By law Terah was compelled to bring his son to the authorities for heresy. Before the court, the ruler of Ur asked the boy, "Don't you know the king is the Lord of all creation, the sun, moon and stars, and that He must be obeyed in all things?" Abraham answered, "Since the beginning of time, the sun rises in the east and sets in the west. Tomorrow, if it pleases His Majesty, command the sun to rise in the west and set in the east; then I will declare publicly that His Majesty is the Lord of the universe."[1] Ever since, Jews have questioned authority.

The Bible also leads the Jews to believe that they have the right, even a mission, to be different. The Bible says that the Jews are "the chosen people." "I chose you not because you are more numerous or powerful, and not because you are morally, spiritually or intellectually superior. You are not. I chose you out of my unknowable will." (Deuteronomy 7:7)

"Then the Lord said to Abraham, 'Know this for certain, that your offspring shall be aliens in a land that is not theirs, and shall be oppressed for four hundred years; but I will bring judgment on the nation that they serve, and afterward they shall come out with great possessions.'" (Genesis 15:13)

Judaism sets up a framework that permits Jews to act and think differently. As part of their religious education, Jewish children learn Hebrew, a language that is read backwards (right to left) and has a completely different alphabet. That sense of difference, individuality and separateness has been the source of great power for the Jewish people. According to Sam Zell, a Forbes 400 member who acquires troubled companies, "Every situation needs someone who has the conviction to step up to the line when conventional wisdom is going the other way."[2]

JEWISH KIDS AREN'T USUALLY "JUNIORS"

The Jewish wish to raise independent children begins at birth when a name is chosen. Traditionally a child is not named after a living relative, especially not his father. Each child is the master of his or her own destiny and should not live under the shadow of anyone else. Avoiding "juniors" is a more common tradition among Ashkenazic Reform Jews, who stem from Germany and Eastern Europe and who make up the majority of Jews in the United States. There is also the superstitious belief that if you use the name of a living relative you may rob him of a full life.

One notable example strays from this tradition. Edgar Bronfman Jr. took over from his father, Edgar Sr., as head of Seagram Company Ltd. in 1994. Edgar Jr. went on to diversify the company with entertainment investments: Polygram Records ($10.4 billion), MCA ($5.7 billion), Time Warner and Universal Studios. The Bronfmans (whose name means "distiller" in Yiddish) have an interesting history. Edgar Jr.'s great-grandfather, Ekiel Bronfman, emigrated to Canada from Bessarabia in 1889, and built a successful hotel business. Ekiel's son Samuel built a liquor business in 1924 as an adjunct to the hotels. Just before Prohibition, he bought the remaining alcohol inventories from American distillers at bargain prices. In an effort to get rid of the stock, Samuel thinned the alcohol with water and caramel coloring – and invented blended whiskey. In 1928 he expanded and bought the Joseph A. Seagram & Sons distillery in Canada. The business was hugely successful. Seagram sold to distributors who in turn smuggled their products into the U.S. during Prohibition. In 1934 the company introduced its Seven Crown whiskey, which eventually became one of the best-selling whiskeys in the world. Edgar Bronfman Sr. took over for his father Samuel in 1971 and introduced many new products, including gin, vodka, rums and liqueurs, to accommodate the changes in American drinking habits.[3] *Forbes* estimated Edgar Sr.'s net worth at $4.2 billion in 1999.

JEWISH INDIVIDUALISM
AND THE LEADERLESS JEWISH COMMUNITY

For such a strong group, it is an odd phenomenon that the Jewish-American community has no visible leaders. There is no religious head like the Pope or community spokesman like Jesse Jackson. The Jewish-American community is the product of strong individuals loosely bound together. Writing in *Forward* magazine, Leonard Fein endorses this view: "In 1994 the person who was nominally the leader of American Jewry was a man named Lester Pollack. The title belongs to him because he was the chairman of the Conference of Presidents of Major American Jewish Organizations. Not even 1 percent of American Jews could pick Mr. Pollack's name out of a random list of Jewish names as one they recognize, if only vaguely." In short, Jewish Americans like to be their own leaders, and follow others only when it suits them.

When Jewish organizations gather, they must act by consensus. Fein writes that "the urge to consensus begets experts in process and negotiation, people skilled at mediation rather than at initiative." Even in the synagogue itself, the congregation controls the temple. The rabbi is employed by the temple and works at the congregation's behest. Fein goes on to say, "There is God, and then there's the people, no intermediaries getting in the way." The rabbi is supposed to be a very learned man of the Torah and to offer guidance and wisdom, but he does not have a special divine power. Some small Hasidic sects have built personality cults around their rabbis and live in relatively closed communities, but they are the exceptions. In general, the visible leaders of the Jewish community are the active members from the business community who have the financial resources to fund their priorities, be it the perpetuation of the State of Israel or the support of medical research at Jewish institutions.[4]

In a way the Jewish community is similar to the Internet. Structurally it does not have an established hierarchy; it is a network of individuals and independent organizations. There is no beginning or end, no traffic cops, few rules – but its presence is very powerful. If a branch is broken, the message successfully makes its way through another part of the web.

As with all communities, Jews have many organizations to perform the functions of charity, social progress and education. Each one acts independently and has its own agenda. It is only in times of crisis that a unified Jewish community is tested and mobilized. With "overwhelming consensus," Jewish Americans act very well together. During the Arab–Israeli wars in 1967 and 1973, there was a clear enemy and an immediacy that required a concerted effort. As noted earlier, the UJA raised $100 million in cash in one week in 1973. Money was needed to address a pressing military need. After the crisis, the community returns to business as usual and breaks up into its separate parts. Since there has been no major crisis for more than twenty years, the Jewish community has become even more decentralized and independent. When threats to the community take the form of intermarriages or the loss of the next generation, the community is ineffective because the threat is not imminent, concrete or easily solved by fund-raising.

> When President Dwight Eisenhower met with Israeli Prime Minister David Ben-Gurion, the American president said at one point: "It is very hard to be president of 170,000,000 people."
>
> Ben-Gurion responded: "It's harder to be prime minister of 2,000,000 prime ministers!"

A BAR MITZVAH SOLOIST VS. A CONFIRMATION CHORUS

In the Jewish religion, children are recognized in the synagogue as adults at the age of thirteen. The young adolescent is singled out to read from the Torah and lead the Sabbath service. The family holds a reception, and the Bar Mitzvah boy or Bat Mitzvah girl is the center of attention. The parallel in many Christian denominations is the confirmation ceremony for young adults, yet the two rites of passage could not be more different. In a confirmation, all the children in the confirmation class take to the church stage together. They recite together a pledge or prayer that they will follow the rules of the Bible and actively participate in and support the church. Afterwards there may be a reception for the whole group, but the individual child is not singled out. Jewish parents, on the other hand, encourage their kids to stand out and be heard, and they do not raise conformity to a virtue. In the context of Jewish economic success, the ability to strike out on your own helps breed the entrepreneurial spirit that has led to the formation of many businesses and creative enterprises.

THINKING WAY OUTSIDE THE BOX

Albert Einstein was a physicist, mathematician and, at twenty-six, the creator of the Theory of Relativity that ushered in the atomic age. His Jewishness played a critical role in his life. Pursuing a field of study many considered fruitless, Einstein searched for a "unified field theory" that would link energy, matter, velocity and mass. During his childhood he had read popular science books, and through his religious studies he developed what came to be a lifelong belief that the universe is orderly. As the ancient Hebrews put it, "The Lord is one." And if there was one creator, there must be a set of consistent rules that governs how it all works. Einstein had a faith in the ultimate simplicity and beauty of

nature. In his youth he was "intensely religious, both spiritually and rit-
ualistically." The cohesiveness he perceived was the same order described
in the Bible and taught in the tenets of the Jewish religion. Biographer
Banesh Hoffman emphasized the influence of Einstein's spiritual beliefs
on his history-making theories. "When judging a scientific theory, his
own or another's, he asked himself whether he would have made the universe in that way had he been God."

In one year, 1905, Einstein wrote four landmark papers that revolutionized the world of physics. In the first, he worked out an equation that provided direct evidence that molecules exist. In the second, Einstein posited a
theory that light was really a stream of "quanta," later called photons.
When light hits a metal, these "quanta" force atoms to release electrons;
this is called the "photoelectric effect." In the next one, he postulated that
if you traveled at the speed of light, your velocity is "relative" to the
observer; there is no absolute space or time. In his fourth paper published
that same year, Einstein proclaimed what became his most famous idea: the
Theory of Relativity. He stated that mass and energy were different forms
of the same thing. The energy of a quantity of matter equals the mass of
that matter times the square of the velocity of light: $E = mc^2$. In 1916 he
extended his own theory, proposing "that space was curved in the presence
of mass and that gravitation is not a force but merely the result of moving
objects following the shortest possible path in curved space." On May 20,
1919, during a total solar eclipse, Einstein proved his theory by correctly
calculating that light bends. He measured the actual bending of a beam of
light passing the gravitational field of our sun at 1.75 seconds of an arc, a
figure that matched his predicted calculation. The universe was orderly.

At the time, he said, "Today in Germany I am hailed as a German man of
science, and in England I am pleasantly represented as a foreign Jew. But if
ever my theories are repudiated, the Germans will condemn me as a foreign
Jew and the English will dismiss me as a German." He was right. The Nazis
eventually outlawed his theories. They forced him to leave the country, took
his possessions and confiscated his books. He moved to the U.S. in 1933 and
continued his work at Princeton. In 1939 Einstein wrote to President
Franklin Roosevelt encouraging him to launch an atomic bomb project
because the Germans had already begun one of their own.[5]

Sigmund Freud's contributions to civilization were on a human level, not a
cosmic one; his theories provide the basis for modern psychology and psychi-
atry. They have also profoundly affected the fields of education, art, literature

and social sciences. Freud was the son of a Jewish trader and lived in an open-ly anti-Semitic Austria. According to M. Hirsh Goldberg, "As a victim of anti-Semitism, he had already had to deal with rejection; his Jewishness therefore prepared Freud for the exclusions that his theories provoked. As an innovator he was upsetting comfortable ways of thought."

Freud graduated from medical school in Vienna in 1881, and went on to teach at the University of Vienna from 1902 to 1938. In his *Self Portrait*, he wrote that his exposure to anti-Semitism in medical school "produced one important result. At a rather early date, I became aware of my destiny: to belong to the critical minority as opposed to the unquestioning majority. A certain independence of judgment was there-fore developed." Goldberg continues: "Freud's statement points to one good reason why Jews can be found so frequently in movements that challenge preconceived notions. Often placed outside society by religious discrimination, Jews can serve society as intellectual rebels, questioning the theories and exploding ignorances of the past."[6]

In 1900, Freud published *The Interpretation of Dreams*, what many consider his greatest – and certainly his most influential – book. His works have created an entire vocabulary of psychological terms: Freudian slip, Oedipus complex, phallic symbol, sublimation, inhibitions, death wish, behavior modification, pleasure-pain principle, anxiety avoidance and sexual drive. As with Einstein, his theories were attacked at the time as being "Jewish" and his books were burned by the Nazis. They also seized his money, destroyed his publishing house and forced him to flee to England in 1938, where he subsequently died of jaw cancer.[7]

"PERMISSIVE" BUT PROTECTIVE JEWISH PARENTING PROMOTES INDIVIDUALITY, CREATIVITY AND SUCCESS

It might appear that Jewish parents spoil their children. As Charles Silberman says in *A Certain People*, "It is a charge to which Jewish parents freely plead guilty." Sociologist Zena Smith Blau conducted an in-depth study of Jewish parenting to see whether there was a difference between Jews and non-Jews, and there was. Blau studied first- and second-generation Eastern European Jewish mothers in her groundbreaking 1974 work called *The Strategy of the Jewish Mother*. A critical review of the study succinctly stated its importance: "Rather than sketching a stereotypical 'neurotic parent-child relationship' often portrayed in our culture, [Blau] empha-sized the positive consequences of Jewish child-rearing practices."[8] These practices may have been largely overlooked, but they have had a profound impact on Jewish-American success.

Blau identified seven general rules of parenting followed by first- and second-generation Jewish-American mothers. The research for this book confirms that these themes have been passed on to subsequent generations.

- ¤ Refrain from corporal punishment; control in non-punitive ways.

- ¤ Allow complete freedom of expression in the home.

- ¤ Provide children the best of everything, whenever possible.

- ¤ Nurture the strong ego and self-esteem of the child.

- ¤ Reduce the impact of peer pressure by maintaining close family relationships and delaying independence from the home.

- ¤ Set high standards for educational and professional advancement.

- ¤ As a community, reinforce those high standards.

Blau found that Jewish mothers "promote a strong ego structure in their children. And as a result the children find the strength to cope with an environment in which their self-worth will come into question," especially in the face of anti-Semitism. Consequently, Jewish children have a strong belief in their own ability to achieve success in the classroom and eventually in their careers.

The mother of Steven Spielberg said of her son, "His badness was so original there weren't even books to tell you what to do." He peanut-buttered his neighbor's windows as a prank. He got his first camera at twelve, and he filmed his toy trains crashing. He spent his summer vacations hanging around Universal Studios. He wore a suit and carried a briefcase and nobody knew enough to throw him off the lot. He pushed his way in and managed to get hired as a contract director when he was twenty. In short, Spielberg would not give up until he was successful.

The Jewish mothers Blau observed had a distinct parenting style that at first appeared to entail a great deal of self-sacrifice, but ultimately this sacrifice had a higher purpose. "The Jewish mothers appeared far more permissive, indulgent and self-sacrificing than typical Anglo-Saxon mothers. They exerted little pressure on their children to control explosions of feelings and temper, demanding only that they avoid physical forms of aggression.

Toward their fathers and other grown-ups, a Jewish child was expected to behave with respect, but toward their mothers, the children were allowed considerably more leeway to express negative as well as positive feelings.

"Jewish mothers erected no status distance between themselves and their children. They did not stand on ceremony; they did not protect their pride or their self-respect. With no other human being did the Jewish child develop as close, as trusting, as free and fearless a relationship as with his mother, and therein lay the secret of her power to gain their compliance ultimately in those areas of behavior in which she chose to exert pressure during the entire period of maturation."

The married daughter calls on the phone: "Hello, Ma?"

"Darling, is anything wrong?"

"Oh, Ma, everything's wrong!" she wails. "Both kids are sick, the stove is broken, and I am expecting six friends over to the house for a B'nai B'rith luncheon!"

"Darling, don't worry. I'll take a bus into the city, and I'll walk the two miles to your apartment. On the way, I'll buy food for the luncheon, and when I get there, I'll take care of the kids. I'll even make dinner for Sydney."

"Sydney? Who is Sydney?"

"Sydney, your husband."

"My husband is Isaac. Is this 362-7327?"

"No, this is 362-7328."

"Oh ... does this mean you're not coming?"

Blau found that "Jewish mothers seemed singularly unconcerned with 'discipline' and 'independence training.' They allowed their children a greater degree of latitude in acting out at home than was customary among Gentiles, and readily acknowledged that their children were *zelosen* – that is, pampered, demanding, spoiled, not well-behaved the way Gentile children seemed to be in the presence of their mothers. The Anglo-Saxon code of stoic endurance and suppressed emotion was alien to Eastern European Jews."

The parenting style Blau observed most often was accompanied by volatile exchanges between mother and child. Instead of being strict disciplinarians, the mothers were more often "screamers and naggers." Instead of a spanking, they would try to reason, distract and verbally admonish. Tempers would flare to the point of a slap or scream, but as quickly as the explosion came, it was forgotten. "The child was embraced, comforted and peace restored." This ability to engage in conflict and recover quickly has a cathartic effect and is a useful tool for life. Legal debates and business negotiations are by their nature a conflict of wills. Instead of internalizing the tension, Jews are better prepared to do battle and quickly return to normal with few emotional hangovers.

Blau also determined that Jewish fathers, as a rule, were more reserved in their child-rearing. Instead of a mother's expressive outburst, she saw that a father's silence created just as much discomfort and actually resulted in quicker compliance. In both cases, parental disapproval accompanied with guilt and anxiety, rather than fear of coercion, resulted in their children complying with their parents' wishes.

The Jewish parental relationship is even more controlling than it might appear. These parents indulge their children and concentrate on building their children's desire to achieve, which controls the path their adult lives will follow. The parents Blau observed attempted to build their children's self-confidence by providing them with a broad range of experiences that allowed them to succeed or fail and try again. By doing so, parents hoped that their children would not succumb to the limitations placed upon them by other adults later in life. In this environment, high expectations and high standards were not out of step with their philosophy that their Jewish children can do whatever they set their minds to.

Blau went on to write that Jewish mothers saw their child "as a fragile creature whose body and spirit needed to be carefully and assiduously nurtured and protected not only in infancy but throughout childhood and even adolescence. They went to inordinate trouble and expense to provide their children with the 'best and freshest' food, the best medical care, the warmest clothing – at considerable sacrifice of other needs and wants." The infant- and child-mortality rates were lower among Jews than the general population, in spite of the fact that most Jews were working-class people, whose mortality risks are greatest. In those formative years they allowed their children to be free to discover their talents, to develop their own personal style and to build their self-confidence.

It is not surprising, then, that a 1980 study of college students found that Jewish students had more self-confidence. "A significantly larger proportion of the Jewish than of the non-Jewish freshmen, for example, rate themselves 'above average' in academic ability, leadership ability, originality and popularity with the opposite sex."[9] As Geraldine Rosenfield of the American Jewish Committee has pointed out, these findings contradict the stereotype of Jews as ridden with anxiety. "Jewish self-confidence, if not actual brashness, [results] from the eagerness of Jewish parents to admire the remarkable qualities and achievements of their remarkable children."[10] Or as Blau put it, "Second-generation Jewish children lost a good many skirmishes with their mothers, but ultimately they won the war, just as their mothers intended."

Blau observed that the Jewish mothers' ability to nurture their children was further aided by the fact that Jewish families at the turn of the century were smaller than those of non-Jewish immigrants. With fewer mouths to feed, parents could invest scarce resources in a small business, in educating their children, in moving their household from poor to middle class or in providing for the next generation.

One of the most important aspects of the Jewish parent-child relationship has to do with peer pressure. Blau found that by sheltering their children and keeping them at home and busy with their studies, Jewish parents reduced the time children spend with their peers. She believed their reliance on peers may be more hazardous than reliance on parents. The Jewish concept was that the family is the primary socializing agent. In lower-class Gentile families, "children trained to be independent at an early age only became independent of parental influence to become more dependent on their peers." And because education was not a priority for their peers, they adopted the same values regardless of their parents' wishes.

Nowadays, parents of all socioeconomic levels are pursuing a philosophy that encourages early socialization of their children in order to make them independent. Many adopt this parenting style for altruistic purposes and others out of necessity or choice because both spouses have careers outside the home. Parents who pursue this policy encourage many extracurricular activities in an effort to have their child be part of the "popular" crowd, which they believe will lead them successfully to college and a career. Blau proposed, however, that this behavior might have exactly the opposite effect. With parents moving further and further out of their children's lives the values and aspirations of the children's peers become increasingly influential. In the Jewish community, however, this social trend is negated by the fact that more Jewish mothers are stay-at-home moms. The Chiswick study published in *Journal for the Scientific Study of Religion* in June 1986 found that the presence of preschoolers and school-age children in a community has a larger impact on the labor supply of Jewish mothers than on Catholic and Protestant ones. This is consistent with the Jewish tradition of intense parenting.

According to Blau, "Pressure on the child to become self-reliant at home, before there has been time for him to internalize high-achievement norm, and to establish a reliable pattern of scholastic competence in school, makes a child fearful of failure, less persistent and more vulnerable to the influences of peers." If their dependency needs are met at home with strong maternal attachments, children need to rely less heavily on peers for affection and emotional support, making their parents' influence more potent. From the standpoint of building practical skills, deliberately discouraging solitary activities such as reading, practicing a musical instrument and the less-glamorous debate, science and chess clubs, parents may exclude the very activities that hone the skills that build long-term successful professional careers. It has been the Jewish-American experience that the anti-Semitic norms that kept Jews from many "popular" clubs and sports teams in school actually have led them to professional success as an unintended consequence.

The authoritarian styles of discipline that Jewish parents tend to avoid also have unintended consequences. If parents seek to impose their conformity, aspirations and standards with general restrictiveness and by punishment, it will probably have the opposite effect. Blau concluded that "Fear and punishment have a stupefying effect on children. Great anxiety about failure impedes learning and prompts failure. Intellectual motivation is one attribute that cannot be forced."

Ultimately, Blau found that first- and second-generation Eastern European mothers "wanted their sons to 'better themselves' by becoming doctors or lawyers or professionals of some sort." They were keen in judging their children's performance in school and elsewhere. "When her son began to make the first feeble sounds on his violin, a Jewish mother already envisioned another Heifetz. If he showed scientific proficiency, she foresaw another Einstein. Einstein or not, mothers bragged shamelessly to others about their sons' achievements, if only to defend themselves against the bragging of their friends; not to boast was, in effect, to acknowledge that one's child was deficient."

Bragging behaviors served a very useful purpose for the Jewish community; they were an efficient way to transmit vital information about successful strategies for advancement to other mothers. What we take for granted in an era of quickly accessible information was not the norm even in the recent past. How do you apply to college? How do you apply for a scholarship? How do you prepare for entrance exams? Which schools have treated their Jewish students best? Of course, each mother's story would concern her little "genius," but it came with the important message of "the way out of the ghetto." It was a highly effective social mechanism, first for reinforcing parental ambitions, and second for disseminating information about the paths for achievement and mobility open to Jewish youth. Contemporary Jewish-American children obviously already have such information, but their parents' conversations with them clearly convey a desire for their children to have an education, a profession and economic success. And because these are commonly held beliefs within the Jewish community, the entire community pushes the "achievement" message, and it has a potent effect inside and outside the home.

Another important characteristic of Jewish child-rearing is the degree of independence given to children when they grow up. By encouraging elite college education and professional success at all costs, Jewish children are more "free or driven" to move away from their hometowns, no matter how far away from their parents that opportunity may be. This geographic mobility provides a competitive advantage because it allows Jewish professionals to move without the guilt about abandoning their family and community that children from other ethnic groups may feel. Children are expected to repay their parents by achieving the success their parents wanted for them and "showering love and advantages" on their own children – not by staying close to home and taking care of their parents. Silberman observes that "it is not at all uncommon, in fact, for elderly parents to be virtually abandoned by their 'successful' children"; whole neighborhoods in Florida and New York City are filled with such parents.

It is ironic that the successful efforts of Jewish parents to instill in their children the drive to achieve are having a negative effect on the continuation of Jewish traditions. Because the older generation is disconnected from its grown children and grandchildren, the transmission of Jewish cultural traditions to subsequent generations has become more and more problematic. Professional success may be crowding out a rich cultural heritage.

JEWISH CREATIVITY SHINES ON BROADWAY

Jewish success is not limited to the traditional officeplace. Jews have had tremendous impact on the arts, especially music. There is probably no other area that requires such a huge leap of faith and confidence in one-self as the performing arts. Succeeding in these creative professions takes a strong will and determination that have to be nurtured from an early age. In the Jewish community, pursuit of the arts and humanities has held an equal footing with other business-oriented professions. If Jewish youths show musical talent, parents encourage them to cultivate it with zeal in an effort to become the "best" in their chosen field. The Broadway musical, largely a Jewish-American invention, is a case in point. As Silberman points out, "With the notable exception of George M. Cohan and Cole Porter, the composers and lyricists who have given the Broadway musical its distinctive shape have almost all been Jews – artists such as Jerome Kern, George and Ira Gershwin, Lorenz Hart, Richard Rodgers, Oscar Hammerstein II, and, more recently, Alan Jay Lerner and Frederick Loewe, Stephen Sondheim, Leonard Bernstein and Marvin Hamlisch.[11] Even the exceptions have to be qualified to some degree: Cole Porter, who came from an upper-class Anglo-Saxon family, was powerfully drawn to Jewish liturgical music; "the secret of my success," he once told Richard Rodgers, "is that I write Jewish tunes."[12]

Just mentioning their names does not do justice to the impact these men had on Broadway and the musical history of America. You can hardly see a high school musical production today that was not written by a Jew. Jerome Kern is credited as "single-handedly" inventing the American musical. "He transformed the operetta of his day into a new theatrical form graced with ageless sing-along melodies."[13] His credits include:

Nobody Home (1915), the "first" American musical.
Oh, Boy! (1917), with the song "Till the Clouds Roll By."
Showboat (1927), with the classic "Ol' Man River."

Other Kern songs include:

"Look for the Silver Lining" (1920),
"Smoke Gets in Your Eyes" (1933) and
"The Last Time I Saw Paris" (1941).

George (Jacob) and Ira Gershwin (Israel Gershvin) produced timeless works that fused popular and classical styles into their own unique sound:

Porgy and Bess (1935) and the songs "Swanee" (1919), "The Man I Love" (1924), "I Got Rhythm" (1930), "Rhapsody in Blue" (1924), "An American in Paris" (1928).

Another famous collaboration was that of Richard Rodgers, composer, and Lorenz Hart, lyricist. Together they wrote some of the early Broadway hits:

> *Love Me Tonight* (1932), which included the song "Isn't It Romantic?"
>
> *Jumbo* (1935), with "The Most Beautiful Girl in the World."
>
> *Babes in Arms* (1937), with "The Lady Is a Tramp."
>
> *Pal Joey* (1940), with "Bewitched, Bothered and Bewildered."

Rodgers then teamed up with Oscar Hammerstein II, whose father owned theaters. Together they achieved tremendous success by creating an unprecedented string of blockbusters:

> *Oklahoma!* (1943), with "Oh What a Beautiful Morning."
>
> *Carousel* (1945), with "You'll Never Walk Alone."
>
> *South Pacific* (1949), with "Some Enchanted Evening."
>
> *The King & I* (1951), with "Getting to Know You."
>
> *The Sound of Music* (1959) with "The Sound of Music" and many more.

Alan Jay Lerner composed and Frederick Loewe wrote the lyrics for several well-known plays:

> *Brigadoon* (1947), with "Almost Like Being in Love."
>
> *Paint Your Wagon* (1951), with "They Call the Wind Maria."
>
> *My Fair Lady* (1956), with "I Could Have Danced All Night."
>
> *Gigi* (1958), with "Gigi."
>
> *Camelot* (1960), with "Camelot."

Stephen Sondheim has had a long career as a composer and lyricist, sometimes collaborating:

> *West Side Story* (1957), including the song "Maria" (music by Leonard Bernstein).

Gypsy (1959), (with Jule Styne) and the song "Let Me Entertain You."

A Funny Thing Happened on the Way to the Forum (1962).

A Little Night Music (1973), with "Send in the Clowns."

Sunday in the Park with George (1984).

Into the Woods (1987).

A gifted conductor, songwriter and composer, Leonard Bernstein made his mark on Broadway as well:

West Side Story (1957), and the song "I Feel Pretty" (lyrics by Stephen Sondheim).

Candide (1956), a comic operetta.

On the Town (1944), with "New York, New York."

Marvin Hamlisch, composer and pianist, wrote the music for *A Chorus Line* in 1975. He also wrote award-winning music for the films *The Sting* (1973) and *The Way We Were* (1973).

There are even more. Jule Styne was a gifted songwriter who wrote songs for eighteen productions including *Gentlemen Prefer Blondes* (1949), with "Diamonds Are a Girl's Best Friend," and *Funny Girl* (1964), with "People."

Frank Loesser wrote the music and lyrics for two big hits among the ten plays he wrote: *Guys and Dolls* (1950), with "Luck Be a Lady," and *How To Succeed in Business Without Really Trying* (1961), with the song "I Believe in You."

Howard Ashman has written songs for the stage and the screen. For Broadway he wrote the music for *Little Shop of Horrors* (1982). With composer Alan Menken, he wrote the songs for Disney's *The Little Mermaid*, *Aladdin* and *Beauty and the Beast*. *Beauty* was a great success as both an animated film and a Broadway musical.

Many of the producers and theater owners on Broadway are Jewish as well. David Geffen was the producer of *Cats* (1983). The Schubert family owned the theaters by the same name, and in the 1960s it was estimated they owned half of America's opera houses and showplaces. Florenz Ziegfeld was the ultimate showman, producing the popular Ziegfeld Follies from 1906 to 1931. Many Jews, in addition, have taken part as the investors who financed Broadway productions.

JEWISH PLAYWRIGHTS SUCCEED ON BROADWAY AS WELL

Musicals are not the only contributions Jews have made to Broadway. There are several notable Jewish dramatic and comedic playwrights. Arthur Miller wrote about working-class people and the ethical and social issues of living in the modern world in such plays as: *Death of a Salesman* (1949), a Pulitzer Prize winner; *The Crucible* (1953); *A View from a Bridge* (1955) and *All My Sons* (1947).

Neil Simon has been just as successful with lighter fare that points to the comic incongruities of everyday life, typically by showing conflict, often with serious undertones, between two opposing personalities. Born in the Bronx, he wrote for television comedians, including Sid Caesar and Phil Silvers, before turning to the stage and becoming one of the most successful Broadway comedy writers. The popularity of his works and his television roots allowed him to make equally successful film adaptations of many of his stage productions:

> *The Odd Couple* (1965)
>
> *The Sunshine Boys* (1972)
>
> *Plaza Suite* (1968)
>
> *Barefoot in the Park* (1963)
>
> *Lost in Yonkers* (1991): Pulitzer Prize-winner
>
> *The Goodbye Girl* (1977)

More recently, Wendy Wasserstein has also made her mark. She won what is called the "Holy Trinity of Broadway": *The Heidi Chronicles* (1989) won a Tony Award, a Pulitzer Prize and the New York Critics Award. She also wrote *The Sisters Rosensweig* (1992), which met with great success.

As a footnote to the Pulitzer Prizes, Joseph Pulitzer was a Hungarian immigrant whose father had been Jewish. A veteran of the Civil War, he settled in St. Louis and bought the bankrupt *St. Louis Dispatch* in 1878 for twenty-five hundred dollars. His papers stressed "muckracking, yellow journalism" to drive circulation. In 1903, he endowed the Columbia School of Journalism (1903) and the prize that bears his name today. The Pulitzer family had a published net worth of $1.6 billion in 1998.

JEWISH SONGWRITERS AND MUSICIANS STAND OUT

Jewish musical creativity has become mainstream far beyond Broadway. It is hard to tell whether Jews influenced the American musical scene or whether America influenced Jewish composers. Irving Berlin (Israel Baline) wrote some of America's most popular songs. Berlin never learned to read music, so he hummed and improvised pieces on the piano while associates wrote down the tunes. Although he never walked in an Easter parade or dreamed of a white Christmas, he wrote songs for a predominantly Christian America to enjoy:

"God Bless America" (1938)

"White Christmas" (1942)

"Easter Parade" (1933)

"There's No Business Like Show Business" and "Anything You Can Do I Can Do Better" from the play *Annie Get Your Gun* (1946)

"Alexander's Ragtime Band" (1911)

A Jew wrote another Christmas holiday standard as well. Mel "The Velvet Fog" Tormé composed "The Christmas Song" ("Chestnuts roasting on an open fire"). Another American religion, baseball, also has a Jewish touch. "Take Me Out to the Ball Game" was written by Albert Von Tilzer.

Aaron Copland also created uniquely American music that blended jazz, folk and classical music. His American-flavored works expressed his ideas in simplest terms. He captured the youth and vitality that characterize America in songs like "Billy the Kid" (1938), "Rodeo" (1942) and "Fanfare for the Common Man" (1942).

Harold Arlen created the songs for one of the most beloved movies of all time, *The Wizard of Oz* (1939), which included "Over the Rainbow." He also composed classic tunes "Stormy Weather" and "That Old Black Magic," and wrote the music for the Broadway show *A Star Is Born* (1954).

The Big Band era had Jewish band leaders such as Benny Goodman, clarinetist and "King of Swing"; Mitch Miller, the "bouncing ball" band leader; Artie Shaw (Arshawsky), jazz clarinetist and big-band leader; and, later, tenor saxophonist Stan Getz. Getz brought together his own cool jazz sounds with a bossa nova beat in the 1950s with "Girl from Ipanema." When it comes to rock 'n' roll, it was Alan Freed who was credited as the first DJ in the '50s to dare to play the "corrupting sounds of the devil's music."

In the 1950s, 1960s and 1970s, many Jewish songwriters excelled in the popular-music scene. Jerry Lieber and Mike Stoller wrote "Hound Dog,"

"Jailhouse Rock," "Stand by Me" and "Love Potion #9." Burt Bacharach, a pop songwriter, wrote for film, stage and the radio: the *Arthur* theme (1982), "Raindrops Keep Falling on My Head," songs for *Butch Cassidy and the Sundance Kid* (1969), and the Carpenters' hit "Close to You" (1973). Paul Simon and Art Garfunkel teamed up to create "The Sounds of Silence," "Mrs. Robinson" and "Bridge over Troubled Water." Just as popular were Neil Diamond, Herb Alpert, Julio Iglesias (yes, Jewish), Billy Joel, Bette Midler, Barbra Streisand, Carly Simon (from the Simon family of Simon & Schuster), Carole King (Kline) and Barry Manilow (Pincus). There are also Jewish musicians with a bit more of an edge: Kiss's Gene Simmons (Chaim Weitz) and Paul Stanley, Joey Ramone, Lou Reed, Iggy Pop (James Osterberg), Guns 'n' Roses' Slash (Saul Hudson) and Counting Crows' Adam Duritz.

And let's not forget Bob Dylan (Zimmerman), a unique individual with a unique voice! "Blowin' in the Wind" (1963) and "The Times, They Are a-Changin'" (1963) were such a departure from the mainstream that they captured the 1960s counterculture's rebellious spirit. His rebellion also was reflected in his religious choices; in the early 1980s he flirted with born-again Christianity, only to return to Orthodox Judaism. Dylan said, "There is no problem. I am a Jew. It touches my poetry, my life in ways I can't describe. Why should I declare something that should be so obvious?"[14]

Jewish people have also been attracted to the business of music. Many successful producers and music promoters were Jewish, including the Beatles' Brian Epstein. Mo Ostin was the CEO of Warner Records, the largest record label, for more than twenty-five years.

Lewis "Lew" Wasserman is a real stand-out who started in music and became a media mogul. He joined MCA, Music Corporation of America, in 1936 and built the company into one of the largest record companies and media powerhouses. He was particularly successful in leading MCA's talent agency, a branch they later had to divest for antitrust reasons. In 1962, MCA bought Universal Studios primarily for its TV production, but the studio went on to distribute some of Steven Spielberg's most popular movies, including *Jaws, E.T.* and *Jurassic Park*. In 1990 MCA paid David Geffen $545 million for Geffen Records. Shortly afterwards, Wasserman sold the entire company to the Japanese conglomerate Matsushita for $6.1 billion. In 1995 the Bronfmans' Seagram Co. purchased 80 percent of the company, maintaining Wasserman as its honorary chairman.

JEWS MAKE THEIR MARK IN CLASSICAL MUSIC AS WELL

In the area of classical music, Jews have excelled as composers, musicians and conductors. Felix Mendelssohn has had a profound effect on the medium as a conductor, music organizer and composer. Although his grandfather was an important Jewish philosopher, Felix's father, a wealthy banker, had his entire family baptized into the Lutheran church to gain social acceptance. Exposure to his father's rationalist philosophy made him somewhat a religious skeptic. As conductor of the Gewandhaus Concerts in Leipzig, Germany, from 1835 to 1847, Mendelssohn departed from tradition by "interpreting" orchestral music rather than mechanically reproducing it. He expanded audiences' tastes by rediscovering and reintroducing works of Bach to the classics repertoire. Mendelssohn also developed the modern organization of concerts: an overture, a large scale-work, a concerto, and a shorter piece. Before Mendelssohn, lighter forms of music were played between the movements of a symphony! In 1825, at the age of sixteen, he wrote "String Octet" and at seventeen he wrote the concert overture, "Midsummer Night's Dream."[15]

Many experts consider Vladimir Horowitz the premier pianist of the twentieth century. At the age of three, he began taking lessons from his father. Other extraordinary talents include Arthur Rubinstein and the violinists Yascha Heifetz, Isaac Stern, Yehudi Menuhin and Itzhak Perlman.

Many Jews have become preeminent conductors. André Previn, Gustav Mahler, Otto Klemperer, Eugene Ormandy and Arthur Fiedler have pleased thousands of audiences. Fiedler's leadership of the Boston Pops from 1930 to 1979 introduced three generations of Americans to classical music, through his accessible and fun "classical light" concerts.

At the New York Metropolitan Opera, some of the most famous singers are Jewish. Roberta Peters is famous for her performances in *La Traviata* and *La Bohème*. Robert Merrill originally wanted to play professional baseball before taking his talents to the opera. Beverly Sills, Jan Peerce (Jacob Perelmuth), Regina Resnik and Richard Tucker, the "American Caruso," all have made their artistic marks on the operatic stage.

JEWISH ARTISTS GO THEIR OWN WAY

Jewish creativity can be seen in the works of numerous influential artists who decided to defy convention and go their own ways. Being a full-time artist is like being an entrepreneur: the canvasses serve as a storefront and the inventory. Impressionist Camille Pissarro (1830–1903) is considered the most important of all Jewish artists; his work heavily influenced Cézanne, Monet and Renoir. In fact, Cézanne referred to Pissarro as "the first impressionist." By using patches of color instead of concise lines, Pissarro's images created a soft feel and look. He rejected traditional painting techniques and subject matter. At a time when biblical and historical themes dominated the art world, he chose to concentrate on nature instead.

Marc Chagall (1887–1985) was one of the few Jewish artists to pursue Jewish themes and cultivate Jewish patrons. One of his most famous stained-glass windows is of the Twelve Tribes, located at the Hadassah Medical Center in Israel. Chagall did not restrict himself to one medium; he created mosaics, graphics and etchings on large and small scales, all with his distinctive soft, colorful, realistic style.

Most of the other famous Jewish artists have been pioneers in the modern movement. Best known for his colorful, expressionistic portraits of the destitute and decadent of New York City's social scene, Max Weber spearheaded the introduction of modern art in the United States. Mark Rothko (Rothkovich) (1903–1970) was a modern abstract expressionist who used large blocks of color or an intricate splattering technique on large canvasses. Louise Nevelson (1899–1988) (née Leah Berliawsky) was a modern sculptor who popularized a style that incorporates found objects, such as boxes, furniture and wood scraps, into massive sculptural walls. Her most famous works were painted flat black and appear as stacked modular structures. Her inspiration was her father, who was a junkman; as a child she would collect things and display her found treasures in boxes. George Segal (born in 1924) casts life-size white plaster images of human figures and places them in everyday urban settings, such as buses, to show the anonymity of modern living. Amedeo Modiglianni (1884–1920), an early modern painter, led a life of extremes that included excessive drinking, drug use and sexual promiscuity. His distinctive impressionist paintings of human subjects had a sculptural quality that elongated his subjects' faces like masks. Peter Max popularized his own "Cosmic '60s" psychedelic style with brilliant colors and bold linear outlines. Robert Rauschenberg (born in 1925) uses common objects in his artwork and creates silk-screen photographic collages. Franz Kline (1910–1962) was an abstract painter who used broad black brush strokes on a large white canvas. Roy Lichtenstein (1923–1997) created large-scale comic-strip pop art paintings that sometimes included captioned dialogue.

A largely unknown Jewish artist, Victor Brenner (1871–1924), designed the first American portrait coin, the Lincoln penny, in 1909. His influence has gone pretty much unnoticed, although we handle his work every day.

The business of fine art is also heavily influenced by Jewish people through their ownership of galleries and trade publications. Milton Esterow owns *Art News*, the largest fine art magazine in the world, which he bought from *Newsweek* in 1972.

JEWISH CARTOONISTS HAVE FUN

It's a bird, it's a plane, no, it's a Jewish cartoonist! Although cartooning isn't considered as prestigious from an artistic standpoint, it is a small, profitable niche that provides entertainment for the masses. Even Lichtenstein reproduced comic-strip art to create some of his famous pieces. And Jewish cartoonists have created some of the most famous comic-book and animated characters of all time.[16]

Al Capp	Li'l Abner (1934–1977)
Max Fleisher	Popeye, Betty Boop
Isadore "Fritz" Freleng	Warner Brothers characters: Bugs Bunny, Daffy Duck, Porky Pig, Tweety Pie, Speedy Gonzales and, separately, the Pink Panther.
Mel Blanc	"The Man of 1,000 Voices" gave the voices to most of Freleng's Warner Brothers' characters including: Bugs, Daffy, Porky and Tweety. Mel also was Woody Woodpecker and Elmer Fudd.
Bob Kane	Batman
Stan Lee	Spiderman, The Hulk
Joe Shuster and Jerry Siegel	Superman

In addition, the Rugrats, those impossibly precocious infants, are the Jewish cartoon creation of Arlene Klasky and Gabor Csupo. The Rugrats' Passover special with Grampa Boris and Gramma Minka is drawn from the real lives of its creators.[17]

Jewish people are represented in the world of animated pictures in the same high percentage they are in the rest of Hollywood. Krusty the Clown

(Hershel Krustofsky) gives only a clue to the number of Jewish writers behind *The Simpsons* and many other cartoons.

JEWISH PHOTOGRAPHERS PIONEER NEW ART

In yet another artistic medium, Jewish artists have made their mark. Alfred Stieglitz is credited with establishing photography as a legitimate art form, worthy of display in museums and galleries. He is noted for his striking portraits of his wife, artist Georgia O'Keeffe (not Jewish), as well as many photographic studies of New York City. Alfred Eisenstadt (1898–1995) is recognized as the first modern photojournalist. His most famous photo is of a World War II sailor kissing a nurse in Times Square. Richard Avedon (born in 1923) turned his fashion photography into art and created a distinctive look by including the negative's markings on the borders of his photos. He is also recognized for his celebrity portraits and his daring photos of snake handlers and crossdressers.

Annie Leibovitz (born in 1949) is also known for her celebrity portraits. She became chief photographer for *Rolling Stone* in 1973, then moved on to *Vanity Fair* in 1983. Two of her most famous photos are of a naked John Lennon curled up like a baby beside a clothed Yoko Ono and of a pregnant and nude Demi Moore (all not Jewish). Leibovitz's career started after a stay in Israel, where she had worked and photographed an archaeological dig. She resumed her studies at the Art Institute in San Francisco, but pursued photography as a new hobby and took a few photos capturing the protest scene of the '60s around San Francisco. Leibovitz sold one of Allen Ginsberg to *Rolling Stone*, for which they paid her twenty-five dollars. When they sent her to shoot Grace Slick (not Jewish) and began paying her forty-seven dollars a week, her professional career had begun.[18]

On the scientific end of the photography business, in 1948 Edwin Land invented the field of instant photography with his Polaroid Land camera and film.

THE "PEOPLE OF THE BOOK" WRITE AS WELL AS READ

Jews have been their own very best customers. It is not surprising that many creative talents behind their products are Jewish as well. With a higher level of education, a tradition of literacy and a creative spirit, Jews make up a disproportionate share of successful authors and winners of Nobel Prizes for Literature and Pulitzer Prizes. A very short list includes literary giants as well as best-selling authors. Some have been award-winning and others distinctively commercial for poolside reading. The list includes: Isaac Asimov (*I Robot*, 1950, a sci-fi classic); Saul Bellow (*Humboldt's Gift*, 1976, Pulitzer Prize, Nobel Prize-winner); Beat Generation poet Allen Ginsberg (*Howl*, 1956); Arthur Frommer (travel-on-a-budget guides); Joseph Heller (*Catch-22*, 1961); Erica Jong (*Fear of Flying*, 1973); Franz Kafka (*The Metamorphosis*, 1912); Judith Krantz (*Scruples*, 1970); Ira Levin (*The Stepford Wives*, 1972); J. K. Lasser (income tax guides); Norman Mailer (*The Executioner's Song*, 1980, Pulitzer Prize); Ayn Rand (*The Fountainhead*, 1943); Harold Robbins (*The Carpetbaggers*, 1961); Margaret Rey (*Curious George* series); Philip Roth (*Portnoy's Complaint*, 1969); Erich Segal (*Love Story*, 1970); Maurice Sendak (children's author and illustrator, *Where the Wild Things Are*, 1963); J. D. Salinger (*Catcher in the Rye*, 1951); Sidney Sheldon (*The Other Side of Midnight*, 1990); Shel Silverstein (*Falling Up,* 1996); Isaac Bashevis Singer (*A Crown of Feathers*, 1974, Nobel Prize); R. L. Stine (*Goosebumps*, 1990s mega-best-selling children's series); Alvin Toffler (*Future Shock*, 1970); Leon Uris (*Exodus*, 1957); and Herman Wouk (*The Caine Mutiny*, 1951, Pulitzer Prize).

THE TOY INDUSTRY

There is no industry like the toy industry for pure creativity. To capture a child's attention and desire is truly a Herculean task. It may seem like a fun industry to work in, but in reality it is a very competitive, cut-throat business. If you have something great, there are a dozen imitators at your heels. By the time you have enough inventory to meet the demand of a hot product, the craze cools, leaving you with a warehouse full of last year's Furbys, Tickle-Me Elmos or Cabbage Patch Dolls.

Jewish people are heavily involved in all aspects of the toy business, from inventing to manufacturing and retailing. The $16 billion toy industry has two major players: Mattel, with 19 percent of the market, and Hasbro, with 12 percent. Both companies were founded by Jewish entrepreneurs. A distant third is Little Tykes with only 2.8 percent, followed by many other minor players. When a company does manage to grow out of obscurity, "The Big Two" gobble it up.

Mattel was founded by Elliot and Ruth Handler (née Moscowitz). In 1939, the Handlers began a small toy company that produced trinkets. To expand their lines, the Handlers teamed up with Harold Matson, who produced frames, doll furniture and other toys (Matson and Elliot = Mattel).

The business took off in 1955 with their first big product, the Burp Gun. In 1956 Ruth came up with the idea of selling a doll with a bust after she saw a doll called Lilli in a shop window in Switzerland. At that time in America, children's dolls had no obvious busts or shapeliness. In the conservative air of the late 1950s, the Handlers developed the marketing pitch that Barbie would prepare little girls to become proper young ladies by teaching them how to dress and apply makeup. Otherwise, Barbie would have been viewed as risqué. Barbie, named for Ruth's daughter, was later joined by her friend Ken, named after Ruth's son. Barbie was born and so was Mattel.

Mattel went on to create Hot Wheels, develop toys for Disney characters and buy Fisher-Price in 1993.[19] According to one Mattel CEO, basic play patterns are universal. "Little girls like to comb hair; they like to change clothes. Boys like to race cars across the table or across the floor. They like to have fights between bad guys and good guys."[20]

In 1996 Mattel had a chance to buy Hasbro for $5.2 billion. At first, the talks were friendly, and Hasbro's chairman, Alan Hassenfeld, favorably commented, "Here you would have a six- or seven-billion-dollar company not shooting each other in the foot, but shooting others down."[21] Hasbro, however, rebuffed a heavy-handed offer because of financial and antitrust concerns, and the merger quickly turned into a hostile takeover. Mattel eventually gave up when they realized they could not win. As a consolation prize, Mattel bought Tyco Toys – then the No. 3 toy maker – in 1997 because it owned Matchbox and Sesame Street toys.

In 1997, the Jewish Jill Elikann Barad became chairman and CEO of Mattel. Until her sudden resignation in February 2000, she was one of only two women to head a Fortune 500 company in 1998. (In fact three of the seven female CEOs of the Fortune 1000 were Jewish.) Barad received her degree at Queens College and held jobs in the cosmetics industry. She was hired in 1981 to work on the Barbie brand. Insiders compare her drive and energy to the drive of Mattel's founder, Ruth Handler. Because of her aggressive style, a boss once told her that she "shouldn't pretend to know all the answers" and that she "wouldn't go far."[22] He was proven wrong. She moved up the ranks, and under her direction Barbie grew from $200 million to $1.7 billion in sales. In 1999, Barad expanded Mattel into educational computer software with the $3.5 billion acquisition of The Learning Company. However, it was her undoing as the company suffered great losses and forced her resignation. Today, Mattel is the largest toy manufacturer in the world with $5 billion in sales.

Henry and Hillel Hassenfeld of Rhode Island founded Hassenfeld Bros. Inc. (Hasbro) in 1920. The company was founded as a scrap textiles (i.e., rags) company. Stuck early on with a load of book-binding cloth, Henry thought of using the cloth to create pencil boxes. With orders from Woolworth and Kresge, the Hassenfelds set up their first factory in 1922. They soon began including pencils, rulers, notebooks and other school supplies in their boxes. At first they bought the contents from others, but soon started manufacturing their own pencils, which evolved into the Empire Pencil Co. Henry's son Harold ran Empire, while his other son, Merrill, ran the "box" business. Because the boxes were a back-to-school item, Hasbro started including paints, clay and crayons to appeal to customers throughout the year. In the 1940s the company began making junior doctor and nurse kits complete with kiddie stethoscopes and pill bottles in a box. During the war they produced junior air-raid warden kits.[23]

In 1951 George Lerner, a Brooklyn toy inventor, brought Merrill a box of plastic noses, ears, eyes, mustaches, hats, hair and pipes. Children were to stick these pieces on fruits and vegetables to create wacky characters. All the other toy companies turned the idea down because they thought it was a waste of food and the characters would rot and stink if lost behind the sofa. With the addition of a plastic body Mr. Potato Head was born, and Hasbro was launched as a major toy company. Mr. Potato Head was soon followed by Mrs., son Spud and daughter Yam. Lerner received a $500 advance and 5 percent royalty.[24]

In 1963, when Larry Lerner (not related to George) was working as a games designer for Ideal Toys, he thought that a soldier doll for boys would be a winner if it could strike realistic poses, handle weapons and fit into armored vehicles. Toy soldiers at the time were all inflexible plastic or metal, good for display and not much else. "Boys will never play with dolls" was Ideal's reaction. Believing in his idea, he took it to Merrill Hassenfeld, who liked it because, just as with Mattel's Barbie, you could sell a lot of extra gear to go with the soldier. GI Joe, America's "Movable Fighting Man," had arrived. Hassenfeld paid Lerner one hundred thousand dollars for his idea without any ongoing royalties.[25]

In 1984 Stephen Hassenfeld (Merrill's son) headed Hasbro and acquired Milton Bradley games and Playskool, doubling the size of the company. After Stephen's untimely death, his brother Alan took over. In 1991 Alan doubled Hasbro by acquiring Tonka, which had been saddled with debt from its own acquisitions of Kenner (Star Wars and Batman toys) and Parker Brothers (Monopoly and other games). In 1998 Alan acquired Tiger electronic games and Galloob, with its Micromachines and mini–Star Wars figures. Today Hasbro, under the leadership of Alan Hassenfield, is the second-largest toy manufacturer, with sales of $3.3 billion. With Mr. Potato Head, Star Wars, Teletubbies, Furby and Play-Doh, Hasbro is the continuing nemesis of Mattel.

Jews founded other famous toy makers as well. The Weintraub family owned Ideal. The Greenberg brothers founded Coleco, which popularized the Cabbage Patch Doll and later became part of Mattel.[26] Louis Marx started the Marx Co., known for its action figures, and David Abrams founded Mego. Russell Berrie's Russ Berrie & Co. became synonymous with stuffed animals.

On the retailing side of the business, as I mentioned in an earlier chapter, Charles Lazarus pioneered discount toy retailing with Toys 'R' Us. Lazarus started in 1948 and today is the largest toy retailer in the world with $11 billion in sales and more than one thousand superstores.

With so many Jewish leaders concentrated in the toy industry, many of the executives, managers, designers and inventors are also Jewish, in no small part because this relatively small industry requires specific experience, temperament, creativity and connections.

WHAT SHOULD I DO TO GENERATE THE CREATIVE SPARK WITHIN MY CHILDREN AND MYSELF?

1. Be "permissive" but protective parents

2. Reward venturing

3. Build your own creative engine

BE "PERMISSIVE" BUT PROTECTIVE PARENTS

As Zena Blau found in her studies, Jewish parenting is different. It is a mixture of tight family bonding and a lax parenting style. How lax is up to the individual parents, but an authoritarian style is not the way to go. The whole idea is to keep them close to home so they can be infused with the values of hard work, education and the desire for professional and financial success. The lack of overbearing parental discipline allows children to create a strong ego and sense of self that will immunize them from negative outside influences. Conformity is not taught as a virtue. Instead, being your own person and going your own way are encouraged. This form of parenting develops a brashness of action and spirit that allows Jewish children to find their own way in professional careers, as pioneers, rule breakers and entrepreneurs. It may not make for the best-behaved children, but it does sow the seeds for their success as adults.

REWARD VENTURING BY YOUR CHILDREN AND YOURSELF

Succeeding is very important, but success cannot happen every time. One needs to have the courage to try different things. Doing the same thing each day, meeting the same people, traveling the same route, one will rarely encounter new challenges. Ironically, staying in your comfort zone should become increasingly uncomfortable. You should not set up situations or conditions for your children or yourself that are so difficult that the penalty of failure is greater than the penalty of doing nothing. Reward yourself and your child for trying something different, even if there is some initial hesitation.

If stuck in a pattern of behavior, ask why. Fear is a strong force perpetuating the status quo. In counseling, therapists often ask fearful people to take their fearful thoughts to their most drastic conclusions, a therapy often called "Burst the Worst." Often, the worst results are not that bad. Rarely could something result in imminent physical demise. Another technique involves rating feelings of anxiety on a scale of 1 to 10. Place the most stressful situation ever experienced as a 10, then compare it to the current situation. Again, more times than not, it will rate below a 5, and one should press ahead and take action. Make that phone call. Join that club. Go to that convention. Investigate that opportunity.

If you think the task is too large or difficult, ask for help. A first step dispels paralysis, and motion produces momentum. Reduce the perceived risk of acting. Plan your actions and develop contingency plans. And, last but not least, use the visualization techniques that athletes often use. Visualize yourself successfully and actively pursuing your goal. Visualize success. Combine the techniques and forge ahead.

BUILD YOUR OWN CREATIVE ENGINE

Everyone needs to nurture a creative attitude. Be open to new ideas, try new things, and think in new ways.

Here are a few other tips for encouraging creativity, individuality and an open mind:

IGNORE "KILLER PHRASES" AND SENSELESS RULES

"Killer phrases," according to the book *What a Great Idea!* by Chic Thompson (not Jewish), are the enemies of ideas. A successful idea must be a good idea and must be presented properly in order to be adopted or implemented. However, many people use "killer phrases" to stop new ideas in their tracks:

"Yes, but . . ."

"We tried that before."

"Don't rock the boat."

"Put it in writing."

"Let's stick with what works."

"I'll get back to you."

"It isn't your responsibility."

The worst killer phrases come from ourselves. We doubt our own abilities to do something new, so we do nothing. We make excuses about resources and do nothing. We procrastinate and do nothing. We fear what the reaction to a new idea will be and do nothing. Even more self-defeating is, "If the idea is successful, can I handle it?"

Jews have always rocked the boat. Having an outsider mentality has allowed Jewish people to work outside the mainstream and create new ideas, inventions and businesses. To have different results, people must act differently. Just remember that the definition of insanity is doing the same thing over and over and expecting a different result.

In the chapter about spending and saving, I made the point that, as dependent workers, employees need to create their own capital base. Without capital, employees are at the mercy of their employers to pay their bills. The fear of upsetting the boss prevents employees from being truly creative and productive. If the idea is really such a good one, you can make the big leap with your own capital and pursue your dream yourself. As an entrepreneur, anyone can create real wealth. The Forbes 400 is filled with Jews who did just that.

CHALLENGE WIDELY HELD ASSUMPTIONS

Remember Ideal Toys' assumption that "boys would not play with dolls"?

"Girls want to be mommies and only want baby dolls to feed and care for."
With that thinking, both Hasbro's GI Joe and Mattel's Barbie would not exist
today. Assumptions stifle creativity just like killer phrases. The best thing
about assumptions is that everyone else follows them. If they turn out to be
wrong, you will be all alone pursuing that new product or new method.
Breakthroughs contradict history. It was once thought that peptic ulcers were
caused by excess stomach acid, but it has been proven that ulcers are caused
by a bacterial infection called *Helicobacter pylori*. The acid was just a symp-
tom, but doctors accepted it as the cause for years because the old assumption was so ingrained. According to a 1997 study by the Centers for Disease
Control and Prevention, half of all doctors continue to treat ulcers with drugs
to combat stomach acid. As Irl Hirsh, an endocrinologist at the University of
Washington, points out, "When a major medical advance in medicine occurs,
it takes about ten years to change the way doctors practice."[27]

A good creative exercise is to think in opposites. If you want to improve
something, think about what you would do to really mess things up. It may
lead to a new perspective that can be productive!

Problem solving and idea generation are also stifled because our
assumptions preclude possible options. A Harvard Business School case
study presented a problem about an ice cooler manufacturer who needed a
new manufacturing plant. The company had a factory in Georgia, but
when its products were shipped to its customers out west, the coolers often
became damaged during the long trip. A whole series of facts and figures
were presented to the students indicating where the new plant optimally
should be placed. All the facts led students to assume the problem required
building a new factory, when in actuality the coolers might just have needed some better packaging for shipment. As Jonas Salk said, "Find the right
questions. You don't invent the answers; you reveal the answers."

BE A GOOD COPYCAT

Estée Lauder once said, "Being interested in other people's ideas for the
purpose of saying, 'We can do it better,' is not copying. Innovation doesn't
always mean inventing the wheel each time; innovation can mean a whole
new way of looking at old things."[28]

New ideas do not need to be revolutionary to be great. They can be
incremental improvements or applications of a good idea borrowed from
one industry and applied to another. Ms. Lauder (née Josephine Esther
Mentzer) saw that when new foods were being introduced, free samples

were given out so people could try them. She realized that "if you put the product in the customer's hands, it will speak for itself if it's something of quality." She made her breakthrough in 1946 by giving a vast number of free samples and "gifts with purchase" to introduce new cosmetics to new customers. It is commonplace now, but it was a revolution in the cosmetics industry. The Lauder fortune totaled $8.1 billion in 1999 and is still in the hands of her sons Leonard and Ronald.[29]

KEEP CURRENT: KNOW THE TRENDS
Jewish people read a lot. Reading can provide enjoyment, but it can also provide information about what's going on in the world, so that you can find your own way. Of course the *Wall Street Journal* and the *New York Times* are great newspapers, but most Americans read more mainstream publications. *USA Today* is great for quick news recaps and popular culture. The *National Enquirer*, the largest circulation newspaper in the country, provides insights into what Americans are really interested in, what they buy and what they wish for. Tour the local book superstore and check out the magazine racks. Catalogs can also be a great source of inspiration. For industry-specific information, attend the related trade association's annual trade show.

When reading something exceptionally interesting, save it in a clipping file for future reference. I am not talking about extensive indexing, but rather a simple box with some folders for general topics. New trends and opportunities are not always clearly defined. A seemingly unrelated event or personal experience may later make one of your exceptional clippings germane. Suppose one day you save an article about Jewish billionaires and the next day you think about writing a book about Jewish success while watching the last episode of *Seinfeld*.

CREATE AN IDEA-FRIENDLY HOME
Good ideas are precious, yet many evaporate as soon as they are created. Be prepared to capture them when they emerge. The more ideas you generate, the higher the probability that a great one could be developed.

Become aware of your most creative time of day and your most creative environment. Do you do your best thinking:

- in the shower?

- while commuting?

❏ at the gym?

❏ while shopping?

Dreams, which are a mix of reality and fantasy, often contain creative thoughts that can prove very valuable. Here are three basic steps to remembering your dreams:

1. When falling asleep, tell yourself you want to remember your dreams.

2. When waking up, keep your eyes closed for a minute and try to remember your dreams.

3. Have paper and pencil by your bed to immediately record "brilliant" thoughts, images and dreams.

It is important to capture an idea when you get it. If you are a shower genius, you better have a grease pencil and slate handy. If shopping is an inspiration, carry a little pocket memo book or a small tape recorder.

Generate ideas freely without filtering them. Filtering is the next stage of creativity. Generate the idea, then evaluate it. Is it feasible? What are the economics? By leaving the idea-generation process as free-wheeling as possible and being critical later, you can develop a greater number of creative and innovative ideas.

But most importantly, thinking is not enough; you need to follow through with the good ones. Kenneth Tuchman, the founder of TeleTech, described it best: "I am a finisher in a society of starters. I want to see something through and get a sense of completion. I have this vision that is constantly evolving in my head. I go to sleep thinking about it, and wake up thinking about it, and have the shower beating on me on the back while I am thinking about it [then I go out and do it]."[30]

CHAPTER 7

Have Something To Prove:
A Drive To Succeed

Motivation is the elusive quality that transforms good ideas into reality. Without execution, the most creative person would remain the next "potential" Michael Dell or Steven Spielberg. The question is, what motivates Jews to succeed? Although Jews have reached the top in a variety of fields, they are still considered the outsiders of Western civilization. Jews have always been trying to gain acceptance, while at the same time maintaining their cultural identity. This causes a great deal of internal conflict, but it also serves as a drive to succeed. Here is Steven Spielberg's version of the experience: "I didn't have any Jewish friends growing up in Phoenix. I felt like I was the only Jewish kid in my high school. [I remember feeling] ashamed because I was living on a street where at Christmas, we were the only house with nothing but a porch light on."[1]

Even in the U.S., where Jews encounter less anti-Semitism than in any other country, they still psychologically live apart. They struggle for acceptance, yet they do not want to walk all the way through the doorway to the mainstream. Jewish people need to prove to themselves, their families and the world that, if they wish, they are worthy to sit down at a table with anybody. Or, as Mary Rodgers Guettel (Richard Rodgers's daughter), puts it, "I realized I never disliked being Jewish. I just didn't like being disliked for being Jewish."[2]

During their struggles, Jews have always believed that things could change for the better, and that individuals had the power to create change. A long history of persecution, combined with an enduring ability to survive, has resulted in a "restless optimism" that drives Jews to find new answers. It has pushed them to pursue alternate paths, many of which have produced extraordinary results.

Mark Twain, a Gentile, asked the same questions about the source of Jewish motivation. He saw the Jews' small numbers, how they were forced to move from place to place over the centuries, and how they managed to succeed when given a little bit of freedom. He recorded his observations in *Harper's* magazine in September 1899:

"If the statistics are right, the Jews constitute but one quarter of one percent of the human race. It suggests a nebulous dim puff of stardust lost in the blaze of the Milky Way. Properly, the Jew ought hardly to be heard of; but he is heard of, has always been heard of. He is as prominent on the planet as any other people, and his importance is extravagantly out of proportion to the smallness of his bulk.

"His contributions to the world list of great names in literature, science, art, music, finance, medicine and abstruse learning are also way out of proportion to the weakness of his numbers. He has made a marvelous fight in this world, in all the ages; and has done it with his hands tied behind him. He could be vain of himself, and be excused for it. The Egyptian, the Babylonian, and the Persian rose, filled the planet with sound and splendor, then faded to dream-stuff and passed away; the Greek and the Roman followed, and made a vast noise, and they are gone; other peoples have sprung up and held their torch high for a time, but it burned out, and they sit in twilight now, or have vanished. The Jew saw them all, beat them all, and is now what he always was, exhibiting no decadence, no infirmities of age, no weakening of his parts, no slowing of his energies, no dulling of his alert and aggressive mind. All things are mortal but the Jew; all other forces pass, but he remains. What is the secret of his immortality?"

McCLELLAND AND THE NEED FOR ACHIEVEMENT

David McClelland, a Gentile, observed in Jews an "achievement drive" that motivates them to pursue academic, professional and creative excellence. In *The Achieving Society* (1961), McClelland studied motivation in what textbooks often refer to as one of the cornerstones of psychology. He believed that many motivations or "needs" are acquired from the person's culture. He outlined these prime motivators as the need for achievement, the need for affiliation and the need for power. "For example, having a high need for achievement encourages an individual to set challenging goals, work hard to achieve goals, and use the skills and abilities needed to accomplish them," he wrote. Using a test he created called the Thematic Apperception Test (TAT), McClelland asked subjects to write a story based on a set of pictures. Evaluators analyzed the stories to reveal the subjects' drives.

In a finding that is excluded from our politically correct, ethnic- and gender-neutral psychology textbooks today (but appears in his original studies), McClelland found that "Jews have a high need for achievement on religious grounds." Max Weber's prior research confirmed this; the Jews' motivation was the strongest of any ethnic group measured. Weber noted especially "the emphasis in Jewish religious teachings on individual responsibility for personal actions and extensive self-education."[3] In order to prove their individuality and mastery of their own destiny, Jews are motivated to achieve and succeed. In a related 1959 study, Rosen and D'Andrade found that Jewish family norms are conducive to stimulating the motivation for high achievement in their children. Now consider Michael Palmer's 1971 research outlining five indicators of the need for achievement:

- Interest in making long-range plans
- Tendency to work harder at tasks requiring mental manipulation
- Preference for decisions taking prudent risks
- Working hard for tangible and intangible rewards
- Desire to take personal responsibility for decisions and see the results[4]

Also consider a 1969 study by Shapero, who saw two additional factors closely correlated to this achievement drive:

- Accepting other entrepreneurs as role models
- Belief in self-determination of his or her own destiny[5]

The list is striking because on every count, Jewish culture, values and actions closely correlate with the research. And I have discussed most of these points in past chapters. Jews are active participants in their long-range goals such as education and their personal savings. Stressing intellectual pursuits, less than 1 percent of Jewish workers in America are physical laborers. Jews choose professions that have a higher probability of higher incomes. When they choose entrepreneurial careers, it is often with a good education or related work experience that reduces their chance of failure. And while most Jews concentrate on lucrative professions, many others choose careers that produce rewards beyond money, such as science, the fine arts and teaching. And when looking for Jewish role models, they have more than their share to choose from.

JEWS BELIEVE THEY CONTROL THEIR OWN DESTINIES

Ethnic background plays a significant role in the way groups regard their futures. It is an issue of control. Jews think people can significantly change the outcomes of their lives through their own actions. In 1960, at about the same time as McClelland's studies, Fred L. Srodtbeck reported in *Family Interaction, Values and Achievement* that Jews in particular were less fatalistic about their situations than other ethnic groups. The study compared Jewish men with Italian men to try to explain their divergent immigrant experiences and outcomes in America. Researchers posed statements to the subjects that were very telling about the effects of their ethnicity on their social advancement.

"Planning only makes a person unhappy since your plans hardly ever work out." When asked about how they felt about this statement, 90 percent of Jews disagreed while only 62 percent of Italians disagreed.

"When a man is born, the success he's going to have is already in the cards, so he might as well accept it and not fight against it." Ninety-eight percent of Jews disagreed while 85 percent of Italians disagreed.

The next statements gauged the men's motivation to break with their family in order to achieve success. "Even when teenagers get married, their main loyalty still belongs to their fathers and mothers." Sixty-four percent of Jews disagreed and 46 percent of Italians disagreed.

"Nothing in life is worth the sacrifice of moving away from your parents." Eighty-two percent of Jews disagreed and 59 percent of Italians disagreed. It has been shown that Jewish parents historically have not imposed mobility restrictions, especially in the pursuit of higher education. On the contrary, they encourage pursuing the best education possible, as Blau confirmed in her studies of Jewish mothers.

As I've said before, being an individual and proving yourself are closely held Jewish values. The last statement tested by Srodtbeck revealed an even larger difference between Jewish men and their Italian counterparts.

"The best kind of job to have is one where you are part of an organization all working together even if you don't get individual credit." Fifty-four percent of Jews disagreed and 28 percent of Italians disagreed.[6]

This statement clearly taps into the achievement drive that each Jew has to be his or her own person. Experience has shown Jewish people that dependence on others can be dangerous because the politics of the day may change. If you are independent, at least you succeed or fail based upon your own performance. In the context of corporate America of the 1980s and '90s, this quest for independence has been exceptionally valuable. Corporate downsizing, restructuring and mergers have displaced many competent but misguided employees who had placed their futures in the hands of large, faceless corporate bureaucracies. Those who maintained their independence have come out ahead.

JEWS ARE RARELY SATISFIED WITH THE STATUS QUO

It's a Jewish axiom that "Everything is so right that something must be wrong." Even if things are good, there is always room for improvement and a reason to be on guard. If a business is doing well, it could still be more profitable. Competitors could overtake the company, and there might be a recession. Do you see the bagel or the hole in its middle? Things never seem to be right. This kind of thinking drives Jewish people to push for new and better ideas in order to secure their place in the world.

> Mr. Simon: How is business on Halstead Street?
>
> Mr. Katz: How can the men's clothing business ever be good in Chicago? The weather is against us.
>
> Mr. Simon: Just what do you mean?
>
> Mr. Katz: Here's the situation. In summer it is so hot that people hesitate to venture out, while you stay in the store and lose money. In winter it is so cold that people are afraid to leave their homes, while your expenses go on and you lose money.
>
> Mr. Simon: Why then leave your store open?
>
> Mr. Katz: If I close up, how will I make a living?

At home, this restlessness is part of a child's education. Good grades are not enough. "All A's and a B+ in math? Why the poor showing in math?" Things can always be done better. The Jewish community is a tough audience to please because there are so many successful students from successful families. A good performance is taken for granted. To stand out you must do something really big. With each improving grade, the child proves himself to be the bright Jewish child his parents and community expect. This stereotypical expectation keeps the pressure on throughout a Jew's life.

A REAL SCENE FROM THE ACCOUNTING WORLD: JEW MEETS NUN

I was assigned to head an audit of a chain of charity hospitals run by the Sisters of Charity. When I met with Sister Rosemary, we discussed our plans for the assignment. In between the dollars and the cents she interjected, "You know, Steve, I know a Jew who lives in California."

"Oh really," I replied, thinking about how many Jews there must be in California.

"Yes, his name is Michael Goldberg. Do you know him?"

"No, I haven't had the chance to meet him yet," I politely answered, pondering the vast secret network linking all Jews around the world.

"He's also an accountant like you; he is very bright, and especially good with figures," Sister Rosemary said.

"I am sure he is. Give him my regards the next time you speak to him," I told her.

The race for admission into the best college encompasses both scholastic and judgmental hurdles. Excellent grades and honor roll status are a given. In a student's sophomore year, the results of the PSAT provide the first brush with reality about his or her ability to enter college. Perhaps extra effort to improve grades or a tutorial in test-taking will produce the desired result. The SAT taken in the junior year will to some extent determine the caliber of schools the student should aim for. Third- or fourth-generation Jewish-American families take it for granted that their children will go to college. Which schools accept their child is "the" question Jewish parents will be answering repeatedly for their Jewish friends.

PROGRESSIVE JEWISH UNION LEADERS
AND THE LABOR MOVEMENT

At the dawn of the industrial revolution, workers were exploited and abused by their employers. However, Jews have long believed things can change if you are willing to stand up and take action, and so it is hardly surprising that Jewish union activists have been driven to spearhead the movement for social change.

Jews were some of the first workers to collectively stand up to management. In 1909, twenty thousand Jewish women garment workers went on strike against their Jewish factory owners. It was called the Great Revolt. With the help of financier Jacob Schiff and U.S. Supreme Court Justice Louis Brandeis, all parties agreed to the "Protocol of Peace" in 1910. In this settlement many of the cornerstones of unionism were created, including the concept of a union shop with shop stewards, a grievance committee, a board of sanitary control and a board of arbitration. The labor movement became legitimate.[7]

Like his father, Samuel Gompers worked as a cigar maker in London. In 1863, Gompers came to America and joined the cigar makers' union in New York. In 1886 he became one of the founders and the first president of the American Federation of Labor (AFL). His contribution to the labor movement was his focus on wages, benefits and working conditions rather than general social change. He remained at the AFL's helm for thirty-seven years.

David Dubinsky rose to the presidency of the Ladies Garment Workers Union in 1932. Sidney Hillman, a former garment worker himself, led the Amalgamated Clothing Workers of America union from 1914 to 1946. He also was one of the founders of the Congress of Industrial Organizations (CIO). After mid-century, Jews had a diminishing role in the unions because most of them left the blue-collar rank-and-file to achieve greater success elsewhere. A notable exception was Jackie Presser, who negotiated the merger of the AFL-CIO and Teamsters in 1987.[8]

In the related topic of workers' rights, Jewish radical thinkers were at the center of the Marxist and communist movements beginning in the mid-1800s. In 1848 Karl Marx and Frederick Engels (not Jewish) wrote the *Communist Manifesto,* which served as the basis of Communist Party platforms. Marx's *Das Kapital* (1867) described the exploitation of the workers and how it would bring the eventual demise of capitalism. Leon Trotsky (Lev Bronstein) was a communist thinker and a leader of the Russian Revolution in 1917. He was opposed to Stalin's brand of authoritarian communism and was assassinated in the power struggle.[9]

Even more recently, in the 1960s, Jewish activists fought for justice and against what they saw as wrong with America. Abbie Hoffman and Jerry

Rubin were the leading radicals protesting against "the system" and the war in Viet Nam. Hoffman said to a gathering of student leaders in 1988, "The decision to be blindly obedient to authority versus the decision to try and change things by fighting the powers that be is always, throughout history, the same decision." He was driven to make a difference.

NACHES MACHINES

A variation on "the family as a motivation" theme is the concept that Jewish children are *naches machines*. *Naches* (see pronunciation notes, p. 203) is the Yiddish word for "joy," especially joy from children. There is a theory that Jewish children strive to satisfy their parents' own need to be successful. It is a very powerful motivator, but it is also a heavy burden. Alexander Portnoy in Philip Roth's *Portnoy's Complaint* (1969) said of his father, "He saw in me the family's opportunity to be as good as anybody, our chance to win honor and respect."

Dennis Prager, a popular Jewish radio talk-show host and author, puts it this way, "Because of my work, I meet people of all backgrounds. After speeches, people come over to talk, and in Los Angeles, because of my radio show, strangers frequently stop to say a few words. Jewish strangers often tell me about the professional accomplishments of their children, yet I do not recall any non-Jewish strangers telling me about their children. The Jewish desire to have children well-educated and professionally successful is praiseworthy, but it often entails a price."

One price is that many Jewish children pursue professions that they wouldn't necessarily choose. Prager went on to say, "I suspect that the number of baby-boomer Jewish lawyers who don't want to be lawyers is not small. These people became lawyers because their options beyond medicine were so limited."

The other downside for these *naches machines* is that their self-worth is dependent on their professional success. If they do not achieve material success and receive their appropriate kudos, they do not believe they are worthy of love and live unhappy lives. With their definition of success being a moving target, it is difficult for these *naches machines* ever to be satisfied.[10]

JEWS SELLING SELF-ESTEEM TO ALL AMERICANS

Trying to gain social acceptance is a subject that Jews have had vast experience in. Perhaps being an "outsider" in society provides a clearer perspective about what being an "insider" is like. This has been especially true for Brooklyn-born Ralph Lifshitz. Using his new name, Ralph Lauren, he captured and packaged a whole upper-crust lifestyle. He created the Polo brand of clothing, bedding, fragrances and decorative accessories for people who aspire to look and feel as if they are part of an elite circle. "If I pay seventy dollars for that thirty-dollar shirt, it will announce to everyone that I have arrived too." Ralph really has arrived; his fortune was estimated at $1.8 billion in 1999.

Like fashion, the cosmetics industry is filled with many Jewish entrepreneurs who have converted "hope in a jar" into fortunes. In addition to Estée Lauder, many of the pioneers of the cosmetics industry were Jewish. Helena Rubinstein created her own fortune in 1908 when she opened the first modern beauty salon. Until then, women made their own beauty aids. She also performed a skin analysis to determine each customer's skin type, and was the first to offer different formulations for the various types of skin. At her death in 1965, her estate was estimated at $100 million.

Jewish men have also played their part in the cosmetics industry. Samuel Rubin founded Fabergé Inc., a perfume and cosmetics company. Max Factor moved to Hollywood in 1909 and became famous for his products and his consultations to the stars. His contributions include Max Factor lip gloss, introduced in 1930, and the first "waterproof" makeup, which was introduced in 1971. His company grew well beyond Hollywood, and today Procter & Gamble sells his products. Charles Revson started Revlon with his matching lipstick and nail color in 1939. Vidal Sassoon formulated new shampoos in the 1980s and invented the premium salon shampoo category. Later he too sold his business to Procter & Gamble.

REMAINING AN OUTSIDER IS GOOD

When is enough enough? George Soros has emerged as one of the most successful international financiers of all time. His fortune was valued at $4 billion in 1999. His speculations have been blamed for manipulating the value of the British pound in 1992 and other Asian currencies in 1997. His Quantum Fund has made him far richer than he could have possibly imagined when he hid from the Nazis in his family's attic. Even with this success, he had difficulty for many years feeling comfortable about himself and his Jewish identity. In *Soros on Soros: Staying Ahead of the Curve*, he gave great insight into his and other Jews' drive to succeed:

"I am proud of being a Jew – although I must admit it took me practically a lifetime to get there. I have suffered from the low self-esteem that is the bane of the assimilationist Jew. This is a heavy load that I could shed only when I recognized my success. I identify being a Jew with being a minority. I believe that there is such a thing as a Jewish genius; one need only look at the Jewish achievements in science, in economic life or in the arts. These were the results of Jews' efforts to transcend their minority status, and to achieve something universal. Jews have learned to consider every question from many different viewpoints, even the most contradictory ones. Being in the minority, they are practically forced into critical thinking. If there is anything of this Jewish genius in me, it is simply the ability to think critically. To that extent, Jewishness is an essential element of my personality and, as I said, I am very proud of that.

"I am also aware that there is a certain amount of Jewish utopianism in my thinking. With my foundations, I am part of that tradition. That is why the European Union excites me so much. There, every nation is in a minority, and that is what makes the concept so appealing."[11]

The problem for Jewish Americans' minority status is that it is rapidly deteriorating. This may sound like good news, but it may also signal the erosion of the uniquely Jewish characteristics that are the subject of this book. Clarence Page (not Jewish) of the *Baltimore Sun* noted that "where anti-Semites failed, assimilation is succeeding. By eliminating barriers, Jewish success is eliminating Jews. Since the mid-1980s, more than half of Jewish marriages are to non-Jews."[12] Alan Dershowitz's *The Vanishing American Jew* (1997) laments that, in one or two generations, the only Jews left will be either the very observant Orthodox ones or the assimilated Jews whose "Jewishness fades into some vague family memory."[13] That is why it is so important to convey to this new generation the definite link between Jewish success and the Jewish culture and traditions discussed in this book.

INDUSTRY EXCLUSIONS AND THE DRIVE TO SUCCEED ELSEWHERE
Many industries are still reluctant to promote Jews. This reluctance has become a motivating force for Jews. Jewish participation in the executive ranks of the Fortune 500 is estimated at between 6 and 8 percent, about three times the Jewish population in the U.S. In a 1986 study Korn/Ferry, the leading executive search firm, found that 7.4 percent of executives at major corporations were Jewish. This is a very positive number – however, the percentage differs widely among industries. It appears that when the industry is characterized as a "hard industry," with large, capital-intensive

corporations with well-defined markets, Jews have not been as prominent. In hard industries, conformity to the established corporate norm is as important as the ability to rise through the ranks. Anti-Semitism can therefore play a far bigger role in such environments. Industries with rapid change and higher risk have attracted and created more Jewish executives. This was confirmed by a study published in 1988 by Abraham Korman in *The Outsiders: Jews and Corporate America*.

PERCENTAGE OF JEWISH SENIOR EXECUTIVES IN FORTUNE 500 COMPANIES BY INDUSTRY

Low Participation		Average Participation		High Participation	
Petroleum	0.7	Appliances	5.0	Publishing	9.5
Utilities	1.9	Forest products	5.2	Financial services	9.7
Chemicals	2.3	Metal products	5.6	Textiles	9.9
Transportation	2.3	Industrial equip.	6.5	Retail chains	20.9
Commercial banking	3.4	Aerospace	7.8	Supermarket chains	21.2
Building materials	3.5	Soap & cosmetics	7.9	Apparel manufacture	26.7
Mining	3.9				
Rubber and plastics	4.3				
Beverages	4.3				
Automobiles	4.4				
Metal manufacture	4.5				

The low, average and high classifications are in relation to the 6 to 8 percent appearance of Jewish executives in the Fortune 500, not the 2 percent of Jews in the general population.

(Adapted from data in *The Outsiders: Jews and Corporate America*, Korman, 1988)

Ironically, when two of these "hard" industries – oil and mining – were young and the rules not well defined, Jews were key players. Louis Blaustein started as a kerosene peddler and developed the forerunner of the modern tanker rail car. His son Jacob started Amoco in 1910 and went on to invent metered gasoline pumps and anti-knock gas. Eventually Amoco merged into Standard Oil in 1954. The Blaustein holdings had grown to $2.8 billion by 1999. In 1881, Meyer Guggenheim was a pioneer with silver and lead mining in Colorado and took control in 1901 of Asarco, the country's largest smelter. The Guggenheim Museum in New York City is his legacy.

In one of the few studies of its kind, R. M. Powell of Ohio State studied the impact of religion on the advancement of executives in 1969. He measured the degree that supervisors considered being of a certain religion a positive or negative. It was a rigorous study that had three phases. The first phase included intensive work with two companies over five years. This was followed by in-depth interviews of executives from a variety of industries, as well as community leaders and leaders of major social organizations and clubs. The final phase included questionnaires plus more intensive interviews with 239 executives. The results revealed that Jews were regarded negatively three times as often as the nearest groups, Mormons and Roman Catholics.

PERCEIVED IMPACT OF RELIGION ON JEWISH EXECUTIVE PROMOTIONS

Impact on Promotability

Religious Group	Helps	Hinders
Episcopal	43.1%	1.8%
Presbyterian	42.2	1.8
Methodist	36.7	1.8
Lutheran	34.9	2.8
Baptist	31.2	8.3
Roman Catholic	28.4	20.2
Mormon	30.3	23.9
Jewish	8.3	63.3

(R. M. Powell, *Race, Religion and the Promotion of the American Executive* [Columbus, Ohio State University, 1969], pp. 67, 107, 109)

In addition, Powell explained the main hindering traits for Jews. His findings give further credence to the belief that the best path for aspiring Jews is an independent, entrepreneurial one.

REASONS FOR HINDRANCE OF JEWISH EXECUTIVE PROMOTABILITY

	% Citing Reason
General public prejudice toward group	10.1
Feelings of distrust	9.2
Clannishness, lack of fellowship with majority	7.3
Fear of customer prejudice	3.7
Not socially accepted in company	2.8

(Powell, *Race, Religion and the Promotion of the American Executive* [1969], p. 118)

In rapidly changing industries, the rules change quickly, personnel turnover is more frequent and individual executive decisions have dramatic impacts on results. These industries are thus more receptive to Jewish participation. One example is retailing, in which the choice of merchandise, its pricing and the level of inventory greatly affect sales and the bottom line. As discussed in the chapter about Jewish entrepreneurs, from Donald and Doris Fisher's the Gap stores to the Lazarus family's Federated Department Stores, Jews have been heavily involved in all types of retailing.

DRIVEN JEWISH JOURNALISTS

Until the 1930s newspaper reporting was considered an undesirable job. The pay was low and the job consisted of writing about local politics, fires and crime. Journalism today is a well-respected profession where some reporters are now as famous as the people they cover. Instead of just reporting facts, insightful journalists can affect public opinion and gain considerable power and notoriety for themselves. It makes sense, then, that Jewish people have been attracted to this profession.

Actually, the Jewish connection to print journalism in the U.S. goes back to its early days. After getting his start in St. Louis, Joseph Pulitzer (Jewish father) bought the *New York World* in 1878.[14] He sent his reporters on crusades to expose local political corruption and ran provocative headlines to gain readership. Herbert Swope, one of Pulitzer's most outstanding reporters, investigated the Ku Klux Klan and the criminal world, and he won awards for his series titled "Inside the German Empire during World War I." As I mentioned in an earlier chapter, Pulitzer founded the Columbia School of Journalism in 1903 and created and funded the annual Pulitzer Prizes. Since Joseph's days, the family has assimilated away from the Jewish faith, but the Pulitzer name now encompasses a media empire of newspapers, TV stations and radio stations with an estimated net worth of $1.6 billion in 1998.

Adolph Ochs bought the nearly bankrupt *New York Times* in 1896 for seventy-five thousand dollars.[15] His mission was to make it an objective newspaper in a market where "yellows" such as Pulitzer's *World* prevailed. Those papers, selling for only one cent, emphasized wild headlines, editorial bias and partisanship. The *Times* sold for three cents, and its managers wanted to raise the price to five cents to further distinguish it as the quality publication. Ochs thought the opposite. He dropped to a one-cent price, reasoning that working people were buying the "yellows" because they were more affordable. He was right, and circulation tripled in a year. The *New York Times* was reborn as the nation's distinguished paper of record.

Instead of being a model for Jewish employment, the *Times* went out of its way to keep Jews out of its highest editorial positions for fear of being labeled a "Jewish" paper. "We never put a Jew in the showcase," said Arthur Hays Sulzberger, Adolph's son-in-law, who took over the paper in 1935.[16] He recommitted the paper to honest, objective and "non-Jewish" reporting. Reporters with Jewish-sounding names were forced to use their initials to disguise their ethnicity. A young Abraham Rosenthal became A. M. Rosenthal when he got his first byline. Grandson Arthur Ochs "Punch" Sulzberger took over in 1963 and diversified the company by buying twenty other papers, ten magazines and six TV and two radio stations. In 1976 he appointed A. M. Rosenthal as executive editor, shattering the Jewish glass ceiling. Arthur Ochs Sulzberger Jr., who is not actively Jewish, succeeded his father in 1992. The remaining stake of the Sulzberger/Ochs family in the *Times* and other family investments was valued in 1996 at $600 million. The *Times* has been the home of many outstanding Jewish journalists over the years, including Max Frankel, Arthur Gelb, Arthur Krock, Anthony Lewis and William Safire.

Financier Eugene Meyer bought the *Washington Post* in a bankruptcy auction in 1933 for $825,000. He was not an experienced newspaperman, but shared the same convictions Ochs did about publishing a paper guided by principles of truthfulness, objectivity and genteel decency. Circulation as well as advertising soon tripled. Meyer married a Gentile, Agnes Ernst, and maintained a secular household in which religion was not even discussed, according to his daughter Katherine's memoir, *Personal History*.[17] In 1948 his daughter's Lutheran husband, Philip Graham, succeeded Meyer and went on to add TV stations and *Newsweek* magazine to the company. After Philip's suicide in 1963, Katherine Meyer Graham became president of the company, and still serves as chairman today. She is affiliated as a Lutheran. The value of the Graham/Meyer family's stake in the *Washington Post* and its properties grew to $1.4 billion in 1999.

In the 1970s, the *Washington Post*'s dedication to the truth, despite the consequences, was put to the test by reporters Bob Woodward (not Jewish) and Carl Bernstein. Their reporting exposed the Watergate scandal and pitted the *Post* directly against the Nixon White House. In 1998 Michael Isikoff followed in the footsteps of Woodward and Bernstein and shook the White House by exposing the stories of sexual misconduct that led to the impeachment proceedings against President Bill Clinton. First as a reporter for the *Washington Post* and then for *Newsweek,* Isikoff broke the Monica Lewinsky story. The *American Journalism Review* said, "It's clear from grand jury testimony that Isikoff's tireless reporting was often the significant factor in the decisions of the major players."

Other outstanding Jewish journalists who have worked at the *Post* include I. F. Stone, David Broder and Shirley Povich (Maury's father). In a 1982 study, Jews made up less than 6 percent of the national press corps, but 25 percent of the media elite at the *New York Times, Washington Post, Wall Street Journal, Los Angeles Times, Newsweek, Time, U.S. News and World Report* and the news divisions of the three major television networks.[18] Many have risen to the highest ranks of management without owning the company, such as Norman Pearlstine, editor-in-chief of Time Warner's magazine group, whose holdings include *Time, Sports Illustrated, People* and *Money* magazines. Peter Kann is the chairman and CEO of Dow Jones & Co. and publisher of the *Wall Street Journal.*

THE MYSTERIES OF NATURE REVEALED:
JEWISH SCIENTISTS ARE DRIVEN TRAILBLAZERS

Einstein said, "The cosmic religious experience is the strongest and noblest driving force behind scientific research."[19] You might imagine that scientists would be the most skeptical individuals when it comes to religion. On the contrary, when scientists discover the laws of nature, many of them find that the complex and structured universe serves to reinforce their beliefs in a higher being. They feel they have been driven to find God revealed in nature.

For example, many of the scientists involved in the Manhattan Project, including J. Robert Oppenheimer, Leo Szilard and Einstein, saw nature's ultimate power and had misgivings that they might have revealed more than humanity could handle. These and other Jewish searchers have been awarded 30 percent of all the American Nobel Prizes in science. Inquisitive and resourceful, the following scientists have been on the vanguard of intellectual discovery.

Otto Frisch – In 1939, he described the process in which uranium bombarded by neutrons can be changed into lighter elements. He named the process *fission*, the basis for nuclear energy.

Jerome Friedman – Friedman conducted experiments on a linear accelerator and demonstrated that neutrons and protons were formed from quarks, the fundamental energy packets of which all matter is composed. (Nobel Prize, 1990)

Hans Bethe – He published the theory in 1938 that solar energy comes from a thermonuclear reaction called the carbon cycle. Hydrogen nuclei fuse to make helium nuclei. (Nobel Prize, 1967)

Niels Bohr – Bohr was the founder of the theory of atomic structure in 1913. In quantum theory, atoms radiate energy only when there is the movement of electrons. (Nobel Prize, 1922)

Melvin Calvin – Calvin gained the understanding of how photosynthesis works. He used radioactive carbon and traced it through the entire process. (Nobel Prize, 1961)

Carl Sagan – Sagan was the popular astronomer and writer of *Cosmos* (1980), the book and TV series. His evangelical mission to teach science reached 500 million viewers. "Everyone starts out as a scientist," he said. "The job of a science popularizer is to penetrate through the teachings that tell people they're too stupid to understand science."

Gabriel Lippmann – Lippmann won a 1908 Nobel for developing the Lippmann Process, the first permanent color photographic process.

Franz Boas – Boas was the father of modern anthropology. He studied the previously unknown societies, languages and cultures of the Eskimos and American Indians (*Race, Language and Culture*, 1940). His method of statistical analysis and scientific method built the foundation of anthropology.

George Dantzig – Dantzig invented linear programming, the predecessor to modern computer programming.

Daniel Nathans – Nathans created the first genetic map of DNA. (Nobel Prize, 1978)

Lias Reiss – He invented the first practical converter of alternating electric current. This made the electrification of the railroads possible. In 1923 he invented a device to add sound to film.

HOW DO I KINDLE MY OWN DRIVE?

If you are part of a minority group, the motivation to gain acceptance is easy to draw upon. You can tap the "outsider" perspective and use it to your advantage. Define what the basis is for your group's exclusion. Learn in which fields or professions your ethnic group already has a foothold. Use your ethnic tradition as a foundation.

What can you do if you are not part of a defined ethnic group? Learn to focus your personal drive. Here are seven ways to set the stage for success.

1. MAKE LONG-RANGE GOALS

You need to set goals for yourself. Do a short exercise: Think about your life and what you want to accomplish. First, write down the three things you value most. Then write down your goals for the next six months, one year, five years, ten years, keeping in mind your values. The goals have to be concrete ones, such as obtaining a law degree or writing a *New York Times* bestseller. And then, more importantly, take the next step and write three concrete things that you will have to do to make each of these goals happen. To get a law degree, you will need to take the LSAT admissions tests, investigate schools and fill out applications. Keep this life planner in your address book or daily planner and check on it periodically.

2. WORK HARDER AT TASKS REQUIRING MENTAL MANIPULATION

Understand that real wealth creation is a product of your head, not your hands. To get big jobs accomplished, you need to multiply your efforts many times over. That can't be done within the limits of one person's time or physical and mental abilities. Learn to delegate work to others. Teach others and move on. Be the planner, the strategist, the leader. Save your efforts and time for value-added activities.

3. TAKE PRUDENT RISKS

Evaluate your actions on a risk-and-reward basis. Successful entrepreneurs do take risks, but they do it with their eyes wide open. Run the numbers. Make a business plan. Develop contingency plans. You should become familiar with all the disciplines of business, finance, accounting, economics, etc., because all of them will pose challenges to you.[20]

4. WORK FOR TANGIBLE AND INTANGIBLE REWARDS

Choose something that you are passionate about. Money for money's sake is a dead end, but a reinforcing reward can be helpful to push you to an ever-higher level in your career. Remember the section about being "selectively extravagant"? For example, your passion may be golf and your career goal may be to become a marketing vice president. On the way to the corner office, you should positively reward yourself with rounds of golf and good clubs.

5. TAKE PERSONAL RESPONSIBILITY FOR DECISIONS, AND CREATE RESULTS

When possible, take assignments in which your personal contribution is evident. Excellent job evaluations and promotions are easier to give to those who create results. It makes sense, as you have earned them. In addition, if an entrepreneurial career is one of your ambitions, only your results will matter, not how well you navigate corporate politics.

6. ACCEPT OTHER ENTREPRENEURS AS ROLE MODELS

Read the *Wall Street Journal* and *Inc.* and *Fast Company* magazines. Read about success stories. If you come from a particular ethnic group or minority group, investigate success stories within that group.

7. BELIEVE IN YOUR OWN SELF-DETERMINATION

Things are within your control. Get unstuck! Perform this experiment: For one day, try to do all your daily routines in a different way. You do not need to go as far as a "do-the-opposite-day," such as the character George Castanza once did on *Seinfeld*. In that episode, George went against his better judgment at every corner and was very successful. For the average person, it may be as simple as going to work a different way. Eating out at a different restaurant. Choosing the sixth number listed in the phone book just to be different. Why? Just to do something different. Go out of your way to meet with people that you normally do not. Call an old friend whom you have not talked to in a long time. It is all about creating new situations and new possibilities. As Jewish philosopher Maimonides said,

> "Free will is offered to all men. If they wish to follow the path of goodness and become righteous, the will to do so is in their hands, and if they wish to follow the path of evil and become wicked, the will to do so is also in their hands."

PULLING IT ALL TOGETHER

As I stated in the introduction, the Jewish-American story is a history of outstanding individual and collective accomplishments and wealth accumulation.

The seven "secrets" are very straightforward. Get a good education. Support your community. Be a professional or entrepreneur. Speak up. Be creative. Save your money and selectively enjoy it. And above all, be driven to be your own person. Perhaps you cannot manage all of the secrets, but if you succeed at four or five out of seven, you are well on your way. Throughout the book, each secret has been revealed as it relates to Jewish success stories past and present. Notice that Jewish success is not represented by just a narrow slice of doctors, lawyers and businesspeople; Jews have also made their mark in such unconventional careers as comedy, art and music. Moreover, these success stories do not tell the whole story; they are only the tip of the iceberg. A more exhaustive accounting of the achievements of accomplished and influential Jews would fill many volumes. Again, this remarkable success comes from a tiny minority of relatively recent immigrants who comprise only 2 percent of the American population. That is what makes the Jewish-American story such an amazing and compelling study.

Each chapter was written to lead you to your own action plan for self-improvement. For my Jewish readers, this book was intended to contribute to your own personal and financial success as well as highlight and encourage you to maintain your Jewish heritage. To paraphrase Ralph Waldo Emerson, you are the conveyance on whom all your ancestors ride. For my general audience, the Jewish successes outlined in this book serve as proof of the enduring power of a few basic "secrets" that anyone can emulate. Make the effort to incorporate the seven secrets of *The Jewish Phenomenon* into your daily life, and you can create your own success story!

Yiddish—"Can't Spell It, Can't Pronounce It and Don't Get It."

A cover story of the *Wall Street Journal* in June 1998 announced what many Jews already know: that many non-Jews frequently misuse Yiddish words. Jews have also been known to get them wrong. With so many third-generation Jewish Americans and Gentiles using Yiddish words in their conversations, it is no surprise that many unknowingly misuse the language. If you work on Wall Street, in a courthouse, in the garment industry, in Hollywood or in the jewelry business, you will inevitably run into Yiddish. In your effort to adopt the "seven secrets," you might want to "talk the talk" as well as "walk the walk" yourself. This chapter serves as a Yiddish primer.

Yiddish is a combination of German, Slavic languages and Hebrew that developed over a thousand years. It began in central Europe and spread to Eastern European Jews. Yiddish was brought to America by great numbers of Jewish immigrants at the turn of the twentieth century. It entered the American vernacular when Jews in Hollywood and on the stage introduced Yiddish words in their schtick while entertaining a broader audience. Leo Rosten, author of *The Joys of Yiddish*, called it the "Robin Hood of languages." "It developed a phenomenal variety of comic uses, an extraordinary range of observational nuances, a striking skill in delineating psychological insight, and remarkable modalities of sarcasm, irony, paradox and mockery." Isaac Bashevis Singer, the Nobel Prize–winning Yiddish author, said in a lecture in 1979, "One can find in the Yiddish tongue . . . expressions of pious joy, lust for life, longing for the Messiah, patience and deep appreciation of human individuality. There is a quiet humor in Yiddish and a gratitude for every day of life, every crumb of success, each encounter of love."

Many Yiddish words have been so popularized they have made it into the English dictionary. Maven, klutz, bagel, chutzpah and schmooz are just a few of the most popular words that have crossed over. What is so wonderful about the language is that it conveys the speaker's state of mind and emotions. Yiddish is a collection of words, but words with an attitude.

With the rampant assimilation of American Jewry, Yiddish is becoming an endangered species. Many people use a word or two, but few speak, read and write in Yiddish. Because many of the words are transliterations of the Hebrew language, which has a completely different alphabet, the spellings of Yiddish words with English letters vary widely. Pronunciations vary as well, depending on the area of Europe that the Jewish family comes from or how that family has inadvertently mispronounced the words for years. Outside the Orthodox Jewish communities, fewer than fifty thousand American Jews speak the language. According to the *Wall Street Journal*, "the Yiddish-language newspaper *Forward*, once a daily, now publishes just once a week, and many of its 9,000 readers are over 70. The English-language edition of the same paper has three times as many readers."[1] Yiddish as a spoken and living language is dying out with the immigrants who brought the language with them.

As the use of the entire language has dwindled, individual words or phrases are used to spice up conversations in English. If you want to enter such a conversation, it is best that you know what you are saying, or you risk embarrassment. You might be using a curse word and not even know it. The *Wall Street Journal* article reported on a few misused and misunderstood common Yiddish phrases:

"Tracy Uzzell loves to shout, 'I'm schvitzing!' when things get tough at work. The 30-year-old African-American picked up the word from a Jewish co-worker and counts it among her favorite expressions. What does it mean? 'To be under pressure,' ventures Ms. Uzzell, president of the Reid group, a New York computer consulting group. 'Isn't that right?' In a figurative sense, yes. Informed that *schvitz* literally means 'to sweat,' Ms. Uzzell is taken aback. She confesses she also has 'no clue' about the woe-betiding meaning of *oy vey* either – although she uses it often.

"In New York's diamond district, with its high concentration of Jewish dealers, non-Jews out of necessity have learned to salt their conversations with Yiddish. Shekhar Parikh, the Indian-born president of Renaissance Diamonds, says that he and other Indians have adopted the Jewish custom of closing a deal by saying *mazel*, the word for luck. Michael Bouregy, a dealer from Turkey, has also adopted the custom of calling his friends *meshuga*, which he thinks means being 'in love.' Love, however, only sometimes can make you *meshuga*, which actually means crazy."

Yiddish is difficult for many American mouths, both Jewish and non-Jewish. If you want to pepper or salt your chicken soup with Yiddish, check the pronunciation and its proper use. The back-of-the-throat "ch" sound, found in *chutzpah*, is particularly tough. "Ch" is pronounced like a heavy "h" sound by closing the back of the throat, as in the name of the composer Bach. In the listing that follows, the "ch" will be underlined to signal this special pronunciation. Even the pronunciations provided are not set in stone. With so many Jews living all over the world, some words may be pronounced slightly differently depending on the location or background of the speaker. No doubt, which is the "true" pronunciation could be debated by Jews like the Talmud. When my grandmother visited America from her home in Brazil in 1961, she insisted that the Jews from New York City did not speak Yiddish correctly no matter what anyone told her.

The following list includes about 150 of the most common words and expressions used in Jewish-American conversations. It goes well beyond the few words that Jewish parents and grandparents have passed on to their increasingly secular children. For those who require it, a more detailed guide for pronunciation is provided. For others, the word is used in a sentence to make its meaning clearer.[2]

YIDDISH	ENGLISH TRANSLATION
aidel	(A-del) refined, cultured or finicky
	"The aidel girl could never order off the menu; she had to special order."
Alevei!	(a-le-VEYE) It should happen to me (to you)!
	"Your cousin won the lottery? Alevei, I should win anything."
alter kacker	(ALL-ter cock-er) an over-the-hill man, past his prime.
	"The alter kacker could only find fault, but not do it himself."

Azoy?   (a-ZOY) Really?
                   "The president is fooling around in the White House. Azoy?"

baitsim   (BAIT-sim) gumption, chutzpah (literally, "testicles")
                   "That man has such baitsim to stand up to his boss like that."

balebosteh   (bal-BOOS-te) housewife, hostess, capable homemaker

bashert   (ba-SHERT) fate, destined, inevitable
                   "I met my wife on the subway. It was bashert."

bilik   (BILL-ik) cheap, inexpensive (merchandise)
                   "Those delicious chocolates are bilik, indulge, buy a dozen."

bisel   (Bih-SELL) a little bit, often related to food
                   "May I try a bisel of your cake?"

boychik   (BOY-chick) little boy

brech   (BREH-ch) throw up

broyges   (BROY-ges) angry

bubee   (BU-bee) friendly term for anyone you like, often term for grandmother

bupkes   (BUP-kess) small things, nothing, triflings, worthless, often used to
                   display disgust. Also said as "bubkes" (BUB-kess).
                   "You know what kind of raise I got? Bupkes is what I got."

Chap nit!   (CHOP-nit) Take it easy! Not so fast! (literally, "Don't grab")
                   "There is enough cake for everyone. Chap nit!"

chazzer   (CHAHZ-zer) a pig, anyone who is greedy
                   "Although it is an all-you-can-eat buffet, it's no reason to be a chazzer."

chazzerei   (choz-zair-EYE) pig's feed, anything bad, rotten

chotchke   (CHAHCH-keh) or (CHAUCH-key) a knickknack, toy, little decorative
                   things that serve no purpose.
                   "I had nowhere to place my coffee, the coffee table was filled with
                   chotchkes."

chuchem   (WHO-chem) wise man, or sarcastically used for "wise guy"

dray   (literal) to twist, to twist things around to make things work out
                   "He had to dray a little so that he could pay for his merchandise after
                   his customer paid him for it."

drek	human feces (curse word), inferior merchandise, insincere talk or excessive flattery "I will not buy those damaged goods, they are drek."
druchus	(dru-<u>ch</u>US) or (dru-KUS) out in the sticks, the wild "He moved from the city to druchus."
eingeshpahrt	(EYEn-ge-shpart) stubborn ("ei" as in height) "He's so eingeshpahrt, he will not wear a coat that his mother wants."
farbissener	(far-BIS-se-ner) an embittered person, always the pessimist. "The farbissener's facial expression expressed her bitter attitude toward life."
farblondghet	(far-BLAWN-jit) lost, confused ("gh" = j) "He lost his map; he was farblondghet."
farmisht	(far-MISHED) befuddled, confused "The farmisht woman in the nursing home did not know what day it was."
farpotshket	(far-POT-shket) messed up "She didn't handle scissors well; the material was farpotshket."
farputst	(far-PUT-st) dressed to kill "She wore her best dress and all her jewelry; she was all farputst."
Farshtay?	(far-SHTAY) Understand?
ferbutzit	(fer-BOOTZ-it) upset "Nothing was going right, so he was ferbutzit."
ferklempt	(fer-KLEMPT) choked up with emotion, mixed up temporarily "She became ferklempt when her son received his doctor's diploma."
Feh!	"It stinks," either literally or figuratively "How's the fish? Feh!"
flaishig	(FLAY-shig) meat dishes, term used in discussion of kosher foods
foiler	lazy man "That foiler, he never mows his lawn."
frailech	(FRAY-le<u>ch</u>) happy "Look at the frailech baby. She's laughing."
fress	eat like a pig, eat a big meal "We stayed in Miami Beach. We fressed and played shuffleboard."

ganef   (GON-iff) thief
                   "The ganef stole my money."

Gedainkst?   (ge-DAIN-kist) Remember? ("ai" as in main)
                   "You already did that. Gedainkst?"

gelt   (like "melt") money

gesheft   (ge-SHEFT) business

geshmak   (ge-SHMOCK) very tasty, delicious, in good taste (figuratively)
                   "The bagels were geshmak."

Gey feifen   (GAY FIFE-en AH-fen YAM) Go peddle your fish elsewhere! (literally, Go
ahfen yam!   whistle over the ocean.)
                   "I hate door-to-door salesmen, gey feifen ahfen yam!"

Gezunterheit   (ge-ZUN-te-HATE) Go in good health (said often when giving a gift)

glik   luck

Got sie dank   (GOT SEA DANK) Thank God!

goy   non-Jewish person

goyim   non-Jewish people, gentiles

groisseh   (GROY-se) big, great

grub   (like "rub") crude, rough, rude
                   "The sailor's grub manners needed improvement."

gruber yung   a crude, rough, rude young man, uneducated
                   "The gruber yung eats with his hands."

Gut yontev   Good holiday. (In Hebrew "yom tov" means holiday)

haimish   (HAME-ish) warm and cuddly, friendly (person)
                   "Because she was a haimish person she had many friends."

Halevei!   (HAL-ev-eye) If only _____ would come true!
                   "Halevei! I can go to Israel next year."

handle   (HAN-dle) to bargain
                   "You need to handle to get the best price."

himmel   (HIM-mel) heaven

hitsik   (HIT-sick) or (HEAT-sick) hot-headed

"Don't be so hitsik; forgive and forget."

hoyzik   (HOY-zick) trouble

hoyzik   (HOY-zick MAH-<u>ch</u>er) a troublemaker
macher   "The big sister was the hoyzik macher; she always started fights with her sister."

Ich vais   (I<u>ch</u>; "ai" as main) I know
                    "Ich vais, Ich vais, don't tell me how to do it."

ipish   (IP-ish) a bad odor, a stink

Ish kabibble   Who cares? No matter

kibbitz   (KIB-its) to meddle, to offer unsolicited advice as a spectator
                    "He didn't play bridge, but he always kibbitzed other people's hands."

kinderlech   (KEEN-der-le<u>ch</u>) affectionate term for children
                    "I love my kinderlech."

kishkes   (KISH-kes) the deepest part of the body, soul, intestines
                    "She was so mad at him; she felt it in her kishkes."

klop   (like "plop') a hard punch, or hit
                    "The thief gave him a klop on the head and he took his money."

k'nacker   ("a" as in water) a big shot

kouved   (KOO-ved) respect, honor, reverence for elders, parents and wise people
                    "Although he disagreed, he showed kouved for his parents by listening."

krenk   a sickness, a chronic physical complaint
                    "What's your krenk today, old lady? Arthritis or constipation?"

k'vel   (k-VELL) to glow or beam with pride and happiness, to enjoy good fortune
                    "The mother k'veled when she heard that her son married a Jewish girl."

k'vetch   (like "fetch") to complain or nag
                    "Constant k'vetching leads to divorce."

lantsman   ("a" as in water) countryman, from same town or country

leiden   (LAY-den) to suffer

macher   (MA<u>CH</u>-er) or (MOCK-her) a big shot, man with influence and contacts

maven   (MAY-ven) an expert
                    "The maven knew everything about profiting in the stock market."

mazel   (like "nozzle") luck (said to close a deal with a hand shake)

mecheiah   (Meh-<u>CH</u>IGH-a) great pleasure

mensch   (like "bench") a respected man, who does things the right way
                   "He's a real mensch. He does what is right."

meshuga   (mah-SHU-ga) crazy

meshugeneh   (mah-SHU-geneh) a crazy woman, often demonstrating obsessive behavior

meshugener   (mah-SHU-gener) a crazy man, often demonstrating obsessive behavior
                   "Why do keep washing your hands? Are you a meshugener?"

mishegaas   crazy activities done by a crazy person
                   "That type of mishegaas will land you in the mental hospital."

mishpucheh   (MISH-pu<u>ch</u>-heh) family
                   "How's your mishpucheh?"

mieskeit   (MEASE-kite) ugly person
                   "The mieskeit could not get a date."

naches   (NA<u>CH</u>-has) or (KNOCK-us) joy, especially from children
                   "My children give me a great deal of naches."

narishkeit   (NAR-ish-KITE) foolishness
                   "Driving recklessly is narishkeit."

Nebech!   (NE-be<u>ch</u>) It's such a pity! (said to respond to someone's else's
                   bad fortune)

nebbish   (NEB-ish) a simpleton, a weakling, an inept loser
                   "The nebbish could never get ahead."

Nifter-shmifter What difference does it make anyway?

nishtikeit   (NEESH-ti-kite) a nobody
                   "The nishtikeit lived next door, but we did not know he existed."

nosh   to snack, to seriously nibble
                   "At the party I noshed on all types of pastries."

nosherei   (NOSH-rye) snack foods
                   "There was so much nosherei, I couldn't help but overeat."

Nu?   (NEW) Well? So?
                   "Nu? Tell me what happened today at the office."

nudge

(Noodj, like "book") a pesterer, one who badgers you
"The nudge wouldn't stop asking for another try."

nudnik

(NOOD-nick, like "book") a pest, nuisance

ongeblozzen

(ON-ge-blozen) conceited, also brooding and upset
"She was so ongeblozzen, the world revolved around her."

ongepatshket

(ON-ge-PAHTCH-ket) cluttered, sloppy, muddled, overly done
"The decorator put so many things in the room it looked ongepatshket."

opgekrochen

(ON-ge-CROCK-en) shoddy (merchandise)
"The opgekrochen gadget doesn't work any more."

Oy gevalt!

(OY geh-VAULT) A cry of suffering
"Oy gevalt! I almost cut off my finger!"

Oy vey!

Oh, my! Oh, God! I can't believe it!
"Oy vey! I have a disease!"

Oy vey iz mir!

(OY VEY IS MEAR) Woe is me!
"Oy vey iz mir! My child is hurt!"

patch

(like "watch") a slap on the face
"Because she was insulted she gave him a patch."

plotchik

(PLOT-chick) matted, flat, beaten down
"My pillow was plotchik and needed to be fluffed up."

plotz

to bust your guts, to faint from exhaustion, sit down with a thud
"After walking all day in the sun, I plotzed down in the shade."

punim

(POO-nem) face
"What a beautiful punim that baby has!"

pushkeh

(PUSH-keh) little tin box for collecting coins, particularly for charity
"Please put some gelt in the pushkeh for the poor."

putz

a stupid person, a dunce, a fool (very strongly, curse word), also slang
word for penis

saichel

(SAY-chel) common sense
"He never has saichel and gets into trouble."

schmaltz

chicken or goose fat, also theatrically anything that is very corny or
overly emotional, maudlin

schmooz	chat, mingle "He schmoozed with the boss at the party."
Sha	Keep quiet. (gently said)
Shabes	(SHAH-bes) Sabbath
shadchen	(SHAHD-ken) matchmaker, marriage broker
shaineh maidel	(SHAY-neh MAY-del) pretty girl
shanda	(SHAWN-da) a thing that brings deep embarrassment "His dropping out of school, it's a shanda to the family."
shep naches	(SHEP NA<u>CH</u>-has) to experience joy, especially from children "The mother shepped naches at the wedding of her daughter."
shikker	(SHICK-er) drunk
shikseh	(SHICK-sa) non-Jewish girl
shlecht	(SHLE<u>CH</u>T) bad (often as a response to a question) "How was the meal? Shlecht."
shlemiel	(shleh-MEAL) clumsy bungler (the shlemiel spills the soup on the shlimazel)
shlep	to drag, carry or haul, particularly unnecessary things "She shlepped her large purse with her on the tour."
shlimazel	(shleh-MAZEL) luckless person (the shlemiel spills the soup on the shlimazel)
shlock	(like "clock") cheapest, lowest of anything, especially merchandise. "I don't buy anything off of TV; it's all schlock."
shmaltz	chicken fat (literal), excessively sentimental, flattery
shmatte	(SHMOT-ta) rag, cheap clothing, often used sarcastically "Oh, this shmatte? I got it at Neiman-Marcus on sale."
shmear	to coat with butter (or cream cheese), to bribe, also "the whole thing" "Please shmear some cream cheese on my bagel."
shmegegi	(shme-GEG-gi) buffoon "The shmegegi made a fool of himself."
shmuck	a strong curse word for fool, stupid person, also for penis.

shmutz	(like "book," SHMOOTZ) dirt
shmutzik	(SHMOOTZ-ick) dirty "They never cleaned; their house was shmutzik."
shpilkas	(SHPILK-as) "to be on shpilkas," to be very nervous, (Literally, pins and needles) "I am oyf (on) shpilkas; I am waiting for my report card."
shrei	(SHREYE) yell
shtarker	(SHTAR-ker) brave, strong person "Moses was quite a shtarker to climb Mount Sinai alone."
shtikel	(SHTICK-el) a small piece, especially bread "Can I try a shtikel bread?"
shul	(SHOOL) synagogue
shvitz	to sweat "I shvitz when I do hard work."
shvitzidik	(SHVITZ-eh-dick) sweaty
simchah	(SIM-<u>ch</u>ah) party, joy, joyous holiday
toyt	(TOYT) dead
tsedrait	(TZEH-drate) crazy
tsuris	(TSOOR-is) troubles ("u" said like book) "I can't pay the rent. I have tsuris."
tuchus	(TU<u>CH</u>-ess) or (TUK-hess) buttocks My tuchus hurts from sitting so long.
Tuchus ahfen tish!	(TU<u>CH</u>-ess OFEN TISH) Put up or shut up! (Literally, Behinds on the table! (crudely used in business)
tummel	(TOO-mel) an uproar, confusion, commotion "They started to talk on *Jerry Springer*, then there was a great tummel."
tzaddik	(TZAH-dick) pious person
tzimmis	(TZI-miss) a big deal or fuss, a big noise, also a dish of mixed cooked fruit and vegetables "She made such as tzimmis over the wedding list."
ugerbutzit	(uger-BUUT-zit) very upset

Vos machstu?   (VOS MA<u>CH</u>-stew) "How are you?"

yenem's   (YEH-nems) someone else's (said often in a derogatory way)
"You never do anything wrong; it's always yenem's problem."

yichus   (YEE-<u>chus</u>) ancestry, prestige gained from scholarship, money, class
"He married into yichus."

yiddin   (like "written") Jewish people

yoisher   (YOY-sher) fair, decent, done in the correct way
"He did not take undue advantage; he's a yoisher man."

yontif   (YON-tif) holiday

zaftig   (ZOFF-tig) plump, full-figured, buxom (about a woman)

YIDDISH DAYS OF THE WEEK

Sunday	Zuntik (ZUN-tick)
Monday	Montik (MON-tick)
Tuesday	Dinstik (DIN-stick)
Wednesday	Mitvoch (mit-VO<u>CH</u>)
Thursday	Donershtik (DONER-shtick)
Friday	Fraytik (FRAY-tick)
Saturday	Shabes (SHA-bas)

YIDDISH NUMBERS

one	eyns (EYE-ns)
two	tsvay (TSVAY)
three	dray (DRAY)
four	feer (FEAR)
five	finf (FIN-if)
six	zeks (ZECKS)
seven	ziben (ZIE-ben)
eight	acht (A<u>CH</u>T)
nine	nein (NINE)
ten	tsen (SEN)
twenty	tsvonsik (TSVON-sick)
fifty	fuftsik (FOOFT-sick)
hundred	hundert (HOON-dert)
thousand	toyzent (TOY-zent)

Hebrew—
Fifty Helpful Vocabulary Words

Yiddish is a very rich language for colorful conversation, but here are about fifty Hebrew words that you should know. You may encounter them in reference to the Jewish religion.

HEBREW	ENGLISH TRANSLATION
afikomen	(ah-fe-KOE-men) the matzah that is hidden for the children to find during the Passover seder meal. The finder gets a prize.
aliya	(a-LEA-ah) immigration to Israel, reading the Torah during a ceremony
bimah	(BEA-mah) the podium in a synagogue, center stage
bris	(BRIS) circumcision ceremony
chai	(CHIGH) life, 18, word formed by the combination of Hebrew letters meaning 18, often seen depicted in gold jewelry
chupah	(CHOO-pah) the canopy for Jewish wedding ceremony
daven	(DAH-ven) to pray
dayenu	(DIE-ai-new) "It would have been enough," a popular Passover song
dreidel	(DRAY-del) a spinning top used in a children's gambling game for Hanukah

Eretz Yisroel	(ER-etz yis-ROYEL) Land of Israel
Hagadah	(hah-GAHD-ah) the Passover prayer book
Hashem	(HA-shem) *God* (used in place of using the Hebrew word for *God* in literature)
Hasidic	(<u>cha</u>-SID-ick) of the revivalist movement of Judaism founded in Eastern Europe
Hatikvah	(ha-TICK-vah) national anthem of Israel
Kabbalah	(ka-BALL-ah) Jewish mysticism movement begun in the 12th century
kaddish	(KAH-dish) the mourners' prayer
kashrut	(KASH-root) kosher (milk and meat separately prepared and eaten, no shellfish)
kiddush	(KID-dush) the ceremonial blessing over the wine
kippah	(KEY-pah) skullcap for men
klezmer	(KLEZ-mer) Jewish folk musician
latkes	(LAT-kiss) potato pancakes served on the Hanukah holiday
Le' chaiyim!	(le <u>CH</u>IGH-em) To life! (a traditional toast)
Mazel tov!	(MAH-zel TOVE) Good luck! Congratulations!
megillah	(me-GILL-ah) any very, long story, "Megillah" is also the name of the Purim storybook, the Book of Esther.
menorah	(me-NOR-ah) candelabra used during Hanukah holiday
mezuzah	(me-ZOO-zah) doorpost ornament with Hebrew blessing inside
mitzvah	(MITZ-vah) a good deed
Mogen David	(MOE-gen DAY-vid) (also Magen David) Shield of David, Star of David, a six-pointed star. Its usage as the Jewish symbol began in 1897 when the Zionist conference convened by Theodore Herzl chose it as the insignia of the movement. None of the Twelve Tribes used the Star of David. It is an ancient magical sign that has been traced to Mesopotamia and ancient Britain, and as far back as the Bronze Age 4,000 years ago.
moyel	(MOY-el) a person who performs circumcisions

moytzi (MOY-tzea) the ceremonial blessing over bread

pareve (PAR-eh-vah) foods that are not dairy or meat. Fish, eggs, can be eaten with any food under kosher laws

Rosh Hashanah (ROESH ha-SHAH-nah) Jewish New Year (one of the two High Holidays)

Sabra (SA-bra) native-born Israeli

Shabbat (shah-BAHT) the Jewish Sabbath starting on Friday evening and ending Saturday evening

shalom (SHAH-loam) hello, goodbye and peace

Shavuot (SHA-voo-oat) holiday commemorating receiving the Ten Commandments at Mount Sinai

shiva (SHI-vah) the seven days of mourning

shofar (SHOW-far) the ram's horn sounded during Rosh Hashanah and Yom Kippur

siddur (SI-der) prayer book

sukkah (SUE-kah) a temporary hut built for living and dining during Sukkot holiday

Sukkot (SUE-coat) the harvest festival holiday

Talmud (TALL-mood) Book of Jewish laws for daily living

Tisha B'Av (TISH b-AV) holiday commemorating the destruction of the two ancient Temples in Jerusalem

Torah (TORE-ah) first five books of the Bible

treife (TRIFE) non-Kosher foods, shellfish, pork, mixtures of dairy and meat ("ei" as in height)

Tu B' Shevat (TOO BISH VAHT) Jewish arbor day. Jews plant trees on this holiday and donate money to have trees planted in Israel.

tzadic (TZAH-dick) a righteous man

Yad Va Shem (YAD VA SHEM) the institution and monuments dedicated to the Holocaust

yamulkah (YAH-mul-kah) skullcap for prayer

yeshiva   (yeh-SHEAVE-ah) a Jewish academy for religious study

Yom Kippur   (YOME KEY-poor) The Day of Atonement holiday (one of two High
                   Holidays)

Ten Yiddish Proverbs

An example is not proof.
A moshel iz nit kain reyeh.
(A MOY-shel IS NIT KAIN RAY-eh)

One can't fill a torn sack.
Alecherdiken zack ken men nit onfillen.
(ale-<u>CH</u>AIR-deak-en ZACK KEN MEN NIT on-FEEL-en)

A wise man hears one word and understands two.
A kluger farshtait fun ain vort tsvai.
(A KLUE-ger far-SHTAIT FUN AIN VORT ts-VEYE)

When does a rich man starve? When the doctor orders him to.
Ven hungert a nogid? Ven der doctor haist im!
(VEN HUN-gert ah NO-gid? VEN DER DOCTOR HAIST IM!)

I trust you, but send cash!
Bist a botuach ober shik arein m'zumonim!
(BIST A bau-TU-a<u>ch</u> OBER SHICK AIR-en m'zu-MORE-um!)

Better one friend with a dish of food than a hundred with a sigh.
Besser ain freint mit gekechts aider hundert mit a krechtz.
(BESSER AIN FRY-nt MIT ge-KECKS AI-der HUN-dret MIT a KRECK-tz)

The door to evil is wide, but the gate back is small.
Arein iz di tir brait, un arois iz zi shmol.
(ARE-ine IZ DEE TEAR BRAIT, UN ar-ROYSE IZ ZEE SHMOLE)

A slap heals but a harsh word is remembered.
A patch farhailkt zich un a vort gedenkt zich.
(A PAHTCH far-HAIL-kit ZEAK UN VORT ge-DENKt ZEAK.)

Some want to live well and can't; others can live well and will not.
Aineh villen leben un kenen nit, un andereh kenen leben un villen nit.
(ANEH VIL-en LE-ben UN KE-nen NIT, UN AN-der-eh KE-nen LE-ben
UN VIL-en NIT.)

When does a hunchback celebrate? When he sees a hunchback with a
bigger hump.
Ven frait zich a hoiker? Ven er zet a gresseren hoiker far zich.
(VEN FRAIT ZICK A HOY-ker? VEN ER ZET A HOY-ker FAR ZICK.)

These are only 10 of 1,001 from *1001 Yiddish Proverbs* by Fred Kogos,
Citadel Press, 1997. It is an excellent reference.

The Jewish Calendar and Jewish Holidays

The Jewish or Hebrew calendar is "luni-solar." The years are solar and the months lunar. The Jewish month is based on the orbit of the moon of twenty-nine days and twelve hours rather than the days used by the Gregorian or Roman month. The Jewish calendar has 354 days, but every two to three years, an extra month (Adar II) is added to reconcile the Jewish and Gregorian years. Therefore, year to year holidays fall on different days because the months vary from year to year. Jewish holidays begin at nightfall the night before the holiday and end at sunset on the last day of the holiday. Accordingly, the Sabbath begins Friday night and ends at nightfall on Saturday. Year 1 of the Jewish calendar began when God created Adam and Eve, not the creation of heaven and the earth. The Gregorian calendar began with the birth of Jesus.

HEBREW MONTHS OF THE YEAR

Name	Period Covered	Duration
Tishre	September to October	29 days
Cheshvan	October to November	29 or 30 days
Kislev	November to December	29 or 30 days
Teyvet	December to January	29 days

Name	Period Covered	Duration
Shevat	January to February	30 days
Adar	February to March	29 or 30 days
Nissan	March to April	30 days
Iyar	April to May	29 days
Sivan	May to June	30 days
Tammuz	June to July	29 days
Av	July to August	30 days
Elul	August to September	29 days

In Jewish leap years the Hebrew calendar has two months called Adar: Adar Aleph (I) with 29 days and Adar Beyz (II) with 29 days.

EIGHT-YEAR JEWISH HOLIDAY CALENDAR

The nine most popular holidays fall on the following days during the next eight years. The holidays begin at sundown before the dates listed. Traditionally some holidays are celebrated for more than one day. Reform and Reconstructionist Jews usually celebrate those holidays for one fewer day, except for Hanukah. For example, a Reform Jew will celebrate one day of Rosh Hashanah and seven days of Passover.

ROSH HASHANAH, JEWISH NEW YEAR (1 TO 2 DAYS)

Gregorian Calendar Year	Beginning Date	Jewish Calendar Year
2000	September 30	5761
2001	September 18	5762
2002	September 7	5763
2003	September 27	5764
2004	September 16	5765
2005	October 4	5766
2006	September 23	5767
2007	September 18	5768

YOM KIPPUR, DAY OF ATONEMENT (1 DAY)

Gregorian Calendar Year	Beginning Date	Jewish Calendar Year
2000	October 9	5761
2001	September 27	5762
2002	September 16	5763
2003	October 6	5764
2004	September 25	5765
2005	October 13	5766
2006	October 2	5767
2007	September 22	5768

SUKKOT, FALL HARVEST FESTIVAL (7 TO 8 DAYS)

Gregorian Calendar Year	Beginning Date	Jewish Calendar Year
2000	October 14	5761
2001	October 2	5762
2002	September 21	5763
2003	October 11	5764
2004	September 30	5765
2005	October 18	5766
2006	October 7	5767
2007	September 27	5768

HANUKAH, FESTIVAL OF LIGHTS (8 DAYS)

Gregorian Calendar Year	Beginning Date	Jewish Calendar Year
2000	December 22	5761
2001	December 10	5762
2002	November 30	5763
2003	December 20	5764
2004	December 8	5765
2005	December 26	5766
2006	December 16	5767
2007	December 5	5768

TU B' SHEVAT, JEWISH ARBOR DAY (1 DAY)

Gregorian Calendar Year	Beginning Date	Jewish Calendar Year
2000	January 22	5761
2001	February 8	5762
2002	January 28	5763
2003	January 18	5764
2004	February 7	5765
2005	January 25	5766
2006	February 13	5767
2007	February 3	5768

PURIM, COMMEMORATES THE JEWISH VICTORY OVER HAMAN (1 DAY)

Gregorian Calendar Year	Beginning Date	Jewish Calendar Year
2000	March 21	5761
2001	March 9	5762
2002	February 26	5763
2003	March 18	5764
2004	March 7	5765
2005	March 25	5766
2006	March 14	5767
2007	March 4	5768

PASSOVER, COMMEMORATES JEWISH FREEDOM FROM SLAVERY BY THE EGYPTIAN PHARAOH (7 TO 8 DAYS)

Gregorian Calendar Year	Beginning Date	Jewish Calendar Year
2000	April 20	5761
2001	April 8	5762
2002	March 28	5763
2003	April 17	5764
2004	April 6	5765
2005	April 24	5766
2006	April 13	5767
2007	April 3	5768

SHAVUOT, COMMEMORATES MOSES RECEIVING TEN COMMANDMENTS FROM GOD AT MOUNT SINAI (1 TO 2 DAYS)

Gregorian Calendar Year	Beginning Date	Jewish Calendar Year
2000	June 11	5761
2001	May 31	5762
2002	May 17	5763
2003	June 6	5764
2004	May 26	5765
2005	June 13	5766
2006	June 2	5767
2007	May 23	5768

(Calendar source: Abramowitz, Yoseph, and Silverman, Rabbi Susan, *Jewish Family & Life*, Golden Books, 1997, p. 291.)

END NOTES

INTRODUCTION

1. Getlin, Josh, "Leaving an Imprint on American Culture," *Los Angeles Times*, April 24, 1998, p. A1.

2. Jacoby, Russell, and Glauberman, Naomi, *The Bell Curve Debate*, Random House, 1995, p. 376.

3. Halberstam, Joshua, *Schmoozing: The Private Conversations of American Jews*, Perigree Books, 1997, p. 16.

4. Garelik, Glenn, "America's Jewish Billionaires, How Rich? How Charitable?" *Moment*, December 1996, p. 35.

5. Halberstam, p. 16.

6. Stanley, Thomas, and Danko, William, *The Millionaire Next Door*, Longstreet Press, 1996, p. 22.

7. Dershowitz, Alan, *The Vanishing American Jew*, Simon & Schuster, 1997, p. 16.

8. Wilder, Esther, and Walters, William, *Journal of Economic & Social Measurement*, 1997, p. 198.

9. Bush, Lawrence, "American Jews and the Torah of Money," *Tikkun*, July 17, 1998, p. 31.

10. Lipset, Seymour, and Raab, Earl, *Jews and the New American Scene*, Harvard Press, 1995, p. 27.

11. Silberman, Charles, *A Certain People*, Summit Books, 1985, p. 145.

12. Sowell, Thomas, *Ethnic America*, Basic Books, 1981, p. 5.

13. Karp, Abraham, *A History of the Jews in America*, Jason Aronson, Inc., 1997, p. 374.

14. Sowell, p. 98.

15. Telushkin, Rabbi Joseph, *Jewish Humor*, Quill/William Morrow, 1992, p. 23.

16. Council of Jewish Federations (CJF), *Highlights of the CJF 1990 National Jewish Population Survey*, 1990, p. 32.

17. *New York Times*, American Jewish Committee advertisement, December 22, 1996.

18. Halberstam, p. 95.

19. *CJF 1990*, p. 28.

20. *CJF 1990*, p. 28.

21. Dornin, Rabbi Hayim, *To Be a Jew*, Basic Books, 1992, p. 7.

22. Sowell, p. 72.

23. Telushkin, Rabbi Joseph, *Jewish Literacy*, William Morrow, 1991, p. 337.

24. As cited in Blech, Rabbi Benjamin, *Complete Idiot's Guide to Jewish History and Culture*, Alpha Books, 1999, p. 156.

25. Karp, p. 337.

CHAPTER 1

1. Karp, p. 323.

2. Lipset and Raab, p. 27.

3. Telushkin, *Jewish Literacy*, p. 46.

4. *CJF*, p. 30.

5. Lipset, p. 27.

6. Sowell, p. 89.

7. Lipset, p. 22.

8. Karp, p. 127.

9. Lipset, p. 21.

10. Lipset, p. 22.

11. Lipset, p. 38.

12. Cohen, Leslie, "Lost in Suburbia," *The Jerusalem Post Magazine*, p. 22.

13. Halberstam, p. 100.

14. Hertzberg, Arthur, *The Jews in America*, Columbia University Press, 1997, p. 195.

15. Lyman, Darryl, *Jewish Heroes & Heroines*, Jonathan David Publishers, 1996, p. 225.

16. Garelik, p. 40.

17. Garelik, pp. 36–37.

18. Lyman, p. 232.

CHAPTER 2

1. Halberstam, p. 41.

2. Dershowitz, p. 10.

3. Wertheimer, Jack, "Current Trends in Jewish Philanthropy," *American Jewish Yearbook*, 1997.

4. Halberstam, pp. 41–42.

5. Dershowitz, p. 10.

6. Lipset and Raab, p. 120.

7. "U.S. Jews Refocus Donations," *Wall Street Journal*, October 5, 1998, p. A22.

8. Brawarsky, Sandee, and Mark, Deborah, *Two Jews, Three Opinions*, Perigree Books, 1998, p. 58.

9. Abramowitz, Yoseph, and Silverman, Rabbi Susan, *Jewish Family &*

Life, Golden Books, 1997, pp. 236–237.

10. Auerbach, Jon, "Charity Case: Jewish Loan Societies Rethink the Traditions of Helping All Comers," *Wall Street Journal*, September 11, 1997, p. A1.

11. Cited in Auerbach, p. A1.

12. Marcus, Jacob, *The Jew in the Medieval World*, Sinai Press, 1938, p. 167.

13. Auerbach, p. A1.

14. Sowell, p. 84.

15. "Jewish Philanthropy Facts," Jewish Funders Network Web site, www.jfunders.org/facts, 1998.

16. Miller, Lisa, "Titans of Industry Join Forces for Jewish Philanthropy," *Wall Street Journal*, May 4, 1998, p. B1.

17. Farber, Eli, *Jews, Slaves and the Slave Trade*, New York University Press, 1998.

18. Goldberg, J. J., *Jewish Power*, Addison Wesley, 1996, p. 24.

19. *Black Man* (London), July, 1935, p.5.

20. UCLA, "Marcus Garvey and UNIA Papers Project," Web site, p. 22, www.isop.ucla.edu.

21. "Board of Contributors," *Wall Street Journal*, February 24, 1998, p. A22.

22. Goldberg, p. 314.

23. Goldberg, p. 315.

24. Dershowitz, p. 62.

25. "Rule of Law," *Wall Street Journal*, October 12, 1998, p. A1.

26. Goldberg, p. 14.

27. American-Israeli Cooperative Enterprise Web site, www.us-israel.org/jsource.

28. Goldberg, p. 15.

29. Goldberg, p. 30.

30. Goldberg, pp. 23, 25.

31. Goldberg, p. 35.

32. Goldberg, p. xxi.

33. Goldberg, p. 256.

34. Goldberg, p. 24.

CHAPTER 3

1. Sowell, p. 88.

2. Halberstam, p. 27.

3. Halberstam, p. 11.

4. Silberman, p. 122.

5. Halberstam, p. 25.

6. Halberstam, p. 26.

7. Lipset and Raab, p. 24.

8. Lipset and Raab, p. 52.

9. Dershowitz, p. 300.

10. Rosenberg, Roy, *Everything You Need to Know About America's Jews and Their History*, Plume, 1997, p. 215.

11. Silberman, p. 96.

12. Silberman, p. 124.

13. Goldberg, M. Hirsh, *The Jewish Connection,* Stein and Day, 1976, p. 171.

14. Hacker, p. 125.

15. Shatzmiller, J., *Jews, Medicine and Medieval Society*, Cambridge University, 1994.

16. Beller, S., *Vienna and the Jews, 1867–1938: A Cultural History*, Cambridge University Press, 1989.

17. Hogue, John, *Nostradamus: The New Revelation*, Barnes & Noble Books, 1995.

18. Lyman, p. 49.

19. Halberstam, p. 27.

20. Halberstam, p. 35.

21. Halberstam, p. 28.

22. Vesper, Karl, *New Venture Strategies*, Prentice Hall, 1980, p. 3.

23. Silberman, p. 135.

24. Cited in Silberman, p. 133.

25. "A Gentleman for Four Seasons," *Lifestyles,* Fall 1993, p. 14.

26. O'Brien, Timothy, *Bad Bet*, Random House, 1998, p. 27.

27. Halberstam, p. 34.

28. Geisst, Charles, *Wall Street: A History*, Oxford University Press, 1997, p. 109.

29. Hayes, Samuel, and Hubbard, Philip, *Investment Banking*, Harvard Press, 1990, p. 233.

30. Birmingham, Stephen, *Our Crowd: The Great Jewish Families of New York*, Dell Books, 1967, p. 119.

31. Halberstam, p. 34.

32. Brawarsky and Mark, p. 379.

33. Harris, Leon, *Merchant Princes*, Kodansha International Press, 1994, p. x.

34. Harris, p. 337.

35. Federated Corp. Web site, www.federated-fds.com.

36. *Encyclopedia Judaica*, "Diamond Industry," Coronet Books, 1994.

37. Samberg, Joel, *The Jewish Book of Lists*, Citadel Press, 1998, p. 39.

38. "Forbes 400," *Forbes*, October 11, 1999, p. 414.

39. Hacker, p. 138.

CHAPTER 4

1. Dershowitz, Alan, *Chutzpah,* Simon & Schuster, 1991, p. 18.

2. Telushkin, *Jewish Humor*, p. 17.

3. Goldin, Barbara Diamond, *Bat Mitzvah: A Jewish Girl's Coming of Age*, Puffin Books, 1995.

4. Goldberg, M. Hirsh, p. 28.

5. Etkes, Asher, and Stadtmauer, Saul, *Jewish Contributions to the American Way of Life*, Northside Publishing, 1995, p. 58.

6. "What!? He's Jewish?!" *Lifestyles,* Winter 1993, p. 7.

7. Samberg, p. 86.

8. Birmingham, Stephen, *The Rest of Us*, Little Brown, 1984, p. 83.

9. Birmingham, *The Rest of Us,* p. 254.

10. Birmingham, *The Rest of Us*, p. 260.

11. Lyman, p. 231.

12. Sirvorinovsky, Alina, "Do Jews Control TV?" *Inside*, December 31, 1996, p. 70.

13. Willens, Michele, "The New TV Season," *Los Angeles Times*, September 10, 1989, p. 6.

14. Willens, Michele, p. 6.

15. James Andersen, Sr. V.P. of Publicity, e-mail response.

16. "Partners in TV Comedy," *USA Today*, August 21, 1989, p. 1D. Also see "Can This Team Go 5 for 5," *Business Week*, June 19, 1989, p. 77.

17. Werts, Diane, "Mark Goodson: 1915–1992, Passing of a Game Show Pioneer," *Newsday,* December 19, 1992, p. 20.

18. "Mighty Merv," *LA Magazine*, July 1, 1988, p. 72.

19. Brawarsky and Mark, p. 86.

20. "Larry King," *Lifestyles*, Spring 1993, p. 8.

21. Etkes and Stadtmauer, p. 121.

22. Silberman, p. 156.

23. Goldberg, J. J., p. 280.

24. Sirvorinovsky, p. 70.

CHAPTER 5

1. "Titans of the Tightwads," *Forbes*, November 20, 1995, p. S136.

2. "Shakespeare As Anti-Semite," *Globe & Mail*, April 13, 1989, p. A7.

3. "Putting a Price on Anti-Semitism," *Jerusalem Post*, August 28, 1998, p. 19.

4. Halberstam, p. 11.

5. Silberman, p. 137.

6. *Globe and Mail*, November 28, 1981, p. E16.

7. Etkes and Stadtmauer, p. 174.

8. Hirschman, Elizabeth, "American Jewish Ethnicity: Its Relationship to Some Selected Aspects of Consumer Behavior," *Journal of Marketing*, Summer 1981, p. 102.

9. Hargerty, James, "Home Depot Founders Settle a Few Scores," *Wall Street Journal*, February 19, 1999, p. B1.

10. "As Jewish Divorces Multiply, So Does the Bitterness," *Chicago Tribune*, November 14, 1986, p. 5.

11. Srole, Leo, and Fisher, Anita, *Mental Health in the Metropolis*, University Press, 1978, p. 424.

CHAPTER 6

1. Blech, p. 42.

2. "The Rich List," *Chicago*, March 1, 1994, p. 50.

3. Lyman, Darryl, *Great Jewish Families*, Jonathan David Publishers, 1997, pp. 41–55.

4. Fein, Leonard, "Me, Follow?" *Forward*, November 18, 1994, p. 11.

5. Lyman, *Jewish Heroes and Heroines*, pp. 93–94. Also see Goldberg, M. Hirsh, pp. 81–84.

6. Goldberg, M. Hirsh, pp. 79–81.

7. Lyman, *Jewish Heroes and Heroines*, pp. 124–125.

8. Sklare, Marshall, ed., and Blau, Zena Smith, "The Strategy of the Jewish Mother," *The Jew in American Society*, Behrman House, 1974, pp. 165–187.

9. Drew, David, King, Margo, and Richardson, Gerald, *A Profile of the Jewish College Freshman*, 1980, p. 36.

10. Rosenfield, Geraldine, *Jewish College Freshmen*, The Jewish American Committee, 1984, p. 7.

11. Silberman, p. 142.

12. Rodgers, Richard, *Musical Stages*, Random House, 1975, p. 88.

13. Etkes and Stadtmauer, p. 14.

14. Shelton, Robert, *No Direction Home: The Life and Music of Bob Dylan*, 1986.

15. Lyman, p. 197.

16. Samberg, p. 128.

17. Churnin, Nancy, "Rugrats Rock," *Dallas Morning News*, December 2, 1998, p. 1C.

18. Aguire, Holly, *Lifestyles*, Pre-Spring 1995, p. 8.

19. Mattel, Glenn Barth, Sr. V.P. Corporate Communications, e-mail response.

20. Miller, G. Wayne, *Toy Wars*, Adams Publishing, 1998, p. 215.

21. Miller, G. Wayne, p. 254.

22. Morris, Kathleen, "The Rise of Jill Barad," *Business Week*, May 25, 1998, cover story, BW Interactive Web site, www.businessweek.com.

23. Miller, G. Wayne, p. 21.

24. Miller, G. Wayne, p. 22.

25. Miller, G. Wayne, p. 23.

26. Etkes and Stadtmauer, p. 172.

27. Ross, Philip, "Nine mistakes doctors make," *Forbes*, August 9, 1999, 116.

28. As cited in Krass, Peter, ed., *The Book of Business Wisdom*, John Wiley & Sons, 1997.

29. Lyman, p. 146.

30. Sanders, Adrienne, "On My Mind: Success Secrets of the Successful," *Forbes*, November 2, 1998, p. 22.

CHAPTER 7

1. Brawarsky and Mark, p. 95.

2. Brawarsky and Mark, p. 303.

3. Gerth, H. H., and Mills, C. Wright, *From Max Weber: Essays in Sociology*, Oxford University Press, 1946.

4. Palmer, Michael, "The Application of Psychological Testing to Entrepreneurial Potential," *California Management Review*, Vol. 13, No. 3., Spring 1971, p. 32.

5. Vesper, p. 9.

6. Sklare, Marshall, ed., *The Jews: Social Patterns of an American Group*, Free Press, 1960, p. 160.

7. Lipset and Raab, p. 23.

8. Etkes and Stadtmauer, p. 180.

9. Lyman, *Jewish Heroes and Heroines*, p. 130.

10. Prager, Dennis, "Jewish Children Are Often Naches Machines," *Moment*, February 28, 1997, p. 26.

11. Soros, George, *Soros on Soros*, John Wiley & Sons, 1995, p. 242.

12. Page, Clarence, "Maybe I Don't Want to Give Up Outsider Status," *Baltimore Sun*, March 31, 1997, p. 11A.

13. As cited in Page, p. 11A.

14. Goldberg, M. Hirsh, p. 142.

15. Lyman, *Great Jewish Families*, p. 179.

16. Silberman, p. 153.

17. Graham, Katherine, *Personal History*, Alfred Knopf, 1997.

18. Alba, Richard, and Moore, Gwen, "Ethnicity in the American Elite," *American Sociological Review*, Vol. 47, June 1982, p. 377.

19. Samberg, p. 49.

20. See my book *The Ten-Day MBA: A Step-by-Step Guide to Mastering the Skills Taught in America's Top Business Schools*, Morrow, 1999.

APPENDIX 1 AND 2

1. Auerbach, Jon, "They Can't Spell It, Can't Pronounce It and Don't Get It," *Wall Street Journal*, June 2, 1998, p. 1A.

2. For the information in these appendices, I am especially indebted to the following sources: Kogos, Fred, *The Dictionary of Popular Yiddish Words, Phrases, and Proverbs* (Citadel, 1997); Kogos, Fred, *1,001 Yiddish Proverbs* (Citadel, 1997); Samberg, Joel, *The Jewish Book of Lists* (Citadel, 1998); and Abramowitz, Yoseph, and Silverman, Rabbi Susan, *Jewish Family & Life* (Golden Books, 1997).

HUMOR SOURCES

*For the many jokes sprinkled throughout the text,
I am indebted to the following sources:*

Berger, Arthur Asa, *The Genius of the Jewish Joke*, Jason Aronson, 1998.

Eilbirt, Henry, *What Is a Jewish Joke?*, Jason Aronson, 1993.

Menchin, Robert, *101 Classic Jewish Jokes*, Mustang, 1998.

Mendelsohn, Felix S., *Let Laughter Ring*, Jewish Publication Society of Philadelphia, 1962.

Novak, William, and Waldoks, Moshe, *The Big Book of Jewish Humor*, Harper Perennial, 1981.

Spalding, Henry, *Encyclopedia of Jewish Humor*, Jonathan David, 1969.

Teluskin, Rabbi Joseph, *Jewish Humor*, Quill/Morrow, 1992.

Youngman, Henny, *Take My Wife Please*, Citadel, 1998.

INDEX

Einstein, Albert, 2, 149–150, 151, 191
Einthoven, Willem, 68
Eisenstadt, Alfred, 167
Eisner, Michael, 1, 32, 91, 111, 112
Ellison, Larry, 87, 88
Emerson, Ralph Waldo, 195
Empire Pencil Co., 170
employees, need for independence among,
  95–96
Encyclopedia Judaica, 130
endowments, 55
Engel, Eliot, 55
Engels, Frederich, 183
English, desire among immigrants to learn, 29
entertainment industry, 108–117
entrepreneurial careers, 9, 59–97, 180
entrepreneurial pursuit, 59, 95–96
entrepreneurs, 69–72
Ephron, Nora, 111
Epstein, Brian, 163
Ernst, Agnes, 190
ESPN, 112
Esterow, Milton, 166
Esther, 17
Ethnic America (Sowell), 4, 9, 35
ethnic household income, 5
ethnic pride, 49
ethnic tradition, building on, 192–193
Europe, emergence of Jewish communities in,
  18–19
executives
  by industry, 186–187
  religion's impact on advancement of, 187–188
Exodus, 44, 101
expectations of success, 4
Exponent, 124–125
expulsions, 26–27

F
Fabergé Inc., 185
Factor, Max, 185
factory worker, as one-generation phenome-
  non, 62
fair employment statutes, 50
Falk, Peter, 113
family dynamic, supporting law career, 64
Family Interaction, Values and Achievement
  (Srodtbeck), 180
Famous Players Company, 109
Famous Players–Lasky Corporation, 109
fathers, child-rearing style of, 154
Federal Reserve System, 93
Federated Department Stores, 81, 189
Federation survey (1990), 27
federations, 46–47, 55
Fein, Leonard, 147–148
Feingold, Henry, 62
Feingold, Russ, 54
Feinstein, Dianne, 54

Feld, Kenneth, 91
feminist movement, 24
Fernandez, Giselle, 116
Fiedler, Arthur, 164
Filene's, 81
Filner, Bob, 55
financial support, Jewish-American, 41
financiers, 75–80
fine art, 164–166
Fine, Larry (Louis Fineberg), 105
Fingerhut Cos., 81
Fireman, Paul, 70, 92
first day of school, importance of, 27
Fishberg, Maurice, 13
Fisher, Donald, 82, 88, 189
Fisher, Doris, 82, 88, 189
Fisher, John, 89
Fisher, Lawrence, 89
Fisher, Martin, 89
Fisher, Max, 90
Fisher, Richard, 89
Fisher, Robert, 89
Fisher, William, 90
Fisher, Zachary, 89
Fisher family, 75, 89
Fisher-Price, 169
Flamingo Hotel, 74
Fleisher, Max, 166
Flom, Joseph, 64
Forbes 400, 4, 87–92, 99
  Jewish billionaires in, 3
  prevalence of real estate wealth on, 72
  real estate fortunes, 75
Forbes magazine, 32, 33, 73, 87, 103, 104,
  115, 121, 147
Ford, Harrison, 104
Ford, Henry, 3, 75
Fortas, Abe, 62
Fortune 1000, 169
Forward, 147–148, 198
foundations, 46–47, 55
401(k) plans, 136–137
Four Questions, 101–102
Fourth Lateran Council, 19
Fox, William, 110
France, first European country to grant equal
  rights to Jews, 20
Frank, Barney, 55
Frankel, Max, 190
Franken, Al, 105
Frankfurter, Felix, 62, 64
Franklin Mint, 83
Free Loan Societies, 44–46
Freed, Alan, 162
Freleng, Isasdore "Fritz," 166
Freud, Sigmund, 150–151
Fribourg, Michel, 91
Friedan, Betty, 24
Friedman, Jerome, 191–192